Sectors
and
Styles

Founded in 1807, John Wiley & Sons is the oldest independent publishing company in the United States. With offices in North America, Europe, Australia, and Asia, Wiley is globally committed to developing and marketing print and electronic products and services for our customers' professional and personal knowledge and understanding.

The Wiley Finance series contains books written specifically for finance and investment professionals as well as sophisticated individual investors and their financial advisors. Book topics range from portfolio management to e-commerce, risk management, financial engineering, valuation, and financial instrument analysis, as well as much more.

For a list of available titles, visit our Web site at www.WileyFinance.com.

Sectors and Styles

A New Approach to
Outperforming the Market

VINCENT CATALANO

John Wiley & Sons, Inc.

For general information on our other products and services or for technical support, please contact our Customer Care Department within the United States at (800) 762-2974, outside the United States at (317) 572-3993 or fax (317) 572-4002.

Wiley publishes in a variety of print and electronic formats and by print-on-demand. Some material included with standard print versions of this book may not be included in e-books or in print-on-demand. If this book refers to media such as a CD or DVD that is not included in the version you purchased, you may download this material at http://booksupport.wiley.com. For more information about Wiley products, visit www.wiley.com.

Library of Congress Cataloging-in-Publication Data:

Catalano, Vincent, 1948-
    Sectors and styles : a new approach to outperforming the market / Vincent Catalano.
        p.   cm.—(Wiley finance series)
    Includes index.
    ISBN-13 978-0-471-75882-2 (cloth)
    ISBN-10 0-471-75882-5 (cloth)
      1. Investments.   2. Speculation.   3. Investment analysis.   I. Title.   II. Series.
    HG4521.C374   2006
    332.6—dc22

                                                                    2005037199

10   9   8   7   6   5   4   3   2   1

*To my two wonderful kids, Tess and Bryan,
and their loving mother, Debbie.*

Forever, with love.

Contents

Acknowledgments

This book is as much about how I got to be where I am today as it is about what I do. The hard work involved with going out on my own and starting my own business after 25 years at Merrill Lynch has been a journey filled with joy and challenges. The joy was shared by many, and the challenges were overcome thanks to those whom I am proud to call friends and colleagues.

Many thanks go to Jason and Jane Welsch, Bharath Chandar, Joseph Roccasalvo, George and Andrea Fulop, Emily and Len Brizzi, Gino and Donna Albertario, Vahan Janjigian, Annette and Clint Welch, Don Horenstein, Mark Wachs, John Mihale, Mark and Roberta Aaronson, Rocco Papandrea, Milan Miletic, Maris Ogg, Ed McDonough, Connie Dambra, Maria Rudic, Milton Bakogiannis, Susan Wells, Bill Mahoney, John Lewis, and Gary Wolf. Your kindness, friendship, counsel, and support is greatly appreciated.

My base of business began with my involvement with the New York Society of Security Analysts (NYSSA), culminating in my serving on its board and as president (1997–1999). From this sprang a whole host of relationships, many of which have evolved in lasting friendships. Accordingly, many thanks go to those analyst society leaders and staff who have made the events business I produce all the more rich and enjoyable. To Wayne Whipple, Eileen Budd, Evelina Ioselev, Eileen Stempel, and everyone at the NYSSA, thank you for all the years of support and help. To Greg Hryb, Helen Marshall, and everyone else at the Stamford Society, also many thanks to you for years of help and support. To John Kirby and the staff and board at the Market Technicians Association, I always look forward to doing our programs. To Toonce, Phil Keating, Darin Morgan, Joe Bramuchi, and all my other good friends in the Sunshine State, may your winters be ever so mild. To Roger Muns, Alan Smith, Elee Reeves, and everyone else in Jackson, Mississippi, you have truly redefined the phrase "Southern hospitality." To my new friends at the foothills of the Rockies and the Valley of the Sun, many thanks to Jason Meshnick, TD, Bob Boschee, and Tree Houle. And to Tom Cammack, Eric Boyce, and everyone else at my favorite Lone Star State society, Austin, I have just two words— yee haw!

I also wish to acknowledge and thank the many speakers and panelists whom I have had the pleasure and privilege of getting to know up close and personal at the various events and functions I produced and conducted over the past decade. Special thanks go to Rich Bernstein, Subodh Kumar, Ralph Acampora, Tom McManus, Byron Wien, Jason Trennert, Kathy Camilli, Tom Gallagher, Liz Ann Sonders, Phil (the Thrill) Orlando, Ed Hyman, Mary Ann Bartels, Kari Pinkernell, Ken Tower, Mark Freeman, Chuck Hill, Arnie Berman, Delos Smith, Congressman Christopher Shays, Joe Battipaglia, Dr. Peter Hooper, Don Straszheim, Stephen Biggar, Dr. Rob Atkinson, Dr. Ian Bremmer, Sam Stovall, Justin Dew, Gail Dudack, and Tim Hayes. Your willingness to share your insights has enriched the knowledge of all who attended—especially me.

Finally, I am very grateful to a special person, Deborah Weir, for introducing me to John Wiley & Sons' senior acquisition editor, Kevin Commins, and for Kevin and everyone else at John Wiley & Sons for enabling this book to become a reality. Despite the intensity and level of work that was involved, the experience was all that I hoped it would be—an exploration and exposition of the work that I do for clients. For this, I am both thankful and grateful.

VINCENT CATALANO

Introduction

WHY THIS BOOK? WHY NOW?

To paraphrase a good friend of mine in the public relations business, "Why this book? Why now?" It's a fair question to ask when you consider that there are so many investment-related books available, and some of them are quite good, even invaluable. So, yet another book about investing had better have something to contribute to the discussion. I believe this book does for several reasons.

A CONFLUENCE OF EVENTS

To begin, the timeliness and relevance of this book rest on the confluence of three key developments—two technological and one financial—that have emerged over the past two decades: the personal computer (PC), the Internet, and exchange-traded funds (ETFs). When these are combined with a solid understanding of sound valuation principles and an investment philosophy (a set of concepts and beliefs), an investor has the makings of an investment strategy that tilts investment decision making in an investor's favor. And, just as in real life, gaining competitive advantage almost always makes the difference between success and failure.

The first of the two recent developments, the personal computer and the Internet, are great enablers of information access and processing. The third, the exchange-traded fund, is an investment vehicle that allows investors of all means to engage in the construction of an effective portfolio—a portfolio built and maintained on the principle of diversification. Let's look at each development and see how they have made the world of investing so much more democratic *for all investors*.

THE PC AND THE NET

On so many levels, the personal computer and the Internet were made for each other. The PC is a device through which information captured can be analyzed and created for presentation. The Net is the communications platform over which information is transmitted. It is also the environment within which information is presented in the form of web sites and blogs. When it comes to investing, the combination enables just about any person who has the interest and a good grasp of sound investment principles to access the necessary information to analyze the economy, industries, companies, government, and the markets and, thereby, do quality original investment research.

Thanks to the PC and the Net, an investor has at his/her disposal the essential communications and analytical tools to capture that data and incorporate it into a financial and valuation model that forms the basis for a successful investment strategy. For example, the full text and not someone else's interpretation of an important government report or a speech by a business leader or politician can be easily accessed and downloaded for review and analysis. Whereas in the not too distant past access to this information and the ability to develop it into an investment strategy required special contacts and expensive research tools and services, today this is no longer the situation. Moreover, in most cases, the cost today is delightfully either zero or some modest amount that is very affordable to nearly every investor—certainly much more affordable than in the time before the PC and the Net.

As a result, the ability to capture useful economic and financial information, analyze it, and develop it into a well-thought-out investment strategy has been freed from the constraints of privilege and power. Therefore, I think it's fair to say that the Internet (combined with the PC) has lived up to its bubble-era reputation and changed just about everything.

CONVERTING INVESTMENT STRATEGY INTO AN EFFECTIVE PORTFOLIO

Yet, for all the good that is done by having this information and drawing worthwhile conclusions, an investor needs to convert the investment strategy outcome into a productive use of time. After all, investors are just that—investors. They are not analysts who are being compensated for rendering their advice to others. Rather, investors invest. That is to say, they create and manage portfolios for themselves and, in the case of portfolio managers, for others. Here, once again, the PC and the Internet lend their combined power to enable an investor to build and maintain an investment portfolio, thereby putting that knowledge to good investment use. Portfolio management tools are so readily available from various Internet services that managing one's assets has also been brought into the twenty-first century. And here, too, the costs are most attractive.

The third development that has emerged recently is an investment instrument that enables investors to build effective portfolios—exchange-traded funds (ETFs). ETFs allow an investor to make investment bets precisely in an economic area (economic sector) and in an investment style (by market cap, by growth, by value, and so on). When ETFs are combined with the power of the PC and the Net, investors now have the wherewithal to do what only investment professionals with large resources and large research budgets could do before—build effective portfolios.

Therefore, as a result of the power of the PC, the Net, and ETFs, today's investor, investment manager, and financial adviser can conduct quality research. Together with a solid understanding of valuation principles and an investment philosophy, an investor, investment manager, and financial adviser can then develop a well-thought-out investment strategy and construct and maintain effective portfolios.

Why this book? Why now? Because investing in the twenty-first century just got that much better for all investors.

WHO SHOULD USE THIS BOOK

No one book can be all things to all people. In the case of this book, that is certainly true. Although every investor should find value, this book is written primarily for the more active investor—someone who has a degree of knowledge as to how to analyze the economic and investment climate and how to construct and manage a portfolio. That does not mean that you have to be an analyst or portfolio manager to learn and apply the principles and processes in this book. But it does mean that I am assuming that the reader has some knowledge and, preferably, experience in investing so that a better perspective can be applied.

As for investor types who like to trade a lot, let me clearly state that this not a book for you—unless, of course, you wish to reconsider the need for action and replace it with a more consistent methodology for making money, not to mention the opportunity to live life less stressfully and with more knowledge and clarity on what makes stocks (and portfolios) go up and down.

I am fairly certain that serious investors, professional and nonprofessional, seeking to gain an edge will find their time well spent reading these chapters. Such a person is the audience for this book.

STRUCTURE OF THE BOOK

I have written this book in the same manner in which I teach my equity analysis classes, write my research reports, and conduct my various analyst society events:

- Concepts presented in a (hopefully) logical flow.
- Each point building upon the previous one.
- Constant references to the core concepts.
- Examples to illustrate a given point.
- Real-world situations to bring reality into the equation.
- A conversational style.

I also apply my "critical variable" principle to the information within. What matters most gets the most ink. This point warrants a further word.

The critical variable principle is my attempt to identify what matters most and devote the most time and energy on that point(s). This is especially necessary given the scale and scope of the topics discussed in each chapter. Specifically, the topics and even some of the subtopics discussed in every chapter are so large that entire textbooks are devoted to them. What I have done is distill each topic down to the critical variables that I have determined matter most. A reader may beg to differ with what I have chosen as the critical variables for a topic. But it is hard to argue with the fact that not every aspect of any topic is equally important. Therefore, judgment must be exercised. This is what you will find in every chapter—judgment as to what matters most.

As for completeness, every effort is made to provide the deepest understanding possible. To this end, I also provide information that helps round out the picture. Some of the information may not be central to the theme of a chapter but helps in broadening the context of a chapter and, thereby, making the chapter focus more clear.

CHECKMATE

The last point to be made is the distinctively real-time and real-world feel to the book. Examples and articles are taken from a variety of sources but all are framed in the context of today, for this book is written for those seriously interested in making investment decisions in a world dominated by change and uncertainty—the beginning decade of the twenty-first century. Moreover, given the dynamic change that the real and financial economies are undergoing, an investment book focused on the world we live in today should be more useful than a book about theoretical concepts. In other words, this a practical book written for practitioners and serious investors interested in developing their skills as managers of money. The book is rooted in timeless concepts and principles while at the same time it recognizes that there are many unresolved issues at work in the dynamic, interdependent, interconnected, interactive world of investing. It is a truly dynamic process with answers still be discovered and questions still be raised. It is, in effect, the ultimate chess game—only with live pieces.

With that said, here is the flow of the book:

Start with Valuation Principles

It is necessary to first understand what constitutes good investment principles. For one cannot analyze the real economy (economic environment, both domestic and global) and the financial economy (the financial markets) without first understanding where the analysis is relevant. Put differently, it is the context of the analysis that must be first understood so that the information and analysis can lead you to the useful tools.

Develop an Effective Investment Strategy

Moreover, it is especially relevant to place the analysis in a real-time context. Therefore, this is a book that seeks to combine the principles of sound investment analysis and asset management with contemporary events. The principles act as the foundation, while the contemporary events serve to illustrate the principles in action. The contemporary events of another time (past or future) would serve just as well to illustrate what works. However, thanks to key macro trends such as globalization and technology, the investing environment has changed sufficiently so that spending most of our time in the present-day era should serve our interests best.

As for the analytical process that I use, the approach focuses on government, economy, and the markets (GEM). GEM is a fairly in-depth exploration of the factors that impact government action and economic performance, and the markets' take on both. It is a rich and robust way to analyze all the important aspects of both the real economy (the G and E part) and the financial economy (M) so that our analysis and conclusions about what *should* happen are cross-checked with what *is* happening in the markets. I have found that GEM gives the best chance of getting the investment strategy right, especially the critical asset allocation decision.

Understand the Essential Elements of an Effective Portfolio

Investors invest. That is their purpose. To this end, the creation of an effective portfolio, a portfolio designed to meet an investor's needs, needs to be understood. We explore what goes into creating and maintaining a portfolio that is effective, that works to satisfy an investor's needs.

Give Thanks for the Useful Technological and Financial Tools

With our valuation principles and analytical process and what constitutes an effective portfolio in hand, the investment tools of the Internet and ETFs are then described. There is a great deal of attention given to the practical part of the process: What information web sites are necessary? What data about ETFs do we need to know? What web sites can we use to construct and manage our portfolios? The investment tools to use are the enablers of achieving the goal of building and maintaining an effective portfolio.

Put It All Together: Creating and Maintaining an Effective Portfolio

The final step is when we put it all together. The valuation principles, the investment philosophy, the investment strategy, the elements of an effective portfolio, and the tools that make it all happen culminate in a portfolio construction and maintenance process that results in an effective portfolio. The valuation principles provide the foundation upon which the dynamic aspects of the real and financial economy can be evaluated. The effective portfolio is the end result.

Like the inputs into the valuation model, putting it all together is conceptually easy but extremely difficult to do successfully. Each piece is interconnected to the other. And the failure to get one part of the puzzle right has more than a singular effect on the whole. There is no other way, though, to build and manage an effective portfolio to produce consistent results. Granted, there may be other investment strategy approaches used, but the overall comprehensive approach taken here ensures that all the important bases are touched, priorities are determined, and judgment is exercised. At a minimum, the reader will gain a deeper insight into the process of analysis, investment strategy, and portfolio management. And that is all to the good as it advances the reader's knowledge of sound investment principles. At its best, the reader will be on the path to successful asset management that will last a lifetime.

CHAPTER FORMAT

Most chapters in this book adhere to the following sequence, whether explicitly stated or not:

- For the most part, chapters begin with, in effect, a statement of purpose. This *overview* provides the context or framework of the chapter and sets the tone for what follows.
- The need to grasp the central principles is dealt with next. *Core concepts*, including concepts and principles, definitions, and descriptions are presented—a description of the core principles and practices at work, if you will.
- The economic and financial worlds are not issue-free, however. Established rules and traditions are constantly challenged, new concepts and methodologies emerge threatening the established order, and developments in seemingly unrelated areas that have an impact on the real and financial economy need to be discussed, if not understood, as they often play a role in the valuation model inputs, even if it is not apparent at first glance. Therefore, the *issues* section of a chapter is where the debate exists. Sometimes it is lively and profoundly meaningful and at other times peripheral but important.
- To help illustrate concepts and principles, *real-world examples* are presented in which events—current and past—are reviewed to help put the core concepts and issues into action. Most examples are from the recent past but some reach back over time. Whatever it takes to make clear the concepts and principles is used.
- Most chapters conclude with a summary section. Like the cuffs on a pair of pants, this section puts on the finishing touches by summarizing the key points just discussed and provides the logical sequence to the next chapter. It therefore also serves as a bridge, hopefully ensuring the natural flow of one thought to another.

Throughout the book, intrachapter examples, similar to the real-world examples presented at the end of a chapter, are used to help illustrate the core concepts and issues discussed. Tables and charts serve the same purpose.

A FEW CAVEATS

Here are a few warnings, or more correctly caveats, to bear in mind when reading this book.

This Is Not the Complete Book on Valuation and Equity Analysis

The valuation principles described in this book might lead some to believe that all that is needed to know about investment strategy and equity analysis is contained within. This is not the case, however. Granted, equity analysis is central to the valuation process and to understanding from a bottom-up perspective the investment strategy derived, both of which culminate in the asset allocation decision and portfolio construction and management. Therefore, valuation principles and equity analysis are closely linked. What is covered in this book in regard to valuation will help form the basis on which a reader can do decent equity analysis. But my advice is to then seek out other materials that will enable you to complete the complex process of analyzing companies and their stocks and to fill out your knowledge base. For while it is impossible to write a book about investing without touching upon key aspects of the valuation and equity analysis process, such as financial models, industry analysis, and competitive analysis, the in-depth analysis of companies and their stocks is not the purpose. How to make good sectors and styles investment decisions is.

Nor Is This the Complete Book on Portfolio Management

If constructing and maintaining an effective portfolio is a final goal of this book, then perhaps a reader might conclude that this is a complete exploration of portfolio management. As with equity analysis, this book takes the reader into important areas that lead to the construction and management of effective portfolios but it cannot and does not cover in detail and in depth the myriad of other approaches and styles one could incorporate using the principles, tools, and process described.

Having said that, let me be clear on one point: In both cases—equity analysis and portfolio management—this book provides an important foundation upon which good investment strategy can be developed and practiced. A reader could take what is contained in these pages and put it to good use. But investing is more like a movie than a snapshot. Things change over time. New methodologies will emerge, existing methodologies will evolve, and the timeless principles described in these pages will find new applications. Moreover, the breadth and depth of both equity analysis and portfolio management can and should be explored. For example, an investor could never gain too deep an insight into the impacts of corporate strategy on the competitive advantage principles of Michael Porter's Five Forces and Three Generic Strategies. Nor could an investor understand too deeply the geopolitical circumstances of globalization.

My advice: Take the principles and process in this book and add as much useful depth and breadth to them as you can, and you will be a better investor.

And This Book Is Most Definitely Not about Financial Planning

The discussion of equity analysis and portfolio management does not reach the point of financial planning. Personal finance and financial planning are valuable processes, and all investors should spend time and energy engaged in them. Life planning decisions such as retirement planning, asset and income protection policies (life insurance, long-term care, etc.), and other obligations and needs are the domain of the financial planning and financial adviser expert. Portfolio management is the tool, the instrument through which personal finance goals are satisfied. That is what this book attempts to assist in. For all other personal financial matters, you will have to read another good book.

COMMENTS

With the principles and process expressed in this book, there is no hiding behind the argument that you were right about the sector but wrong about the individual stocks you bought or sold or sold short. Those days are over. With ETFs, the principles of diversification and choice guarantee that an investor will participate in the correct strategy and sector bets made. As for the investment strategy you might use, you don't have to use the investment strategy described—GEM—to reap the benefits of this book. For most readers, the process undertaken in its comprehensiveness will provide ample valuable information. Obviously, I believe in the approach. Perhaps, however, there is another investment strategy approach you prefer. That is just fine. In fact, just about any well-grounded investment strategy approach that works can take advantage of the technological and financial innovations of the past two decades.

There is a related issue that warrants further comment. It has to do with the underlying assumption that following the principles espoused in this book will result in better investment performance. In fact, just about every book written about investments has this underlying theme to it—read this book, practice its principles and processes, and you stand a better chance of generating better investment results than you would have otherwise. A few comments on this line of thinking.

First and foremost, I wrote this book in the same spirit as I conduct my classes and events: to make sure that the buyer feels that he/she got his/her money's worth. To this end, the very least that I can do is increase a reader's investment knowledge, with the assumption being that a more knowledgeable investor should be a better investor. This is my minimum goal: to increase your knowledge base on what constitutes good investment principles and practices. With that knowledge, the odds increase that your investment results should be better than they would have been otherwise *and* the results should be due more to skill and less to luck.

The second point I wish to make has to do with your point of departure. Better performance results depend on what your present approach to investing is, how successful have you been, and, if you have been a successful investor,[1] how consistent those results have been, and what are the true causes of that success. In other words, was success due to skill or luck?

Therefore, this book seeks to achieve:

- An understanding of good investment principles and processes.
- A methodology by which an investor can achieve alpha (returns in excess of the returns he/she would have received investing in an index fund, adjusted for the degree of portfolio risk taken and based on the risk tolerance of the investor).

The principles are timeless. The tools (ETFs, the PC, and the Net) are fairly recent innovations. The combination will empower investors as never before.

Speaking of innovation, let me conclude by noting that this book is as much about *innovation* as it is about the principles and process of good investment management. Take a good look at what is contained within the following pages and you will note that there is nothing that has actually been *invented*, but a whole lot has certainly been *innovated*. By taking advantage of the innovations of past decades, adhering to sound investment principles, and applying well-thought-out investment strategies, investors will be able to construct effective portfolios for the benefit of themselves or, in the case of financial professionals, their clients. It is in that spirit that I encourage you to view this book—as both a guide to making money consistently and an example of what a little innovative thinking can do. Now, what can you innovate with what you will learn on the following pages?

ONE FINAL THOUGHT

In many respects, this book is a point of departure. For some, it is a starting point in which a further exploration of the concepts, principles, practices, and processes will be pursued through further study in each respective area. For example, anyone contemplating pursuing my investment strategy, GEM, should seriously consider the effort it takes to understand the complexities and interactive aspects of such a large-scale research effort. As a result, a deepening of the knowledge in each area is necessary to achieve the critical mass of knowledge to know what to include and what to exclude from the investment strategy equation. In other words, you can't get to the critical variables if you are not capable of knowing what to include and exclude.

For others, this book will act as a refresher of key valuation, investment strategy, and portfolio construction concepts, principles, and practices. This is akin to the practicing investment professionals who attend my equity analysis classes in pursuit of their Chartered Financial Analyst (CFA®) charter. They may know the topic but could always use a different perspective.

And, finally, for the remaining readers, this book will act like a catalyst, a call to investment arms, in which the possibilities presented in this book stimulate one's own approach to investment strategy and portfolio construction and thereby lead to better, more effective ways to make money investing.

Whatever your goals or purposes, a central message of this book is for all investors to not rest on their skills. The real and financial economies are very dynamic places where change and uncertainty are the only constants. Armed with the knowledge, skills, and processes, the odds then get tilted in an investor's favor—kind of like the concept of tilting a portfolio in one's favor using sectors and styles as the core tool.

Valuation Principles, Investment Strategy, and Portfolio Construction

THE VALUE IN VALUE

As suggested by the title, the goal of this book is to describe how the benefits of making investment decisions on a sector and style basis can lead to the creation and maintenance of an effective portfolio, a portfolio designed to satisfy an investor's needs. Knowing how to allocate your investment assets in your portfolio by investing in industries, in economic sectors, and on market attributes (such as market capitalization or quality) is the objective of this book.

But it is essential that an investor understand the valuation process, as it is the base upon which we can then determine what is called the true or intrinsic value of an asset. And that takes us where we want to go: determining whether a industry, sector, or style is overvalued or undervalued and, therefore, whether we should overweight or underweight an industry, sector, or style in the portfolio we own or manage. By understanding the valuation process, an investor is then capable of gaining the necessary knowledge to *begin* making an informed buy/sell/hold decision.

In effect, you cannot be an effective sectors and styles investor unless you have a firm grasp of the core valuation principles that determine the intrinsic value of an asset. Once the principles are understood, a giant step will have been taken toward making good sector and style decisions. And that will then lead to building and maintaining an effective portfolio.

CHAPTER 1

Valuation's Core Concepts

The cornerstone of any investment strategy is the valuation model. The valuation model is necessary to understand simply because an investor needs to know what the true value of an asset is so that he/she can decide if *owning that asset at the current price* is a good thing to do. Therefore, it is the valuation model that is used to begin the investment decision-making process. The phrase "begin the investment decision-making process" is important because, as you will see in subsequent chapters, the better investment decisions depend first on the intrinsic value derived *and then* on incorporation of an assessment of how the marketplace views that asset. It is the concept of good company and good stock. More on the second point later. For now, let's get the valuation basics under our belt.

THE SEARCH FOR INTRINSIC VALUE

Understanding the valuation model means ascertaining the information that goes into the valuation model—the inputs—and then forecasting the future growth and risk factors of those inputs. To help understand the basics of this process, we will do this on an individual company basis. We begin on a company-specific basis for the following several reasons:

- The economic sectors and styles that we will use to build our effective portfolio are composed of individual companies. The valuation determination of each sector and style is the sum of its parts—the individual companies. It is therefore advisable to know what's in the sectors and styles that we are deciding on.
- By conducting quality company analysis, a key component of the valuation process, we may gain a deeper insight into the sectors and styles we are interested in investing in or avoiding. This is because when we view the specifics of a sector or style from a company or bottom-up

perspective, the trends and themes that drive the sector or style become more readily apparent.

- The valuation model for the market as a whole is the same as for individual companies. Therefore, given the greater degree of complexity involved in determining the intrinsic value of the market, the valuation process can be more easily understood if we start on an individual company basis.
- The valuation model for sectors and styles can be more easily explained and understood by studying one company rather than whole industries and sectors, which have layers of complexity.

There is an added reason for being capable of conducting company-specific analysis: the ability to recognize change thanks to leadership companies.

Leadership companies are those companies that are most likely to set the competitive tone for an industry or a sector. A leadership company can be the largest company within a sector, but not necessarily. For example, a leadership company can also be the most innovative one in the group. Such companies can be the trendsetters of the group. Leadership companies can also be defined as companies that act as early warning indicators of change within an industry or sector. In a worst-case scenario, such an early-bird warning (or canary in the mine shaft, if you will) can help tip off an astute investor to a major change in the direction of an industry or a sector.

Having given the justification for placing valuation principles and processes as our starting point and for applying it first on a company-specific basis, let us begin.

VALUATION METHODOLOGIES

There are two primary methodologies used to determine the value of an asset, any asset. One method is *discounted cash flow* (DCF). The discounted cash flow method states that the value of any asset is the present value of its future cash flows. It is an inward look at a company and the environment in which the company operates (its industry, the economic environment) and seeks to determine the company's true or intrinsic value. An investor can then compare the intrinsic value derived with the current market price of the stock of the company and then decide whether to own or not own the stock. In other words, if the return that an investor would receive is an acceptable rate of return for the level of risk and uncertainty involved in owning the stock, then the stock is a buy. If not, it is not a buy.

This is simple to say and even to calculate, as you will see. But it is very difficult to get right, as you will also see.

The other method is known as the *comparables* method. The comparables method involves the comparison of a metric, such as the price-earnings (P/E) ratio of the stock, to other comparable stocks. If the company under review is equal in all respects to other comparable companies, then the P/E ratio of the stock of the company should be equal to the P/E ratio of the stocks of the comparable companies. If, however, the P/E ratio of our company is below the P/E ratio of the comparable companies, then the stock would be considered undervalued and, therefore, would be considered a buy. If the P/E ratio were above its comparables, its peers, then it would be considered overvalued relative to its peers and therefore would not be a buy. Put simply, the comparables method states that the best way to determine the value of an asset is to compare that asset to other similar assets and then judge whether one asset is more or less attractive than the other.

While both methods incorporate measures of corporate performance, there are meaningful differences between the two.

The comparables approach combines a measure of company performance (earnings, sales, and book value being the three most commonly used measures of company performance) with a market metric, the price of the stock of the company in question. This is more of what I call an "outward-looking approach" to determining value simply because you have a market factor—the price—in the valuation equation. As a result, that non-company-specific market factor distracts from the task at hand—what is the economic value of the asset (the company) in question? For at the end of the day, it is the economic potential of an asset that ultimately determines its true economic value. However, and this is a big "however," value is a highly subjective determination made by investors, who are human and therefore subject to all the strengths and weaknesses of being human (read: greed and fear). And here you have the age-old question: Does a good company (good being defined as having an intrinsic value below its market value) *always* equal a good stock (defined as generating a rate of return in excess of the market return, adjusted for its risk)? The answer is obviously no. Not always. And that is the essence of equity analysis and, ultimately, successful investment management: Will our stock (or sector or style) go up, down, or sideways?

So, which method is best—DCF or comparables? Which method will help us get to the answer we seek? The answer is *it all depends*. As explained in Chapter 6, some situations warrant the use of the comparables method over the DCF. However, for the most part, and because an understanding of the company and its operating environment can best be achieved through the DCF method, it is essential that an investor calculate what that economic (intrinsic) value is, as there is a depth and richness of understanding that takes place in the process. I recall a very astute investor once saying that the value in the research process was not in the conclusion but in the value learned from the process. From my experience, the good company, good stock issue belongs in the portfolio management decision process. In fact, most professional investors use both methods—one to determine what the value of the stock should be (its intrinsic value) and the other as a check against what the market says the value should be (as compared to its peers).

CORE PRINCIPLES

Let's begin by determining the intrinsic value of a business.

DISCOUNTED CASH FLOW MODEL

Ultimately, the value of any asset and, therefore, the investment decisions made are based on the cash-generating capability of that asset. It is this cash-generating ability, which comes in the form of the economic profit or cash flows that an asset generates, that determines its economic or intrinsic value. More specifically, it is the *free* cash flows, the net cash flows of a business after factoring in the cash used to maintain and grow the business, available to equity investors that an asset produces that is of primary interest. Since the common stock of a business is an asset owned by investors, the same rules apply—the free cash flows generated by a business determine its intrinsic value.

However, when it comes to determining the intrinsic value of a business it isn't the cash flows of today that are of the greatest interest to investors. Rather, it is the ability of the company to produce cash flows well into the future that matters most. For investing is all about the future. What will I earn from my investment today *and* tomorrow? Since there are many more tomorrows, it is the economic earning power of the company in the future that concerns us most. Therefore, the free cash flows produced for the projected life of the business determine its intrinsic or fair value. Given that the future cash flows matter most, there are three important factors to consider:

1. At what rate of growth will the future cash flows be produced?
2. Are the cash flows earned in the future the same as those earned today?

3. How certain are we that the company will earn the projected cash flows?

As investors, we expect growth into the future. But forecasting that future growth rate is both an art and a science. It requires both skill and judgment. It requires an understanding of the competitive factors within an industry, the competitive position of a company to successfully compete, the quality of management to produce consistent operating results, the financial strength to capitalize on opportunities as they are presented, and the ability to execute in the most effective manner. This is no small task. It is easy to say, but quite hard to do—quite hard to do consistently into the future. And it is just as hard for investors to predict, for there are many obstacles in the way of a company outsider (which is what an investor is) trying to predict what a company is capable of. Therefore, getting the growth rate of our most precious future cash flows right, or as close to right as possible, is an extremely valuable advantage.

On the second point: Clearly, cash flows earned tomorrow are not the same as cash flows earned today simply because of the time value of money and the impact of inflation. Obviously, we invest because we expect income today (usually in the form of dividends) and growth tomorrow (in the form of capital gains). But due to the effects of inflation, a dollar tomorrow is worth less than a dollar today. Therefore, we need to bring back or discount those potential future gains (thanks to rising cash flows) to the present-day value. We do that by discounting the future cash flows back to present value using a basic discounting formula. But what about the uncertainty factor? How does that come into the picture?

Last, we invest because we have a degree of confidence that the future is somewhat predictable. But somewhat predictable is not absolutely predictable. There is a degree of confidence but not an absolute degree of confidence. All well and good, but how does an investor quantify that degree of confidence? By using the same discount tool that brings the future cash flows back to the present value.[1]

Well, there you have it—the essence of the intrinsic valuation model:

- Free cash flows produced by the company today.
- Growth of the free cash flows into tomorrow.
- Uncertainty or risk of not generating the projected free cash flows.
- The present value of the future cash flows.

Put another way:

- How much profit does our investment produce today?
- How much profit will our investment produce tomorrow?

- How certain are we that the company will produce that profit?
- What is the current value of the profits of the company?

Since the last two points, uncertainty and present value, are captured in the same formula, we can reduce our intrinsic value model to its three inputs:

1. Free cash flows
2. Growth
3. Risk

Let's take each in order.

The Free Cash Flows of a Business

The value of an equity investment in a company is the funds that accrue to my ownership interest. The funds that accrue to my ownership interest can come in several forms. One popular form, for example, is that the business can pay dividends and they are the funds that are calculated as my cash flows. It is, in effect, the cash flowing from the business to investors. This is fine if the growth and return prospects of the business are less than what an investor could earn simply by taking those funds and reinvesting them in a broad market index, like the S&P 500 index.[2] But what if a company did have growth prospects that could produce a rate of growth and return that was greater than the stock market as a whole? Then, why would I want to receive dividends from a company that I own shares in if the company is capable of using that money to generate a rate of growth and return greater than what the market has to offer and doesn't? Think of it this way:

Dividends are a dispersal of corporate money. They are a form of cash flows to investors that can be used to calculate the intrinsic value of a company. But they are also a statement about the growth and return prospects of a business. In effect, their very existence says, "Our company cannot find growth and return prospects that exceed the return you, our investor, can receive elsewhere. Therefore, here, take the money and do something more productive with it. We can't."

Pretty powerful stuff, wouldn't you say? And an important point to be made about the productive use of capital—something that I will get to as follows:

If dividends are not the applicable definition of the free cash flows that accrue to me as an investor, what is? The answer lies in the phrase "grow or die."

Ownership in stocks is all about the corporate struggle between growth and death. Dividends are a sign that growth into the future is limited. The company has more free cash flows than it has productive projects and, therefore, dispensing some of that excess cash generated to you, the investor, to do as you please with it makes more economic sense than plowing that excess cash flow into corporate investments that produce a below-market rate of return.[3] Growth, on the other hand, is indicated when a company does not dispense its excess cash (its free cash flows) and instead reinvests it into the business and produces an above-market rate of return. The company could dispense that money but doesn't. The funds that a business could dispense—its free cash flows—are the funds that could accrue to me, the equity investor. Since they are the free cash flows that could accrue to me and that I trust in the company to put those funds to good productive use, I will use that figure as my cash-generating number—my free cash flows.

To recap: Dividends are cash distributed to investors and, as such, are a form of cash flows to investors that can be used in the DCF valuation model to determine the intrinsic value of the business. However, beyond the valuation formula, the larger issue at work is the statement that dividend distributions (and stock buybacks) are a reflection of below-market rate of return opportunities for the company and therefore must be taken into account when viewing the company as a whole—its growth prospects, its risk factors. For most investors who are more interested in the growth prospects of a business (capital gains) as opposed to the income prospects (dividends, stock buybacks), the reapplication of the excess cash flows back into the business is of greater interest. Therefore, we need to understand what goes into the free cash flows of the business.

Let the calculating begin.

Show Me the Real Money

There are several ways to derive the cash-generating power of a business (its free cash flows). One useful way, and the one that I prefer to use, is to start with the company's net income and then adjust that figure for the accounting distortions inherent in arriving at net income. In that way, we can then reach the true cash-generating capacity of firm—its free cash flows.

The basic formula I prefer is:

```
    Net Income
  + Depreciation
  - Capital Expenditures (Capex)
 +/- Change in Working Capital
  = Free Cash Flows of a Company
```

Net income is an excellent starting point in our search for the real money because it highlights two important points:

1. It is the conventionally acknowledged measure of corporate performance.
2. It is a distortion of the real economic profit of a business.

The first point is well known and a given. The second requires a further comment.

Net income is an accrual accounting-derived expression of the economic performance of a business—its bottom-line profit. It is the sum of money earned after all expenses have been factored in and taxes have been deducted. Unfortunately, it is a number that, in most cases, does not reflect true performance reality—the real economic profit of the business. The excellent textbook *The Analysis and Use of Financial Statements* by White, Sondhi, and Fried states:

> *Accrual accounting does have its weaknesses. It is subject to pervasive accounting assumptions such as the going concern assumption. Because periodic statements must be prepared, estimates of the revenues earned and costs incurred during the reporting interval are required. These estimates require management judgment and estimates that are subject to modification as more information about the operating cycle becomes available. Accruals are, therefore, susceptible to manipulation by management's choice of accounting policies and estimates. Furthermore, accrual accounting fails to provide adequate information about the liquidity of the firm and long-term solvency. Some of these problems can be alleviated by the use of the cash flow statement in conjunction with the income statement.*[4]

As you can see, accounting rules allow corporate management a great deal of latitude. And the potential for distortion, intentional or not, exists. The accounting rules allow corporate managements to apply the rules to their situation according to the correct application of a given rule. It also assumes that management will exercise good judgment and accurately reflect the true financial strength of a business and its true operating capability using the accounting rules at its disposal. However, since not every corporate situation fits neatly into the existing accounting rules, problems in determining true economic profit arise. Moreover, some accounting rules, such as depreciation, are meant to provide companies with a tax benefit enabling them to properly reflect the erosion in the productive value of fixed assets and to eventually replace those assets in the future so that a company can maintain and grow its business. The problem arises when the future plans of the business do not match up with the current-day depreciation write-off of the assets. Corporate circumstances can and do change. Additionally, the cost to replace the written-off assets may not match up with the deductions taken. This is the tip of the accounting distortion iceberg. There are other financially derived issues, too numerous to mention here[5] but necessary to at least appreciate.

The bottom-line point to be made here is that accounting rules can and often do distort the true economic profit of the business. The net income number is an accepted measure of corporate performance but it should not be taken as a measure of true economic performance. Accordingly, it needs to be adjusted. Therefore, the usefulness of net income lies in the fact that it is a number that should be used only as a starting point in our quest for determining the true economic profit of the business.

Back to the Formula

The free cash flows formula (net income + depreciation − capex + or − changes in working capital) is elegant and insightful in its simplicity for several reasons. First and foremost, it captures quite nicely the operating essence of the business. It is a formula that in effect describes what it takes to maintain and grow a business.

- Depreciation, a noncash charge, is added back in to reflect the fact that no cash expense was actually made.
- Capital expenditures (capex) are subtracted because they were the actual funds dispensed for fixed assets.
- Working capital is the shorter-term operating lifeblood of the business and is a source or use of funds, hence the plus or minus calculation.

Let's consider several important factors in the three adjustments to net income.

Depreciation   Depreciation is the accounting write-off of an earlier capital expenditure. Because depreciation is a book entry write-off of a previously acquired asset, it is not an actual expenditure. It is a noncash charge. And being a noncash deduction against revenues, depreciation ends up lowering the net income of a business. Accordingly, it should not be deducted from the current cash-generating power of the business as it was not an actual disbursement of funds and needs to be added back to net income. It, in effect, is a source of funds.

Capital Expenditures (Capex)   Capex, on the other hand, is an outlay of money. Capex is the investment in fixed, long-lived assets that are necessary for business growth and development. Capex is, therefore, considered a use of funds. Since it is an outlay of capital necessary for the growth and development of a business, it must be deducted from the free cash flows available to equity investors (that's us).

Working Capital   The textbook definition of working capital is the difference between current assets and current liabilities:

$$\text{Current Assets} - \text{Current Liabilities} = \text{Working Capital}$$

The problem with this definition and its lack of usefulness for our purposes is that both current assets and current liabilities contain nonoperating items such as cash, marketable securities, and short-term debt. Since we are interested in determining the economic profit of the business, we therefore need to exclude those nonoperating items in the working capital equation. In other words, what we are really seeking are those shorter-term operating factors that are either a source or a use of funds necessary to maintain and grow the business. In this regard, there are three components that are of use and value to understanding the source and use of funds for operating a business: accounts receivable, inventory, and accounts payable.

These three components of current assets and current liabilities are of great interest to investors, for they help us determine the free cash flows of a business.

Here are a few salient points on all three:

1. Accounts receivable are sales booked but not collected. They are the funds owed to the firm by customers that will be collected (and received as cash) in the near future.
2. Inventory is products held and ready to be sold.
3. Accounts payable are the mirror image of accounts receivable—they are a calculation of what a business owes suppliers for services or products received that it has been billed for but has not yet paid.

Each of these three components is either a source of funds or a use of funds and, as such, directly impacts the free cash flows of a business. For example, a sale that has been recorded as such but has not been collected is a use of funds (accounts receivable). Revenues have been booked but the cash from the sale has not been received. The sale shows up as an entry on the income statement and thereby inflates the net income bottom-line number. Conversely, a bill that has not been paid but is recorded as an expense is a source of funds (accounts payable). It shows up on the income statement as an expense and thereby reduces the net income figure. In both cases, entries have been made on the income statement (revenues and expenses), a portion of which (receivables and payables) did not generate an actual exchange of money.

As to inventories, the cost to produce products is an expenditure that is recorded not as a direct out-of-pocket expense in the current income statement period but via an accounting rule either on a first in, first out (FIFO) basis or on a last in, first out (LIFO) basis. Either way, the money spent to produce the inventory is not directly lined up with the charge an investor sees on the income statement.

In all three cases, what we are interested in as investors is the change year over year. It is that change, the year-over-year difference, that source or use of funds, that needs to be accounted for in our quest for the free cash flows of the business. And that change impacts the free cash flows of the business. Consider the following example regarding accounts receivable:

- Revenues for a given year are $10 million.
- Of that figure, $2 million was recorded as accounts receivable (funds due).
- The difference of the accounts receivable number on the balance sheet is a $1 million increase.
- Revenues actually received are overstated by $1 million.

"Whoa," you might say. "Why aren't revenues overstated by $2 million as that is the amount of money that was booked but not received?" The reason the overstatement in revenues is $1 million and not $2 million is due to the simple fact that some of the previously recorded accounts receivable have been collected in this statement period. Get it? It is the change (on the balance sheet) that we are interested in—the change from one statement period to the next that incorporates the source or use of funds. Let's do another basic example.

Say that a company's net income was $4 million, its depreciation was $800,000, capital expenditures (capex) were $1.2 million, and the net change in working capital was –$400,000. We can determine our free cash flows as follows:

	Net Income	$4,000,000
+	Depreciation	+ 800,000
−	Capital Expenditures (Capex)	–1,200,000
+/−	Change in Working Capital	– 400,000
=	Free Cash Flows of a Company	$3,200,000

In this very simple example, you can see that by adding back in the noncash charge of depreciation and deducting for the cost of maintaining and growing the business (–$400,000 + –$1,200,000 = –$1,600,000), we obtain a reduction of $800,000. That means that the actual economic profit of the business was not $4 million, as recorded on the income statement, but $3.2 million. By adjusting for these factors, we are one step closer to understanding the true economic capability of the business. Additionally, the process itself helps us to place into focus key aspects of operating the business.

There is a second and perhaps more important reason why the free cash flows formula is so useful to investors: It acts as a basis upon which we can forecast the true growth in sales and economic profit more accurately into the future. As you will see in Chapter 5 on the economy, sales forecasting is the starting point of profit forecasting. That forecast is the product of two well-known methodologies—top-down and bottom-up. Top-down forecasting takes the macroeconomic environment as the key influencing factor in industry and company sales growth. Forecasts for U.S. and international gross domestic products (GDPs) emanate from economists' projections. Bottom-up forecasting, in contrast, relies on the internal capabilities of the business and the dynamics within an industry to determine the price received for the goods sold and the number of units sold (Price × Units Sold = Sales).[6] Most good analysts, portfolio managers, and investment strategists whom I know utilize the information from both sources.[7]

By taking us deeper into the operational performance of the business, the information contained in the free cash flows formula helps an investor predict more accurately the likelihood that the company will achieve its goals. It also enables an investor to weigh the macro environment factors into the equation and thereby make a more accurate forecast. Of course, several other financial measures of performance must be consulted, such as the return on equity (ROE), before an investor can make an informed analysis. Nevertheless, the free cash flows formula is a lot like the discounted cash flow formula—so much for so little. Sometimes less is more.

A Big Caveat

Our quest for the economic profit of a business entails the conceptual understanding of key accounting issues and how they can distort the bottom-line number used to represent profitability—net income. It must be emphasized, however, that the very brief description of the accounting distortion impacts is just that—a very brief description. It points an investor in the right direction, which is toward ascertaining the knowledge necessary to get to that true bottom-line number. But there is so much more depth and so many more details that should be understood about the accounting adjustment process that I strongly recommend that anyone pursuing a thorough analysis of a company must dig much deeper into the process.

In other words, the preceding discussion provides the concept of economic profit and the process by which an investor should go about determining that figure. Depth, details, and accuracy can be achieved only through a thorough analysis of the company involved.

So, let's recap.

Net income is the result of revenues minus expenses. Since both revenues and expenses are accounting-derived numbers, they are subject to interpretation by corporate management as allowed by the rules of business accounting. This latitude is necessary because many businesses have legitimate reasons for such flexibility. But with flexibility comes the potential for distortions and even fraud. We will stick to the distortions issue, as fraud is the domain of the legal profession and cynical analysts.[8]

Accounting distortions are not necessarily some deliberate attempt on the part of management to consciously misrepresent the true operating picture of a company. Accounting distortions can come about simply as by-products of the accounting process in which the true economic profit of a business is not visible. Issues like how and when to recognize revenues and whether to expense or capitalize a given cost contribute to the distortion factor.

Free cash flow is a much more reliable indicator of the cash-generating capability simply because it adjusts for many (but not all) of the accounting distortions that take place when subtracting expenses from income, as it includes adjustments for what it takes to maintain and grow a business.

The Quest for Economic Profit

Now, you might think that there is settled law when it comes to calculating the free cash flows of a firm. *Au contraire.* For there are several variations of free cash flows, some of which are proprietary processes such as Stern Stewart's EVA® (economic value added). Others, such as Holt's cash flow return on investment (CFROI) and the CFA Institute's residual income, also attempt to enable an investor to reach the true free cash flows (the economic profit) of a firm. Moreover, even the basic free cash flows method used earlier has several variations to it, including the idea of factoring in the net borrowing that a firm employs.

Regardless of which approach an investor takes, determining the real economic profit can only lead to, at a minimum, the input number in the discounted cash flow valuation model and, at a maximum, a greater insight into the potential earning power of a business. And that insight is the great enabler of a higher level of valuation analysis.

With this basic understanding of free cash flows under our belt and sticking with our focus on corporate profitability, perhaps it's a good time to take a step back and gain a larger perspective on several of the factors that drive the creation of the free cash flows. For that I have used with great success an innovation of mine, which I call "the Funnel."

THE FUNNEL

The Funnel is a device that I use in the equity analysis classes that I teach that helps one visualize the big picture flow from the macro to the micro. The Funnel is the top-down look at the flow of the macro environment (economic and political) to and through the industry level (competitive factors, growth rates, and profitability). It continues with a view from the company level (products, management, and marketing), which then determines the financial model inputs (profitability, efficiency, and leverage), culminating in the end result—the valuation model (cash flows, growth of the cash flows, and risk). It is the end result of all of the real and financial economy inputs that ultimately impacts future corporate performance and valuation. The Funnel is also a manifestation of the critical variables and judgment principles discussed in the next chapter.

Here is how the Funnel works:

- At the top of our Funnel, we begin with an assessment of the macro environment. The macro environment includes the economic, governmental, and social dynamics at work.
- At the next level down of the Funnel we determine an assessment of what the macro environment might mean for specific economic sectors, industries, and subindustries, placing the emphasis on the impacts to profitability, growth, and risk (uncertainty).
- The impacts from the macro environment to the sector and industry forces are then distilled down to the company level in which products, strategy, marketing, management, and so on are evaluated.
- The fourth level of the Funnel shows the financial results of the company's efforts and provides the inputs into a financial model. The financial model includes the income statement and balance sheet. It also includes a performance analysis using ratios and other key corporate performance metrics.

■ At the very bottom of the Funnel is the valuation model. The flow from the macro environment through economic sectors and industries to the company level results in the inputs to the valuation model.

As with our free cash flow calculations and our valuation model inputs, in the Funnel we have a relatively easy concept—from macro to micro. But getting the individual data items right, which leads to getting the valuation inputs right, is one of the hardest things to do.[9]

We will defer for the moment the macro factors, as they are reviewed in the government and economy chapters (Chapters 4 and 5), and stick with our company-specific focus and the seminal work of one Michael Porter.

PORTER'S COMPETITIVE STRATEGY

In 1980, Harvard professor Michael Porter wrote a book on company analysis titled *Competitive Strategy*. In it, Professor Porter produced what is widely acknowledged as *the* definitive basic tool for industry and company analysis. *Competitive Strategy* described the value chain and how the business process functions—adding value at each stage of product and service development. The book also introduced the perspective of how businesses gain and maintain competitive advantage. Porter calls his approach the Five Forces of Industry Competition and Three Generic Strategies.

Porter's formulation of his Five Forces and Three Generic Strategies has long been the staple of investment basics for aspiring and practicing investment professionals. It is a central component of the Chartered Financial Analyst (CFA®) curriculum and is a simple yet elegant way of capturing the many facets of the competitive forces at work within industries.

Porter describes the value proposition businesses offer and compete for and how profitability, growth, and risk are a function of the quest for competitive advantage. He states:

> *Competitive advantage grows fundamentally out of the value a firm is able to create for its buyers. It may take the form of prices lower than competitors' for equivalent benefits or the provision of unique benefits that more than offset a premium price.*[10]

He goes on to note:

> *Competition is at the core of the success or failure of firms. Competition determines the appropriateness of a firm's activities that*

can contribute to its performance, such as innovations, a cohesive culture, or good implementation. Competitive strategy is the search for a favorable arena in which competition occurs. Competitive strategy aims to establish a profitable and sustainable position against the forces that determine industry competition.[11]

By casting the issue of competition into the subject of how companies gain and sustain competitive advantage, Porter helps investors to keep their eye on what matters most in company performance: Whoever captures the value produced by an industry reaps the greatest benefit. And that quest for competitive advantage to gain the value-capturing prize of better profitability and growth is tied to the degree or intensity of competition between and among firms within an industry. It also is a function of the bargaining position of a company vis-à-vis its buyers and suppliers. All five factors (or forces, as the good professor calls them) are key to determining who will capture the value produced. Let's review Porter's work.

The Five Forces of Competitive Strategy

Most companies operate within a highly competitive environment. A myriad of issues is at play at all times that will either enhance a company's competitive advantage or diminish it. There are:

- Existing firms competing for every dollar spent.
- New firms seeking to enter the space.
- Substitute products seeking to replace the existing ones.

Moreover, the buyers and suppliers are a force to be dealt with as they must be served and managed. Porter has taken these five factors and created his famous Five Forces of competitive strategy, which are classified as:

1. Rivalry among existing firms.
2. Threat of new entrants.
3. Threat of substitutes.
4. Bargaining position of buyers.
5. Bargaining position of suppliers.

The first three forces—rivalry among existing firms, threat of new entrants, threat of substitutes—describe the intensity of competition within an industry. Whoever has the advantage gets the value produced. For example, if Company A has a larger market share and greater profitability, that company is clearly capturing most of the value produced. It has higher margins of profit, lower uncertainty of future profit production, and the potential of further market share gains.

But what if two competitors have an equal or near-equal standing? Who captures the value produced? The answer is it all depends on the state of aggressiveness between the two firms. For example, if the two firms engage in what could be called a "live and let live" approach to competition, then both firms benefit from the competitive situation. If, however, our two companies of equal strength and position engage in a quest for greater market share, then the buyer would benefit and the firms would not as the competitors will likely engage in price cutting or greater marketing expenses, both leading to a potential erosion of profits, margins, and growth rates. In effect, the actions taken can clearly be at the expense of the competitors and to the benefit of the buyer. In this case, the value produced accrues to the buyer.

As a consequence, the more intense the competitive environment is between and among firms, the lower the growth rate and profitability will be for the companies involved. The implications for valuation are clear: The more intense the rivalry, the greater the risk to growth and profitability. All three inputs to valuation are impacted in a negative way. To prove my point, what industries can you think of that fit this description of intense rivalry? And what has been their stock market performance?

In looking at the last two forces—bargaining position of buyers, bargaining position of suppliers—the impact to value can be seen in the following examples:

- Company A is a large and important buyer of goods and services from its supplier, Company X, providing more than 40 percent of Company X's revenues. The odds favor Company A as having the relationship advantage over Company X, and Company A is thereby likely to receive more favorable treatment in both price and contract terms (recall the accounts payable topic).
- Company B is a small buyer of goods and services from Company Y. But Company Y has many competitors and has to fight hard for Company B's business. The odds favor Company B getting the better of the deal, as Company Y knows Company B's switching costs to go to another supplier are likely lower than if there were fewer suppliers.
- Company C is a retailer to a fairly crowded segment of the consumer market. Customer Z will likely gain the value benefit through lower prices because Company C has lots of competitive company.

Each simple example highlights the potential for serious impacts to the valuation model inputs. Cash flows, growth of the cash flows, and risk will be impacted by the competitive climate. Just the kind (positive or negative) and the degree (high or low) of impact matter.

Here are the factors and subfactors that the first three forces face:

Rivalry Determinants
- Industry growth.
- Fixed (or storage) costs/value added.
- Intermittent overcapacity.
- Product differences.
- Brand identity.
- Switching costs.
- Concentration and balance.
- Informational complexity.
- Diversity of competitors.
- Corporate stakes.
- Exit barriers.

Entry Barriers
- Economies of scale.
- Proprietary product differences.
- Brand identity.
- Switching costs.
- Capital requirements.
- Access to distribution.
- Absolute cost advantages:
  - Proprietary learning curve.
  - Access to necessary inputs.
  - Proprietary low-cost product design.
- Government policy.
- Expected retaliation.

Determinants of Substitute Threat
- Relative price performance of substitutes.
- Switching costs.
- Buyer propensity to substitute.

And here are the factors and subfactors that impact buyer and supplier situations:

Determinants of Supplier Power

- Differentiation of inputs.
- Switching costs of suppliers and firms in the industry.
- Presence of substitute inputs.
- Supplier concentration.
- Importance of volume to supplier.
- Cost relative to total purchases in the industry.
- Impact of inputs on cost or differentiation.
- Threat of forward integration relative to threat of backward integration by firms in the industry.

Determinants of Buyer Power

Bargaining Leverage

- Buyer concentration versus firm concentration.
- Buyer volume.
- Buyer switching costs relative to firm switching costs.
- Buyer information.
- Ability to backward integrate.
- Substitute products.
- Pull-through.

Price Sensitivity

- Price/total purchases.
- Product differences.
- Brand identity.
- Impact on quality/performance.
- Buyer profits.
- Incentives for decision makers.

Needless to say, there is a robust dynamic between and among each of these items. The circumstances in one area will almost certainly impact those in several others. Moreover, and most importantly, the forces and strategies directly impact profitability.

Consider the example of Coke and Pepsi:

- Coke and Pepsi are rivals within the soft drink industry. They are the two dominant companies in that industry and set the standard by which competition is measured. If Coke and Pepsi have a "live and let live" attitude toward each other, then the intensity of that rivalry is low. Low rivalry means more money for the two behemoths as the need to cut prices (and thereby profit margins) is reduced.[12]

- For the most part, Coke and Pepsi sell their products to individual consumers. The product is a low-priority, low-cost expenditure for most consumers, and therefore is not a high-cost priority when making a purchase. Therefore, the bargaining position of Coke and Pepsi vis-à-vis their customers is on the side of the companies.
- Several years ago, an alternative soft drink provider emerged on the scene: Snapple. Snapple offered soda drinkers an alternative to their standard fare. This new entrant did, for a time, cut into the profit potentials of Coke and Pepsi. The threat as a substitute was real and thereby created a competitive force that Coke and Pepsi needed to respond to. Had Snapple's growth continued at its earlier pace, the threat could have eventually cut into Coke's and Pepsi's core products in a meaningful way, thereby creating a competitive atmosphere that would have reduced the profitability of the two leaders.

This basic example of the Five Forces at work highlights the common-sense need to understand the competitive environment and the resulting impact on who will retain the value created within the industry.

How Relevant Are Porter's Principles Today?

Although the world has changed quite dramatically since the early 1980s when Porter produced his methodology for analyzing the factors that determine who captures the value of an industry through competitive advantage, most of the factors listed still hold in the twenty-first century. How companies compete and succeed depends in very large part on the ferocity of competition within the industry and the plans and action steps companies take to cope with the competitive situations they are faced with. To state the obvious, the plans and action steps take the form of strategy. To this end, Michael Porter recognized that a solution to the problems and challenges of competition was needed. He offered a basic framework for analysis called the Three Generic Strategies.

Three Generic Strategies

Most companies have very sophisticated strategies that enable them to effectively address the competitive factors they face. However, regardless of how complex a competitive environment might be and how complicated the strategies of a company are, nearly all forms of competitive strategy can be reduced to one of three categories:

1. A company seeks to be low-cost leader.
2. A company seeks to differentiate itself from its competitors.

3. A company focuses its efforts on a defined economic sector—geographic, demographic, or psychographic.

Porter categorizes these three strategies in his response to the five competitive forces as the Three Generic Strategies of:

1. Cost leadership
2. Differentiation
3. Focus

The strategy of cost leadership is defined by Porter as a company seeking "to become *the* low-cost producer in its industry."[13] *Note:* Porter states that for companies competing on the basis of price, it is not enough to be *a* cost leader—for that simply states that an intense competitive atmosphere could exist with other cost leaders, thereby reducing the profit and growth potential for all cost leaders. What Porter states is that a strategy of cost leadership means a company seeks to be *the* cost leader. The difference between being *the* cost leader and being *a* cost leader could be the difference between high profitability and growth versus low profitability and growth.

The other primary generic strategy is differentiation. Differentiation is defined by Porter as a company seeking "to be unique in its industry along some dimensions that are widely valued by buyers. It selects one or more attributes that many buyers in an industry perceive as important, and uniquely positions itself to meet those needs. It is rewarded for its uniqueness with a premium price."[14] Companies that can distinguish themselves from their competitors are in a better position to get customers to pay them a premium price.

Going back to our Coke and Pepsi example, for most people soft drinks are not a necessity (although many parents may beg to differ), soft drinks are a discretionary purchase made on the basis of price and image. "The Pepsi Generation" and "The Real Thing" are just two examples of the imagery that Pepsi and Coke have engaged in over the years. This is a differentiation strategy at work.

Focus is "quite different from the others because it rests on the choice of a narrow competitive scope within an industry. The focuser selects a segment or groups of segments in the industry and tailors its strategy to serving them to the exclusion of others."[15]

Every company must have a competitive strategy that fits the competitive environment in which it operates. Someone is going to gain the economic benefit of a product or service. The only question is who. Will it be the provider of the product or service? A rival company? A new entrant or substitute product? The buyer? Or the supplier?

Having the right competitive strategy increases the odds that a particular company will be able to capture the value being created. And capturing the value created means three things for investors:

1. Greater profit potential.
2. Greater growth potential.
3. A lower uncertainty or risk factor.

An investor needs to gain a good appreciation of the dynamics of the Five Forces and the application of one of the appropriate Three Generic Strategies[16] that companies must employ in order to gain competitive advantage.

THE POWER OF RATIO ANALYSIS

Armed with a foundation in the basics of competitive advantage and headed ever closer to our first goal—learning what the true economic profit of a business is—we can now dig more deeply into the business process with the aid of several key financial statement ratios.

Ratio analysis is an essential element of investment analysis. Ratios help us compare apples to apples by enabling us to look at the level and trend of a company's performance in a clear and comparative manner. For example, if a company's growth in sales revenues and growth in net income from one year to the next were both exactly 15 percent, an investor might correctly conclude that top-line and bottom-line growth were exactly the same. At least numerically they were. But it would be a mistake for an investor to conclude that the performance over that period was even and equal. The expense items between sales and net income may have been anything but even and equal. Consider the following simplified example:

	Year 1	Year 2	Rate of Growth
Sales	$10,000,000	$11,500,000	15.0%
Cost of Goods Sold	3,000,000	3,600,000	20.0
Gross Profit	7,000,000	7,900,000	12.9
Sales, General, and Administrative (SG&A)	−6,000,000	7,000,000	16.7
Earnings before Taxes	1,000,000	900,000	−10.0
Taxes	−400,000	−210,000	−47.5
Net Income	600,000	690,000	15.0

As this very simple example shows, there is a lot of stuff between the top line and the bottom line that we need to know. But this is a rather cumbersome way to view the year-over-year performance of a company, especially when we start looking at multiyear periods. The solution to our problem is what is known as a common-sized statement.

A common-sized statement is simply the listing of each item on a financial statement in relation to one number. In the case of the income statement, the key number is sales. Every item on the income statement is divided by the sales number, which gives us the particular item as a percentage of sales. Therefore, instead of calculating each individual income statement line item on a rate of growth basis, we reflect each item as a percentage of sales. Taking our simple example, we then get the following:

	Year 1	Percentage of Sales	Year 2	Percentage of Sales
Sales	$10,000,000	100%	$11,500,000	100%
Cost of Goods Sold	3,000,000	30	3,600,000	31
Gross Profit	7,000,000	70	7,900,000	69
SG&A	–6,000,000	60	7,000,000	61
Earnings before Taxes	1,000,000	10	900,000	8
Taxes	–400,000	4	–210,000	2
Net Income	600,000	6	690,000	6

Notice how much easier it is to see the performance changes year over year. And while the bottom-line percentage of sales is the same (it would be since the growth rate year over year is identical to the top-line sales number), the differences in operating performance provide a helpful insight into several key aspects of the true economic performance of the company. For example, look at the earnings before taxes figure. In year 2 it actually declined. So did the gross profit figure, on a percentage of sales basis.

Now let's move things a little further and deeper and consider measures of performance that take into consideration the return on the assets of the firm, in particular the return on the equity of the firm.

The assets and liabilities of a company are the stuff of the balance sheet. At this point, what we are most interested in from the balance sheet are the total assets and the equity. With that information we will do a little ratio analysis with the sales and the net income figures from our income statement. The four figures—net income, sales, assets, and equity—will be the basis for another staple of equity analysis: the Dupont formula.

DECOMPOSING ROE: THE DUPONT FORMULA

The Dupont formula is the decomposition of the return on equity (ROE) of a company. ROE is calculated by dividing the equity of the firm (as stated on the balance sheet) into the net income figure from the income statement.

$$\text{ROE} = \frac{\text{Net Income}}{\text{Equity}}$$

Just as the net profit margin (net income divided by sales) is a measure of the profitability of a company, ROE is also a measure of corporate performance: how effectively a company is utilizing its equity. After all, as investors, we are most interested in the asset to which we have a claim: the equity. And the return on that equity is important to us.

Taking our simplified example again, assume that the equity of the company is the following:

	Year 1	Year 2
Equity	$6,000,000	$6,700,000

Then the ROE would be:

	Year 1	Year 2
Net Income	$ 600,000	$ 690,000
Equity	$6,000,000	$6,700,000
ROE	10%	10.3%

ROE increased slightly in year 2, suggesting that the performance of the company has produced results that equity investors would favor. Yet, just as before, we have interesting information that really doesn't tell us much about the true performance of the company. Now, here is where the beauty of the Dupont formula comes into play.

The Dupont formula is a decomposition of ROE. It is the breaking down into several component pieces of ROE thereby enabling us to see what we could not see with the net figure. And once again we have a simple and elegant but insightful ratio analysis at our disposal.

The decomposition of ROE is:

- Net income divided by sales.
- Sales divided by assets.
- Assets divided by equity.

When we represent this information in a formula it looks like this:

$$ROE = \frac{\text{Net Income}}{\text{Sales}} \times \frac{\text{Sales}}{\text{Assets}} \times \frac{\text{Assets}}{\text{Equity}}$$

Notice how with a little simplification we can cancel out sales and assets and we end up with net income divided by equity equals ROE. But the decomposition of ROE enables us to measure three metrics of corporate performance:

1. Profitability
2. Efficiency
3. Leverage

- Net income divided by sales is the net profit margin of the business.
- Sales divided by assets is known as the asset turnover ratio.
- Assets divided by equity is financial leverage of the business.

Profitability × Efficiency × Leverage = ROE

Now let's apply ROE to our example to see if we can gain some insight.

	Year 1	Year 2
Net Income	$ 600,000	$ 690,000
Sales	10,000,000	11,500,000
Assets	12,000,000	12,000,000
Equity	6,000,000	6,700,000

Our formula then works out as shown:

Year 1

$$\frac{\$600,000}{\$10,000,000} \times \frac{\$10,000,000}{\$12,000,000} \times \frac{\$12,000,000}{\$6,000,000} = 10\%$$

$$.06 \quad \times \quad .83 \quad \times \quad 2 \quad = 10\%$$

Year 2

$$\frac{\$690,000}{\$11,500,000} \times \frac{\$11,500,000}{\$12,000,000} \times \frac{\$12,000,000}{\$6,700,000} = 10.3\%$$

$$.06 \quad \times \quad .96 \quad \times \quad 1.79 \quad = 10.3\%$$

In this basic example, we can trace the improved ROE to the better utilization of assets (increase in the asset turnover ratio, sales to assets). At the same time, the company become slightly less leveraged as its financial leverage ratio declined (from 2 to 1.79).[17]

SUSTAINABLE GROWTH

At this point, we are now within a ratio or two of getting to our first goal of calculating the free cash flows of a business, which brings us to the growth of future cash flows. The basic formula for determining the growth of the future cash flows incorporates return on equity and how much of that return is retained by the business. The basic method for calculating this is to take ROE and multiply that figure by 1 minus the dividend payout ratio.

The dividend payout ratio is the percentage of net income that is distributed to investors. One minus that percentage gives us the net amount retained by the firm and, therefore, available for reinvestment by the company into itself.

For example:

ROE	24%
Dividends per Share	$.50
Net Income per Share	$2.00
Dividend Payout Ratio	25% ($1/$2)
1 – Dividend Payout Ratio	75% (1 – .25)

With this data, calculating the amount of money (as a percentage) that the business can reinvest in itself (its sustainable growth rate) is easy:

ROE × (1 – Dividend Payout Ratio)	Sustainable Growth Rate (g)
24% × .75	18%

This means that the business is capable of growing at a rate of 18 percent, and therefore the free cash flows can grow at this rate.[18]

GROWING THE FUTURE CASH FLOWS

With the ability to calculate the current cash flows of a business and its sustainable growth rate, it is now possible to combine the two and project what a company's future cash flow stream will look like. The basic version of this calculation is:

- Determine the current cash flows generated by the company.
- Apply the sustainable growth rate to the current flows.

Before we begin to work our basic example, we need to add one more piece of data to the equation: the duration in years for our projected sustainable growth rate. For illustration purposes, let's assume that the sustainable growth rate of 18 percent will continue for the next two years, after which it will decline to 6 percent to infinity. Going back to our first example, the numbers work out as shown:

	Net Income	$4,000,000
+	Depreciation	+ 800,000
−	Capital Expenditures (Capex)	− 1,200,000
+/−	Change in Working Capital	− 400,000
=	Free Cash Flows of a Company	$3,200,000

	Today	Year 1	Year 2
Free Cash Flows	$3,200,000	$3,776,000	$4,455,680
g		18%	

Easy enough. But cash flows produced in future years are not cash flows in today's dollars. Nor are the future cash flows a guaranteed event. There is the uncertainty factor to consider. The final item to include in our cash flow formula is the uncertainty or risk factor. This factor is known by several names: the discount rate, the cost of equity, the opportunity cost of capital. Whatever the name, calculating the formula is the same.

DISCOUNTING THE FUTURE: THE COST OF EQUITY

Since we are discounting the future equity cash flows of a business, we need a formula that reflects the riskiness of those cash flows. The concept of discounting the future is fairly straightforward: in process, it is the mirror image of our sustainable growth rate. We grow the cash flows through multiplication. We discount the cash flows by division.

Assume for a moment that the future cash flows we projected are to be discounted at a rate below the growth rate. Let's use 12 percent as an out-of-thin-air number. Therefore, the cash flows we grew at an 18 percent rate would be worth the following sum in today's dollars:

	Year 1	Year 2
Free Cash Flows	$3,776,000	$4,455,680
Discount Rate	12%	25.44%

The formula then works out as shown:

Free Cash Flows	$3,776,000	$4,455,680
Discount Rate	1.12	1.2544
Present Value	$3,371,429	$3,552,041

A few quick points:

- To discount the future value of our cash flows, we need to add a 1 to the .12 (12 percent) discount factor to make the formula work. Therefore, for the discount factor in the formula we divide the cash flows by 1.12.
- The 25.44 percent second-year discount factor is a result of multiplying 1.12 by 1.12, thereby getting 1.2544 (1 plus 25.44 percent). This is done because we are discounting two time periods.

But an out-of-thin-air number is not how we get to the appropriate discount factor. We need something that is tied to the risk involved with the cash flows of a business. For that we turn to the capital asset pricing model (CAPM). CAPM is the flawed but widely accepted formula used to discount the future equity cash flows of a business.[19]

The formula to calculate CAPM is:

Risk-Free Rate × Beta × (Expected Return on Market − Risk-Free Rate)

where the risk-free rate is the 10-year U.S. Treasury rate; beta (the volatility of the stock of the company) is used as a proxy for risk; and the expected return on the market is either the expectation of the one-year return for the broad-based market averages (S&P 500 as the proxy) or the historical return for equities.

With CAPM, we have the ability to calculate the cost (the uncertainty) of owning the equity (stock) of a company. Therefore, CAPM is also known as the cost of equity. With CAPM, we can bring our future cash flows back to present value as the discount factor that is connected directly to the company whose cash flows we are discounting. Here's how to calculate CAPM.

Assume the following:

10-Year U.S. Treasury	5%
Expected Return on Market	12%
Beta of Our Company's Stock	1.2

The formula works out as:

$$\text{CAPM} = 5\% + 1.2(12\% - 5\%)$$
$$= 5\% + 1.2(7\%) = 13.4\%$$

Note: Since the stock is 20 percent more volatile than the market (beta at 1.2), it stands to reason that the required return for investing in this slightly more risky stock (as opposed to investing in the market overall via an index fund) would be higher than the market. And that brings us to the highly debatable issue of using beta as a proxy for risk.

RISK

Equities are risky assets. Unlike fixed income investments, they do not have a set maturity. When it comes to business and investing, risk can be calculated in many ways. A very short list includes:

- Everyday operating risks of running a business.
- Opportunity risks of choosing one business investment over another.
- Liquidity risks of not being able to meet the cash needs of a business.

Thanks to the efficient markets hypothesis (EMH), the use of beta in the CAPM as the surrogate for risk is the acknowledged measure of the risk of investing in the stock of a company. The EMH assumes, among many things, that capital markets are efficient and that in their efficiency the volatility of the stock of a company captures the riskiness of the company. Therefore, according the EMH and CAPM, the use of beta as a proxy for risk is acceptable. As I stated, this is a highly debatable subject and a discussion is outside the scope of this book. However, let me bring this point to your attention:

An investor is advised that using a backward-looking metric for risk (beta is the past volatility of the stock), he/she is ignoring the illogic of using the past to discount the future. Therefore, beta is best used as a starting point and, based on an investor's judgment (there's that word again), the investor should adjust beta to project a future beta, which potentially captures more accurately the risk of the future stock performance.

Risk cannot be avoided. It must be managed. As you will note in Chapter 3 on the elements of an effective portfolio, the concept of managing risk is front and center. As it relates to valuation, beta will have to suffice as our risk input. And CAPM will also have to suffice as our discount factor.[20]

THE TERMINAL VALUE OF A BUSINESS

Well, we have finally arrived at the last piece of our valuation puzzle, the one that deals with that fateful day when we have to say good-bye to our investment. After all, nothing lasts forever. No one lives forever. Nor do companies grow forever. In this respect, the life cycle of a business resembles the life cycle of a person: There is an end. And while there may be fewer limits as to how fast a company can grow (at least in its early growth phase), there is most definitely a limit as to how long a company can grow at an above-market rate.

Given that law of nature, investors should consider that there will come a time when a company's above-average growth rate will taper off to a more mature rate of growth. This is not to mention the obvious fact that stocks are held to be sold—eventually. Therefore, when that day comes, the potential sale should be considered a form of cash flow and, accordingly, that cash flow needs to be discounted back to its present value.

The computational aspect of this is no different from the discounting of all the other cash flows. You use the same methodology, viewing the final year as producing two cash flows: one actual, the other from the sale of the stock. That sale value is also known as the *terminal value*.

Let's see how this works.

CALCULATING THE INTRINSIC VALUE OF A COMPANY

At last! We have reached the point in which all the elements of valuation have been presented and described and we are now ready to put them to work in the basic valuation formula used to determine the intrinsic value of a company.

The three inputs are:

FCF	Free cash flows
g	Growth of the free cash flows
k	Risk (in the form of a discount factor)

We take the free cash flows and grow them at an appropriate growth rate. We then take each future period's cash flows and bring them back to the present value using the cost of equity. We then add each period's present value, including the terminal value. (See Table 1.1 through Table 1.3.)

Let's assume that the current free cash flows of the business are $4 million, the growth projected for the next five years is 18 percent, the growth thereafter (until infinity) is 6 percent, and the discount rate is 12 percent (see Table 1.1).

We can then grow our free cash flows at the higher short-term growth for the first five years, determine the terminal value of our company in year 5 (see Table 1.2), discount each to the present value, and add them up as shown in Table 1.3.

Therefore, the intrinsic value of a company producing $4 million in free cash flows today is $115,188,188.

TABLE 1.1 Free Cash Flow Growth Rates

Free Cash Flows	$4,000,000
g (5)	18.00%
g (Forever)	6.00%
k	12.00%

Source: iViewResearch.

TABLE 1.2 Terminal Value

Free Cash Flows in Year 5	$9,151,031
Free Cash Flows in Year 6	$9,700,093
k − *g*	6.00%
Terminal Value	$161,668,215

Source: iViewResearch.

TABLE 1.3 Free Cash Flow Projections

	Year 1	Year 2	Year 3	Year 4	Year 5		Year 5
Free Cash Flows	$4,720,000	$5,569,600	$ 6,572,128	$ 7,755,111	$ 9,151,031	TV	$161,668,215
Discount Rate	1.12	1.25	1.40	1.57	1.76		1.76
Present Value	$4,214,286	$4,440,051	$ 4,677,911	$ 4,928,513	$ 5,192,541		$ 91,734,887
Cumulative	$4,214,286	$8,654,337	$13,332,248	$18,260,761	$23,453,302		$115,188,188

Source: iViewResearch.

VALUATION MATTERS

The valuation model and the inputs that go into it make up the bottom line to all the research and analysis that we will conduct. It is the perspective that an effective investor comes from when analyzing the real and financial economy. It is the final point to which all our research analysis leads. It is the context within which the macroeconomic analysis, the geopolitical analysis, the industry analysis, the company-specific analysis, and all the other aspects of my research process are viewed. For it is not my goal to understand and analyze the three components of my research methodology of government, economy, and the market (GEM) for their individual or collective sake. Rather, understanding the impact to the valuation model is what matters most. It is one of my critical variables.

For the product of the valuation model—the value of an asset—is what the investment game is all about. Do good work in all areas of analysis, work hard, and be thorough, but never lose sight of the fact that what happens in the real and financial economy is valuable to an investor only if he/she can distill that information down to the formula used to determine the value of the asset—the inputs of the valuation model.

But what exactly are the valuation model inputs? And how does focusing on the inputs enable an investor to make better investment decisions?

Three Inputs, One Powerful Tool

As covered in this chapter, the basic valuation model is fairly simple. It is comprised of three inputs:

1. The economic profits of a business.
2. The growth rate of those economic profits.
3. The uncertainty (or risk) of not seeing the projected growth rates come to pass.

There are variations on this theme, which I reference later in the chapter and throughout this book, but conceptually they are the same: What does or can a company earn? At what rate does what the company earns happen? And just how certain can we be that the growth rate will come to pass? Put differently, the three inputs are profitability, its growth, and the risk to that growth. In these three elegant and simple inputs an investor has all he/she needs to understand companies, industries, and markets. Sounds like a stretch? Not really. Let me explain.

At the end of the day, the social science known as investing involves the analysis and opinions of investors who will determine what value to place on assets. In technical terms, it is the present value of the future cash flows (the economic profit) of an asset that determines its value. (This subject and its methodology are covered in detail in the next chapter.) But the concept of value is a human invention—one that requires an understanding of human nature and the conflict between rational and irrational behavior in determining value. As stated earlier, the process for determining what is known as the intrinsic value of an asset is fairly straightforward—you take the economic profit of today and forecast its growth rate. You then reflect that future economic profit in today's dollars (or euros or yen or currency of your choice) by discounting it using a calculation that incorporates the opportunity cost of investing elsewhere and the riskiness (a/k/a uncertainty) involved. This process is call the discounted cash flow method—the most widely accepted formulaic approach to determining the value of an asset. And, as you will see in the next chapter, the process of calculating the intrinsic value is not an overly complicated one. In fact, the most basic version, the Gordon growth model, is so simple to calculate, anyone could do it with a simple three-function calculator (add, multiply, and divide). Actually, the calculating is the easy part. The hard part, the very hard part in fact, is getting the inputs right.

For example, a change in interest rates will have a significant impact on the valuation model inputs because it makes alternative investments like short-term fixed income instruments more attractive vis-à-vis stocks. This then increases the odds of more money being invested in bonds and less money being invested in stocks. A rise in interest rates also raises the cost of capital, which reduces the value of stocks as calculated in valuation models such as the discounted cash flow model. An increase in the cost of capital is an increase in the discount factor of the future economic profit, and that typically results in a lower value for a stock. Lastly, a rise in interest rates increases the borrowing costs for businesses, thereby impacting the income statement of a business; this is likely to lead to a reduction of the company's profitability and growth rate, resulting in a lower valuation.

This example demonstrates the importance of how changes in interest rates can impact a company and its stock in various ways—all of which impact several elements of the valuation model.

Flights of Investment Fancy

A good way to illustrate this issue of simplicity and complexity comes from a book on investment analysis by Robert Higgins, *Analysis for Financial Management* (McGraw-Hill, 2003), in which the author equates investment analysis and valuation modeling to flying an airplane. Higgins states that flying an airplane, be it a two-seat Cessna Skyhawk or a jumbo jet, is based on exactly the same principles of aerodynamics: lift, drag, and thrust. Every plane flies on these three principles—including our small Cessna and our large jumbo jet. The principles that enable one plane to go forward, up, down, right, and left are the same principles for the other; the only difference between the two aircraft is complexity. Well, the same is true of valuation. The only difference between determining the value of an asset and getting the correct inputs to the formula is complexity. There are many moving parts, and some that are interactive, thereby causing an effect on the other. That leads to a great deal of hard work in getting the data for the inputs right. But the core concept of the inputs is beautiful in its simplicity.

Therefore, the first aspect of valuation that must be appreciated is the fact that the simplicity of the model belies the complexity of being right about the inputs. And because the economy (domestic and global) is a dynamic place, a highly interactive place, a place where uncertainty is high, getting the inputs correct is the holy grail of valuation. It's not an easy task, which takes us to another concept that needs to factored into our valuation equation—interactive feedback.

The real economy is highly interactive and interdependent with the financial economy. And while they may appear to act in isolation, the truth is that what occurs in the real economy has a profound impact on the financial economy (the markets). And vice versa. A term that describes this dynamic, interactive, interdependent world we live in is *reflexivity*,[21] coined by billionaire George Soros.

We live in a very dynamic world in which various actors impact each other, producing a fairly highly unpredictable environment at times. It is a world in which companies operate, produce products and services, and manage their resources, and they must understand this world well enough so that they can produce economic profits and growth with the least amount of uncertainty. With so many moving parts, companies have their work cut out for them. For investors, there are the added layers of investor expectations; investor emotions like fear and greed; reliable company, industry, and market information capture and analysis; and macro environmental impacts and influences such as governmental action and monetary policies, to name a few. Turning all this data and information into correct inputs into financial models of companies and industries and then into valuation models is a very, very hard thing to do consistently.

RATE OF RETURN > COST OF CAPITAL

The 1980s marked a key turning point and a power shift away from corporate America and to Wall Street. And while the decade will be most remembered for the scandals of Ivan Boesky, Michael Milken, and other masters of the universe, it was also the starting point for the emergence of independent financial managers with clout—money managers who could demand that the senior management of publicly traded companies adhere to value creation principles and move away from perks.

The demands made to the corporate managers were in the form of earning a rate of return in excess of their cost of capital, thereby *creating and not destroying value*. This revolution, while at times taken to extremes over the past two and half decades, has helped transform how companies are managed. Corporate strategies have been impacted by independent financial managers.

A central component of the independent financial managers' approach was a near obsession with creating value.

Earning a rate of return in excess of the cost of the capital possessed by a firm was the mantra. New methodologies such as Stern Stewart's economic value added (EVA) and Holt's cash flow return on investment (CFROI) became the rage. The value-creation craze even found its way to Wall Street analysts as several major Wall Street firms began incorporating value-based approaches (as they were known) into their research methodologies.

The importance of all this and the value to investors is how the dynamics of managing a business changed. Senior corporate management could no longer ignore the imperative of earning a rate of return on invested capital in excess of the cost of that capital.

Whether in regard to a stock investment or a business investment, the issue is the same: Investing involves a risk/reward trade-off. That trade-off must be made by producing a rate of return that is greater than the required return. If not, value is destroyed, because the opportunity cost of not utilizing that money elsewhere at a rate greater than the required return is a value-destroying proposition. This development is profound as it has changed the economic and investment landscape dramatically over the past several decades and has led, no doubt, to the improved managerial skills of corporate leaders today. Senior management knows that the capability of financial managers, not to mention other more growth-oriented and acquisitive corporate leaders, will step into the picture and take the assets of the business away from existing management in the form of a merger or acquisition and attempt to earn a rate of return in excess of its cost of capital, its required return. This development has literally changed corporate America.

THE ART OF VALUATION

If valuation were a magic potion concocted in a test tube, it could be considered two parts calculation and one part judgment, or some such mixture. No one knows exactly what the formula is. And that is where the next phase of modern finance will take us—into the heart of the investor. Yes, we know the *objective* mind, but we cannot calculate the *subjective* heart. Yes, we know how to calculate the present value of the future economic profit, but we cannot determine with great accuracy how rational investors will be. Nor can we ascertain exactly how the future will unfold—how the economic landscape, the technological landscape, the competitive landscape, the geopolitical landscape, and the like will look years from now. Yet somehow we investors must exercise our best skills and best judgment to determine what the inputs might be.

In the case of investor behavior, the tools at our disposal today will have to do, as they provide us with an imperfect but productive way of making investment decisions. In the following chapters, I describe how to blend the objective and the subjective into the valuation model inputs, thereby producing a comprehensive investment strategy and, ultimately, an effective portfolio.

Investing, as you will see frequently mentioned throughout this book, is a social science. And a social science means people, with all their wants and needs and fears and desires. In other words, it is people and not programs that are at the center of the process. From the early days of the modern finance era, which began in the 1950s, attempts have been made by academicians to divorce the personal or human factors from the valuation process and depict investors as rational, risk-averse, and capable of assessing an investment opportunity and making a dispassionate, unemotional decision to act. That is the basis of the modern portfolio theory (MPT) and the efficient markets hypothesis (EMH). But logic and now facts from the research of a new wave of academics schooled in the principles of behavioral finance have blown holes in the dispassionate investor myth that is based on MPT and EMH. In fact, it is amazing that it took so long to prove that investors are not always rational, not always risk-averse. Sometimes they are irrational, overexuberant, or excessively pessimistic. In other words, when it comes to money and investing, people can and do react to their "animal spirits" of fear and greed and act accordingly. (The story, however, is a little more complicated. Consider the pressures on that breed of investor called the professional money manager, a/k/a portfolio manager, discussed on page 72.)

With a base established in sound valuation principles, we can now move on to our next topic: the development of our investment strategy.

CHAPTER 2

Investment Strategy:
Concepts and Principles

With our valuation principles and processes firmly in hand, we are now ready to take the next step toward building and managing an effective portfolio: the creation of a well-thought-out, well-developed investment strategy.

Investment strategy begins with a set of core beliefs. These core beliefs are our guiding light that enables us to frame the investment strategy issue. The core beliefs are then applied to the conclusion reached from our intrinsic valuation models. The valuation models give us the theoretical intrinsic value of an asset. However, the intrinsic value is a benchmark number upon which other factors must be brought to bear—factors such as various market metrics, investor psychology, and divergences. For it is the investment strategy conclusions, partly derived from our valuation work and partly derived from our market metrics, that give an investor the best chance of implementing the sectors and styles investment approach advocated in this book.

Once we have our investment strategy in place, we can then move on to the single most important investment decision an investor will make: the asset allocation decision. As it is the dominant determinant of investment performance, special attention is paid to getting the asset allocation decision right. At least, that is what we try most earnestly to do.

INVESTMENT PHILOSOPHY

Not to get overly philosophical, but it is our beliefs that guide us in all phases of life. This is true in our outlook on life and relationships and, of course, on money and investing. It's how we frame issues so that we can make intelligent decisions in the highly uncertain world of investing. Therefore, when it comes to matters of money and investing, having a philosophy in the form of a set of consciously decided guidelines is not just helpful but necessary. For, whether we like it or not, whether we are aware of it or not, we cannot make any decisions on any subject without a set of guidelines. This observation brings us to a brief discussion on decision making.

Every moment of every day is composed of acts based on decisions that we make. The simple ones—what to eat, what to wear, which route to drive to work or school, and so on—are made based on our experiences and preferences. The more important and complex ones involve decisions made under uncertainty. Decisions made under uncertainty are the stuff of politics and war. They are also the stuff of business decisions and investing. As to investing, it is where behavioral finance has gone and where modern finance is headed. It is a field of study that would be well worth every investor's while to explore more fully. But not here and not now. Understanding the basic rules and guidelines on decision making is our aim right here.

There are many very good books on decision making that describe the process. One that I have found to be a particularly helpful book for understanding the basics of decision making is James G. March's *A Primer on Decision Making* (Free Press, 1994). In it March classifies decision making into two major categories—limited rationality and rule following. Limited rationality is described as "seeing decisions as based on an evaluation of alternatives in terms of their consequences for preferences." Rule following is described as "the logic of appropriateness by which actions are matched to situations by means of rules organized into identities." And in his book, March introduces the reader to several key concepts, including those developed by behavioral scientists Daniel Kahneman and Amos Tversky. Kahneman won the Nobel Prize for Economics in 2002 for his work in behavioral finance. As noted earlier and as you will see later in the book, behavioral finance is altering the investment landscape in many ways and specifically impacting the investment strategy and portfolio management process.

So, understanding how and why we make the decisions that we do is an important factor that should not be left to our unconscious. Rather, decisions should be thought through and decided upon consciously. When it comes to how I form my investment strategy, I rely on two beliefs:

1. Critical variables
2. Judgment

These two beliefs anchor all that I do and why I do what I do. Let's look at each.

CRITICAL VARIABLES

With apologies to George Orwell and the citizens of Animal Farm, "All things are equal but some things are more equal than others." In other words, knowing what matters most is always a valuable skill to have in life. In my opinion, when it comes to investing, this is especially true.

Some investors believe that more is better: more data, more contacts, more hours worked, more of everything. However, in an age of an abundance of information, more can sometimes be a hindrance to good decision making. It's like the old axiom of failing to see the forest for the trees. Or, as another good friend of mine once said, "getting tangled up in your underwear." Having access to more is better, but more data must be tempered with discretion. Judgment must be exercised in determining just what matters most and we must concentrate most, but not all, of our efforts on those critical variables that have the greatest impact on the subject we are analyzing. In many respects, my critical variable belief is a lot like the asset allocation decision and its impact on performance, or the valuation focus on the impacts to the valuation model. If asset allocation is the overriding determinant of investment performance, then why spend a disproportionate time on matters that do not directly aid in the asset allocation decision? If, when it comes to determining value, what impacts the valuation model matters most, then why spend a disproportionate amount of time studying industry or company data that does not meaningfully impact that valuation model input?

Now, I do agree that more is better. But I also believe that less is more. A paradox? Not really. By concentrating on what matters most, the critical variables, I have found that my analytical time is more productively used, as everything that I study leads me to make more effective decisions more quickly, and therefore frees up my time and energy to consume more data than I could otherwise.

In effect, a focus on the critical variables will enable an investor to concentrate on the key inputs and outputs of analysis *and* create more time to be even better informed and more productive.

It is worth noting that in the parlance of decision making, my critical variables are an attempt to create mental shortcuts that enable me to manage the very large and complex world we live in. Since my investment strategy decisions are based on an understanding and analysis of government, economy, and the markets (GEM), I must distill the world into a more manageable set of guidelines. Relying on identifying the critical variables, the issues that matter most, makes the process manageable and, therefore, the issues understandable. In fact, this is the essence of strategy, as described by management expert Kenichi Ohmae in his book *The Mind of the Strategist* (McGraw-Hill, 1982) when he states, "The first stage in strategic thinking is to pinpoint the critical issue in the situation." When faced with the massive scale and scope of GEM, it is disastrous to not condense the mountain of data. More importantly, however, is the 80/20 rule: 80 percent of anything comes from 20 percent of everything. This is a rule that applies to the asset allocation decision and one that I advocate as just plain common sense. Put another way, failing to see the forest for the trees is a bad way to manage anything.

JUDGMENT

My second core belief is the value of judgment.

The fundamental valuation process described in Chapter 1 produces an intrinsic value that serves as the basis on which a comparison can be made between the market price of an asset and this intrinsic value. Depending on certain important factors (such as risk and correlation), the spread between the market price and the intrinsic value will determine whether the asset should be held, bought, or sold.

Investing can also involve a so-called black box methodology. Quantitative models factor numerous variables, show tendencies and biases, and spew out algorithms designed to identify attractive investment opportunities and capitalize on them.

Both processes, and many others, generate a number that in effect says "go" or "no go." For some, that go or no go decision is a fairly straightforward call using the market price–to–intrinsic value number derived and any portfolio-specific considerations (investor preferences, needs, and obligations). But for me and others who acknowledge that investing is a hard-to-quantify social science, that human behavior is involved, I have chosen to incorporate that all-important subjective factor called judgment.

Investment success comes only through a complete understanding of the principles of good investment analysis. And having the right tools to execute your analysis and strategy puts the average investor on a level playing field with the professional investor. Yet, while the core principles described in this book are relatively easy to grasp and the tools to execute the process have been made available, it is an investor's experience and insights that combine with the data and valuation model recommendations to help an investor ultimately decide how much to invest (asset allocation) and what sectors and styles to invest in.

In my view, when it comes to successful investing, *judgment is king!*

STRATEGY AND PLANNING: THE COACH'S ROOM

I like to think of the creation of an investment strategy as the equivalent of being a football coach. Consider the following:

Developing an accurate investment strategy and creating and maintaining an effective portfolio contains two distinct steps: planning and execution. The planning portion itself consists of two steps, with the first being the analysis of the real economy and all the valuation component inputs that help determine what the true or intrinsic value for the market, sectors, industries, and individual companies *should* be. This is the game plan. We analyze, then calculate what *should* happen. But the game is not played in the coach's room. It happens on the field of battle—in the markets. Therefore, the second step of the process is an assessment of how the game is being played.

Think of it this way: In all endeavors shrouded in uncertainty (war, business, and investing, for example), what *should be* is often not *what is*. For despite all the planning and analyzing about what should be the correct valuation level for the market, sector, industry, and company, the truth may lie elsewhere. It is this disconnect between the intrinsic value derived and the actual price level set by the market that is the essence of famed investor George Soros' "reflexivity"[1] and the value in bringing other measurements—market metrics—into the process. It is therefore essential to the investment strategy process that the field of play (the markets) must come into the equation. But before we get to the actual process, it is worth our while to explore the whole issue of strategy.

WHAT IS STRATEGY?

All the talk about investment strategy begs the question, "What is strategy?" After all, there isn't an investment strategy school that an investor or portfolio manager can attend to earn his/her investment strategy degree. In fact, the primary professional organization for investment analysts, the CFA Institute, does not offer a course, much less a degree, in investment strategy. So, before we go too deeply into the investment strategy forest, let's consider for a brief moment just what strategy is.

One definition that I found particularly helpful in defining strategy comes from the former McKinsey & Company partner and acknowledged strategy and management expert Kenichi Ohmae:

> *Analysis is the critical starting point of strategic thinking. Faced with problems, trends, events, or situations that appear to constitute*

a harmonious whole or come packaged as a whole by the common sense of the day, the strategic thinker dissects them into their constituent parts. Then, having discovered the significance of these constituents, he/she reassembles them in a way calculated to maximize his/her advantage.

In business as on the battlefield, the object of strategy is to bring about the conditions most favorable to one's own side, judging precisely the right moment to attack or withdraw and always assessing the limits of compromise correctly. Besides the habit of analysis, what marks the mind of the strategist is an intellectual elasticity or flexibility that enables him to come up with realistic responses to changing situations, not simply to discriminate with great precision among different shades of gray.

In strategic thinking, one first seeks a clear understanding of the particular character of each element of a situation and then makes the fullest possible use of human brainpower to restructure the elements in the most advantageous way.[2]

These words were written in the early 1980s but are just as valid today. Ohmae goes on to describe the process of strategy and introduces the concept of what I call the critical variables:

When resources of capital, people, and time are as scarce as they are today, it is vital to concentrate them on key functional or operating areas that are decisive for the success of your particular business. Merely allocating resources in the same way as your competitors will yield no competitive edge. If you can identify the areas which really hold the key to success in your industry and apply the right mix of resources to them, you may be able to put yourself into a position of real competitive superiority.

Identifying these key factors for success is not always easy. Basically, the strategist has two approaches at his disposal. The first is to dissect the market as imaginatively as possible to identify its key segments; the second is to discover what distinguishes winner companies from losers, and then to analyze the differences between them.[3]

While Ohmae's words are directed primary to company managers, they are useful for our purposes on two levels:

1. They help us to understand what constitutes good business management.
2. They provide us with a philosophical foundation and process upon which investment strategy can be built.

Let me elaborate on both points.

An essential ingredient of investment strategy is the understanding of what constitutes a successful company. This topic was covered in Chapter 1 on valuation principles. What Ohmae adds to that knowledge base is the process of strategy development for a company:

- "Dissect the market as imaginatively as possible to identify its key segments."
- "Discover what distinguishes winner companies from losers."
- "Analyze the differences between them."

The dissection process allows for a decomposition of a whole, similar to the decomposition of return on equity (ROE) described in Chapter 1. And it makes logical sense. For when you break down a larger entity into its component pieces, you can then clear the path for determining the key factors for success. And you are then an important step closer to determining the critical variables. For example, when analyzing an industry's competitive environment, evaluating each of the Five Forces independently helps an investor to see the dynamics within that one area under review. That enables the investor to then look for the interconnected links that have a cause-and-effect relationship.[4] Applying the decomposition principle to a business helps determine the underlying drivers for success—the critical variables that we want to keep our eye on.

The second value of Ohmae's advice and the decomposition process applies to our goal of creating a successful investment strategy.

While there are some investment strategies that are narrow in focus and scope, the approach described shortly, GEM, is comprehensive, which is to say that it is wide in scale and scope. That's just another way of saying, "There's a lot of stuff to monitor." And whenever we are faced with a mountain of "stuff to monitor," it is very easy to get lost in the forest for the trees. In other words, the threat of information overload is real. Therefore, what is needed is a way to winnow the chaff from the wheat and get to what matters most: our fabled critical variables.

SO, WHAT IS A SUCCESSFUL STRATEGY?

The formulation of a successful strategy rests first in the core beliefs and the process of decomposition. Combining the core beliefs of the critical variables and judgment with the principle of decomposition forms the basis on which a good investment strategy can be created. When used in conjunction with our intrinsic value calculations and key market metrics, we have the solid foundation of an effective investment strategy.

What we must do now is understand the interactive dynamics of the financial markets and their interactive (reflexive) role.

THE FIELD OF PLAY: THE ROLE OF TECHNICAL ANALYSIS AND MARKET METRICS

As stated, assessing the real economy and coming to our conclusions about the intrinsic value of an asset or group of assets are, in my opinion, only the first half of the investment decision-making/portfolio-construction process. The important next step is to take into consideration what the market has to say about this. We may have determined that our intrinsic valuation work points to a rate of return in excess of our cost of equity and, therefore, we should buy the market (or a particular sector or style). But the market may be sending a very different signal.

To be up-front about this, there are a great many fundamental investors who pooh-pooh technical analysis. They call it "voodoo analysis," relying on charts and graphs to predict the future direction of the market and its segments. As noted in Chapter 6, the arguments against technical analysis are rooted in the belief that there is little consistently reliable information in the market trading and investor psychology data. I beg to differ, but let's leave that for Chapter 6 and assume for the moment that technical analysis has value.

There are also a great many closet technical analysts: investors who peek at the charts and give credence to market metrics like investor psychology and fund flows in and out of managed accounts like mutual funds. I prefer to be direct about it and utilize technical analysis, as I believe the market's message carries valuable information that can provide great insight into what investment strategies do work. In this way, technical analysis allows an investor to compare and contrast the real and financial economies to each other.

BACK TO THE COACH'S ROOM

As stated, investment strategy begins with an assessment of the real economy and the valuation model inputs. We figuratively sit in our coach's room planning what should be, based on the intrinsic values we have determined. We then factor into the equation the market metrics provided to us via a technical analysis of the financial economy, the market. We are then ready to finalize our point of view and make our investment strategy call: bullish, bearish, or neutral. After all, stocks move in only three directions: up, down, or sideways. Getting this right drives the base asset allocation decision (which then gets modified for each individual investor according to his/her risk tolerances, goals, and needs).

With the process understood, a brief description of the GEM approach to evaluating both the real and financial economies is in order. Each topic is covered in detail in Chapters 4, 5, and 6.

INVESTMENT STRATEGY: GEM

Every investor must have a research process by which an analysis of the real or financial economy takes place and investment decisions can be made. For me, I have found that it is useful to understand the three components of economic and business life:

1. Role of government (primarily the political aspects).
2. The economy (both domestic and global).
3. The markets.

The government, economy, and the markets (GEM) approach to investment strategy formation is fairly comprehensive. But the value to an investor can be enormous as the interplay between and among each segment and their consequent impact upon the markets themselves is frankly how the world works. For example, to ignore the impact of the loss of political power is to ignore the impact to economic policies of the party whose power is at risk. In today's terms, anything that diminishes President George W. Bush's political power puts at risk his, and his party's, ability to control economic policy. Additionally, from a market's reflexive perspective, the economic power inherent in a higher stock market capitalization impacts consumers (via the wealth effect) and corporate competitiveness (on both a company and a country basis).

In my view, only a GEM approach can capture the issues that impact the direction of the market. And, after all, isn't that what investment strategy is all about—to get the strategy call, the asset allocation call, the sector and style call right? In my view, whatever it takes is what must be done. For me, GEM gets it done.

SUMMARY

Understanding the concepts and principles that underlie an effective investment strategy is a key factor of success. Thinking through what underpins our approach to decision making is not just helpful, it is necessary. Therefore, having a firm grasp on our beliefs enables us to make better decisions. The Socratic phrase "Know thyself" applies.

With our beliefs in tow, we can assess the real and financial economies most completely using GEM, or something like it. That analytical process brings us to our valuation inputs, which are then compared and contrasted with the message of the market. The end result is an effective investment strategy, thereby enabling sound asset allocation and sector and style decisions.

Now let's consider the dynamics involved in creating an effective portfolio.

CHAPTER 3

The Essential Elements of an Effective Portfolio

"Effective: *Having the right effect, or getting the job done.*"
—Jack Lynch
Associate Professor
English Department, Rutgers University

Getting the job done.

An effective investment strategy, one that hopefully forecasts the future with a fairly good degree of accuracy, begets an effective portfolio. What constitutes an effective portfolio and what distinguishes it from an ineffective portfolio lie in the ability of the investor to build and maintain a rate of return that exceeds an investment's required return. This is no small task. For as with the valuation process, the formulations are easy but getting the inputs right—and getting them right consistently—is extremely difficult.

There are always stories of investors with the hot hand. Portfolio managers jump to the top of the media pile with appearances on television to strut their investment stuff, bellowing out advice on what's hot and what's not. Sadly, however, those who follow the prophet du jour generally do not get wealthy in the process. In other words, there are no shortcuts to sustainable investment performance.

The portfolio process described in this chapter, Core Plus, is more tortoise than hare; more quiet confidence versus bellicose braggadocio. Consistency is the effective portfolio mantra. And if an investor adheres to the process described, even if one gets it wrong and screws up the damage is more than tolerable and the loss quite easily recoverable.

With that said, let's proceed.

CREATING AND MAINTAINING EFFECTIVE PORTFOLIOS

Investors invest. And successful investors are very sensitive to what is known as the asset/liability match: the matching of assets and opportunities with need. To this end, let's begin to understand some of the basics of portfolio construction, including the all-important principle of diversification.

THE PC, THE NET, AND THE EFFECTIVE PORTFOLIO

In the Introduction, I presented the justification for this book: the convergence of the personal computer (PC), the Internet, and exchange-traded funds (ETFs). The tools that the trio offers must be applied to a process to be valid. For despite all their wonderful advantages and benefits, personal computers and the Internet, on their own, cannot enable an investor of average or modest means to construct and maintain *an effective portfolio.* Yes, as noted in the Introduction, the PC and the Net do make investment research easier, more efficient, and far more cost-effective. Yes, the PC and the Net do make managing and monitoring a portfolio far more easy and productive. And yes, the PC and the Net do enable investors to get to that all-important asset allocation decision more efficiently. But, there is something that the PC and the Net cannot do: enable an investor to properly diversify his/her assets. To take investment matters to the next step, we need an investment vehicle that will enable us to construct and manage portfolios *effectively.* That's where exchange-traded funds (ETFs) come into the picture.

ETFs TO THE RESCUE

An effective portfolio is one that seeks to minimize risk and maximize opportunities through the intelligent use of the all-important principle of diversification. An effective portfolio is a portfolio designed to give an investor the edge—the competitive advantage—he/she needs to produce consistent investment results. An effective portfolio employs the principles of diversification to its advantage.

Portfolio diversification is an underappreciated aspect of successful investing that most individual and many professional investors fail to fully appreciate. In fact, diversifying within an asset class comes second to the single most important factor in achieving consistent investment performance—the asset allocation decision.

As for diversification, some might ask why it is necessary. Why is it best to build and maintain a well-diversified portfolio? The answer to that question lies in another proven fact: Diversification decreases portfolio volatility while enabling an equal or greater return. Because of the mathematical facts of correlation (the price movement of one asset vis-à-vis another), a well-diversified portfolio is a less volatile and therefore a less risky portfolio. Additionally, a well-diversified portfolio enjoys a rate of return that is often equal to or greater than the return an investor might receive from a less diversified, more concentrated portfolio. Finally, portfolios that are more concentrated and therefore less diversified are destined to be subject to the mercy of overconcentration in sectors, in industries, geographically, and from an investment style perspective, and, therefore, subject to its consequences. As a result, there are two points to make:

1. A less diversified portfolio is almost always a more volatile one than a well-diversified one. (The exception would be a heavy concentration in sectors, styles, and stocks that individually have very low volatilities.)
2. Overconcentration almost always leads to greater risk that hopefully will be rewarded with a greater return—with *hopefully* being the operative word.

The final point I wish to make on the issue of diversification is the issue of playing not to lose. We all want to win, and win consistently. A major part of winning is minimizing the risk it takes to win, and to do that it is most important that investors consider that playing not to lose is an important part of winning. For there are times when the unknowable becomes even more unknowable. That is to say, despite our best efforts to analyze the economic and investment world we live in, there is much that we just don't know. Events occur that are wholly unexpected; exogenous events such as terrorism or natural disasters or uncontrollable circumstances brought about by the lack of transparency of financial instruments, to name a few, produce a situation of making investment decisions with less than perfect information in a highly uncertain environment. Then there is the added issue of human nature.

Buy low, sell high is a wonderful idea but one that human nature often gets in the way of. Many times fear and greed run rampant. And investors, being the less than perfectly rational human beings that they are, become even less rational and often get swept up in the emotion of the moment. That is how bubbles and panics are formed. Moreover, as investors try to outsmart each other, issues like justification for extreme overvaluation or undervaluation get wrapped in phrases like "liquidity-driven markets." Diversification helps counteract the failings of human nature by insisting that no one area is overexposed and, therefore, the risk of being economically adversely impacted is minimized.

Bottom line: A well-diversified portfolio is vital to your financial health. Exchange-traded funds are the everyman's tool for achieving that goal.

Exchange-traded funds, by their very nature, provide the most cost-effective and performance-effective way of constructing and maintaining an effective—that is, diversified—portfolio by enabling an investor to do what heretofore only a person with a considerable amount of money *and* a considerable amount of resources could do. Here's why:

In the time before ETFs, to achieve the all-important diversification necessary for sustainable investment performance, an investor had to mimic professional investors—build and maintain fairly large portfolios with lots of stocks, lots of sector exposure, and lots of style exposure. To achieve this required a considerable amount of money (both within a portfolio and for research services) and the time and skill necessary to monitor the myriad of companies and stocks to make the right portfolio decisions. Few investors and financial managers of more modest means have such time and resources to, in effect, *do the right portfolio thing*. In other words, creating and maintaining a properly diversified portfolio is a hard, but necessary, thing to do. Exchange-traded funds make this possible.

Exchange-traded funds are simple yet powerful investment tools that, above all else, provide investors with the wherewithal to cost-effectively build a portfolio designed to maximize return and minimize risk through diversification. ETFs are the intelligent investor's investment instrument upon which an effective portfolio can become a cost-effective reality. As a recent Merrill Lynch report so aptly describes it:

> *ETFs give investors access to entire portfolios of stocks or bonds through a single exchange-traded instrument. Within the equity universe, ETFs offer investors a wide array of investment choices including the ability to invest based on sector, size & style, as well as a vehicle to easily invest in international equities. While they may be less attractive for investors with strong stock-specific views, ETFs are convenient for implementing diversified top-down investment decisions for investors not wanting to manage large portfolios of individual stocks.*[1]

Therefore, unless an investor can spend a lot of time and money mimicking professional money managers monitoring hundreds of individual companies and their stocks, the ability to benefit from an effective portfolio is beyond their means. That is, until now.

The real power of an ETF-built portfolio rests in the ability of an investor to cost-effectively create a portfolio that provides exposure to the broad economic sectors and styles that comprise the equity markets. But there is something else, something that unfortunately far too many investors often lose sight of, that using ETFs to achieve an efficient portfolio helps to emphasize: *placing the investment focus where it belongs—on strategy.*

In my 30-plus years on Wall Street, I have consistently been amazed at how few investors, mostly nonprofessionals, truly understand the importance of asset allocation and diversification and how they, and not the individual stocks, are the primary forces of investment results. The data I noted earlier on asset allocation is a well-documented fact and speaks volumes for itself. It is where I spend the majority of my research time and effort—focused on the macro and micro environments, from a top-down and bottom-up perspective, from a real economy and a financial economy perspective. When 85 to 90 percent explains anything, it warrants 85 to 90 percent of my time. The side benefit of using ETFs as the core of your investment portfolio (see the next section, "Core Plus") is that it literally forces an investor to focus on strategy and away from the nonproductive exercise of trying to outsmart and outperform the market through stock picking. Stock picking may be good for television ratings and it certainly is a lot of fun when you get it right, but it should not be the center of an investor's attention. When it comes to making money consistently, asset allocation followed by a well-diversified portfolio is the means to that end.

If you have accepted what I have presented thus far, then you are probably now ready to better understand the portfolio construction process I advocate and offer for your consideration. Therefore, let me describe to you my version of the core of effective portfolio managers—overweight or underweight the sectors of the market. I call it "Core Plus."

CORE PLUS

Core Plus is the term that I use when describing the tilting or biasing of a portfolio in a particular direction. It is a portfolio construction process by which sectors and styles are emphasized or deemphasized. It is the weighting process of the 10 economic sectors our portfolio will have. This is where most institutional investors start and where you should, too, particularly if you will follow a sectors and styles approach to investing. In other words, Core Plus is simply the construction of an effective portfolio through diversification by overweighting or underweighting the 10 economic sectors.

The concept of portfolio management guided by the degrees of exposure to the 10 economic sectors is at the root of what most professional portfolio managers do. For example, if an investor is bullish on the Energy sector, he/she would own more Energy than the market weight of Energy (e.g., if Energy comprises 10 percent of the S&P 500, an investor bullish on the Energy sector might invest 15 percent of the portfolio in that sector). Obviously, the opposite applies as well. For example, say an investor is bearish on Technology. He/she would underweight that sector (e.g., if Technology constitutes 17 percent of the market, the investor who is bearish on Technology might own 10 percent of that sector). The same applies from a style point of view. Say an investor believes that mid-capitalization stocks are more attractive than large or small caps. The investor can overweight mid-cap stocks (e.g., if mid-capitalization stocks as reflected by the S&P 400 constitute 7 percent of the total market cap, then an investor bullish on mid-cap stocks might put 15 percent of the equity portion of the portfolio assets in that sector). Then there is the concept of playing one sector against another. Say, for example, an investor believes that U.S. consumer spending is about to rise dramatically; then the investor might own more of the Consumer Discretionary sector and, at the same time, short the more conservative Consumer Staples sector. The investor is betting that consumer spending for big ticket items (cars, durable goods like washers and dryers, furniture, etc.) is on the rise, and then the stocks that comprise the Consumer Discretionary sector will rise more than the stocks that make up the Consumer Staples (food, basic necessities, etc.) sector.

Finally, the ability to apply the concept of creating and managing a portfolio on a global basis exists. Say, for example, an investor believes that after more than a decade of underperformance Japan had finally turned the corner and the Japanese stock market looks more attractive relative to other markets. An investor could reduce his/her ownership of U.S. issues and put money into that market. Of course, the principles of portfolio diversification could begin with a global perspective, and, therefore, the concept of Core Plus could be applied to a globally diversified portfolio. The combinations are many: sectors and styles, domestic and global, sector to sector, even from a quality level (high quality versus medium quality versus low quality). The possibilities and mixtures are almost limitless. And that is all made possible in a cost-effective way thanks to ETFs.

Now that we have introduced the premise of Core Plus, let's look at the top-line driver to Core Plus and the single most important investment decision an investor will make: the asset allocation decision.

ASSET ALLOCATION

Now, when it comes to utilizing the power of the PC and the Net, the asset allocation decision is by far the single most important fruit of that labor. As numerous studies have shown, the *asset allocation decision (the proportion of stocks, bonds, and cash) explains 85 to 90 percent of the investment results of a well-diversified portfolio.* And, as you will see shortly, a well-diversified portfolio is key to an investor's chances of achieving a *consistent rate of return* equal to or greater than the rate of return he/she could achieve otherwise.

By enabling an investor to improve the quality of his/her investment research, the PC and the Internet have changed the face of the investment analytical process. This is to the good; it is very good, in fact. The PC and the Net have empowered all investors with the tools necessary to make better-informed investment decisions and, hopefully, a better and more consistent asset allocation decision. Our job as investors is to determine to the best of our ability the right investment strategy and then to construct and manage the portfolios that incorporate the equity exposure decided upon in arriving at the asset allocation decision.

PUTTING IT ALL TOGETHER:
GEM + CORE PLUS + ETF = CONSISTENT RESULTS

When exchange-traded funds (ETFs) came along and became available to every investor, regardless of the amount of their investable assets, the significant benefits previously reserved for institutional investors—the ability to effectively allocate one's assets by economic sectors and investment styles (by market capitalization, by growth, by value, etc.)—were now within the reach of all investors.

All effective portfolios must have one other ingredient to make money on a consistent basis—an effective investment strategy, one that is rooted in an analysis of both the real economy and the financial economy. The real economy is the world we live in, the place where goods and services are produced and consumed. The financial economy is the place where assets are created and bought and sold—in other words, the markets. Only by studying and understanding *both* economies—real and financial—can an investor understand the assets that we invest in *and* the markets' assessment of those assets. To understand and study one without understanding the other is, in my opinion, a prescription for mediocrity at best and failure at worst.

The more comprehensive your investment analysis and the investment strategy therefrom, the better the odds are of making money consistently. ETFs are my preferred investment tool because they accomplish for me what is needed most—to keep my eye on the investment ball and not get lost in the trees of individual issues.

The problem with owning individual stocks is that because so much can go wrong and the risk (volatility) of owning a relatively low number of stocks is greater than with a large, well-diversified number, the chances of underperforming the market are greatly increased. And even if an investor is fortunate enough to have the right mix for the right moment, that doesn't mean that what's in favor or what's hot will stay in favor or hot. In other words, unless you can construct a well-diversified portfolio like a major portfolio manager does, the odds are stacked against you. The investment version of Murphy's Law (anything that can go wrong will go wrong) works overtime in the stock market.

Consider, for a moment, all the moving parts of investing in individual stocks that must work correctly for you to make money consistently.

- The market must be the right place for your money. Asset allocation is king.
- The economic sector must be the right place for your money.
- The industry must be the right place.
- The company must be the right one.
- The market must agree with you on all of the preceding points.

Talk about a tall order.

SUMMARY

Working off the base or recommended portfolio produced, the creation of an effective portfolio must be tailored to the individual needs of an investor. The assets available for investment (today and tomorrow), the comfort level with loss (risk tolerance), and the obligations to be met in the future (asset/liability match) are three of the most important considerations in the creation of one's effective portfolio. Once they have been determined, the Core Plus strategy can be employed according to an investor's specific needs. The tilting or biasing of the portfolio toward one sector or another, one style or another, one country or region or another can then take place. From that point, maintaining the portfolio and adjusting to the ever-changing GEM factors become the daily operations involved. If the decisions made are correct, there are positive results. The worst-case scenario, however, should be only a modest possible underperformance.

GOOD COMPANY VERSUS GOOD STOCK

In a related field, and one that helps crystallize the distinction between fundamental and technical analysis, lies the issue of the good stock versus the good company.

There is a well-known, but often underappreciated, Wall Street axiom that states that "a good company doesn't always make a good stock." Just because the prospects for the company are positive or the financial strength, profitability, and growth prospects are exceptional, this does not necessarily equate to the stock being a good investment. This is so for a variety of reasons, the most prominent of which is valuation. If a stock price already reflects all the good that the company has to offer, then the stock may not be a timely, worthwhile investment. And what is true for individual stocks is also true for sectors and industries.

A sector or an industry may have terrific growth prospects or exceptional financial strength and stability but may be so fully valued that any increase in market value may be limited or below the required return. As my good friend the ISI Chief Investment Strategist Jason Trennert puts it, "One of the greatest difficulties for both individual and professional investors alike is to keep in mind that some of the best companies can sometimes be the worst investments. The difference between the prospects for a company and the prospects for its stock often part ways due to valuation." Jason goes on to say, "Many market participants employ the greater fool theory of investing, whereby little attention is paid to an asset's intrinsic value as long as there exists someone else, similarly unconcerned about valuation, ready to buy."[2]

However you phrase it and whatever asset you are considering, the issues of value and judgment cannot be avoided. A good stock (or sector or industry or style) may not be a good investment.

JACK OF ALL TRADES, MASTER OF SOME

In the Introduction, I presented a few caveats so that the expectations of what this book can and cannot do were made as clear as possible. I must now take a moment to provide a modest cautionary note on the issue of formulating an investment strategy based on GEM.

The approach to investing advocated in this book does require a considerable amount of ongoing work. It also requires a fairly good level of knowledge in all three areas of GEM. What it does not require, however, is that an investor must be an expert in all three areas at all times. This is not to say that an investor need not have a fairly thorough understanding of each of the GEM components. Quite the contrary. The more and deeper the understanding the better. But here is where the critical variables and judgment factors come into play. This is where determining what matters most comes into play. This is where judgment and not rigid rules comes into play. This is where hard work can really pay off.

Note: The story of portfolio managers and their nonrational motivations directly relates to behavioral finance's loss aversion and regret factors. As a link between the principles of an effective portfolio and the area of behavioral finance (discussed in Chapter 6), it is a story worth telling.

KEEP MY HOUSE IN GREENWICH

Portfolio managers are a competitive bunch. They have to be, for it is the comparative performance of their results matched up against a market benchmark (the S&P 500, for example) or their peers (fellow portfolio managers with whom they are in constant competition) that determines whether they keep the money they have under management (earning money management fees) from going to their competitors and are able to obtain additional money from underperforming portfolio managers. Moreover, the pressures to perform are often measured on the basis of fairly short-term results. The pressure to equal or better their benchmark and their competitor portfolio managers is tracked yearly, quarterly, even monthly. Such pressures may do strange things to a person who has, at a minimum, a lifestyle to maintain (such as keeping their house in tony Greenwich, Connecticut).

This situation reminds me of the story about two guys in the woods who come upon a hungry bear. As the bear begins to chase them, the two men begin to run. One man turns to the other and says, "I hope we can outrun this bear." The other replies, "No, I only have to outrun you." The hungry bear of change is always on the prowl seeking its next meal, which every portfolio manager knows could be himself. The objective, therefore, is to outrun (that is, outperform) the other guy. Well, outrunning the other guy is often not possible, since the act of doing so means placing investment bets that are at odds with what the other guy is doing. And that means risking the chance of *under*performing the competition. Well, why chance that? Why not play it safe and invest in a manner that is close to the other guy but just different enough to give you a chance of outperforming yet not being at risk of severely underperforming the competition should your investment bets be wrong? As you can see, the same applies to a portfolio manager and the benchmark.

If a portfolio manager wishes to beat the market and, at the same time, not want to take the chance of severely underperforming that benchmark (and thereby greatly increase the chances of losing business), he/she might build a portfolio that is close to the benchmark but with a slight tilt in one direction or another—for example, overweighting a sector or two (say Energy and Health Care) and underweighting another sector or two (perhaps Technology and Utilities). The over- and underweighting would, of course, be by a modest amount, even if the portfolio manager is very bullish on Energy and Health Care and very bearish on Technology and Utilities. Why take the chance?

My little story illustrates what behavioral finance experts would call *loss aversion*. Loss aversion is a nonrational, but very pragmatic, aspect of portfolio management life. It is a form of the regret factor, as an investor just does not want to regret the actions he/she takes and, therefore, ensures the avoidance of such pain. What I have described is the antithesis of the rational, dispassionate investor. It is, among other real-world factors, what behavioral finance experts have quantitatively proven, and common sense has dictated, about how the investment world really works. And loss aversion and the regret factor are just two of many examples of how value, like beauty, is very much in the eye of the beholder.

Allow me to introduce the concept of the holding period return. The issue of what to buy must take into consideration its expected return and whether that return warrants the risk taken. This is another manifestation of the earlier-noted earning a rate of return in excess of the cost of capital. In constructing an effective portfolio, the same principle applies: Don't invest in something that does not earn you a rate of return greater than your required return.

CONCEPT CHECK: IS IT A BUY, SELL, OR HOLD?

Premise: A stock is purchased in the anticipation that it will be sold in one year. Given the following data, is this return on this investment a buy, sell, or hold?

Intrinsic Value	$40
Market Price	$30
Gain	$10
Holding Period Return	33%
Required Return	15%

Premise: The same stock is purchased in the anticipation that it will be sold in one year. Given the new data, is this return on this investment a buy, sell, or hold?

Intrinsic Value	$33
Market Price	$30
Gain	$3
Holding Period Return	10%
Required Return	15%

Although both investments are projected to produce a positive rate of return, in the first case the return is a buy. In the second case, the return is a sell. In the first case, at 33 percent the expected return is greater than the required return. In the second case, a 10 percent return is below the required return. Therefore, given the level of risk involved, the second case generates an insufficient rate of return for its level of riskiness.

BEATING THE MARKET

There are three fundamental premises to nearly every investment book—you are reading this book because you want to find a way to (1) make your financial assets produce a return that will enable you to live the lifestyle you aspire to, (2) do this within the risk parameters you are comfortable with, and/or (3) consistently produce investment returns in excess of a return you could receive if you were to manage your money with a neutral asset allocation mix, which is 60 percent stocks, 40 percent bonds. Your investment goals will fall into one or more of these categories.

Implicit in point (3) is a desire to beat the market. And as numerous studies have shown, this is far easier said than done. Take, for example, the comments of Charles D. Ellis in his excellent book, *Investment Policy*:

> The only way to beat the market, after adjusting for market risk, is to discover and exploit other investors' mistakes. It can be done. And it has been done by most investors some of the time. But very few investors have been able to outsmart and outmaneuver other investors enough to beat the market consistently over the long term.
>
> Active investment can work on any or all of the four investment vectors:
>
> 1. *Market timing.*
> 2. *Selection of specific stocks or groups of stocks.*

3. *Changes in portfolio structure or strategy.*
4. *An insightful, long-term investment concept or philosophy.*[3]

Charlie goes on to describe the third investment vector, portfolio strategy:

Strategic decisions—in both stock and bond portfolios—involve major commitments that affect the overall structure of the portfolio. They are made to exploit insights into major industry groups or changes in the economy and interest rates or anticipated shifts in the valuation of major types of stocks such as "emerging growth" stocks or "basic industry" stocks. Each of these judgments would involve what can be described as market segment risk.[4]

The central point in Ellis's comments is that an effective portfolio is one that is effective for your wants and needs and not some arbitrary benchmark.

Creating an Effective Investment Strategy: GEM in Action

THE PREMISE OF GEM: CONNECTING THE DOTS

GEM (government, economy, and the markets) is a concept that I conceived several years ago while producing and conducting the Market Forecast events for the New York Society of Security Analysts. After creating the moderated format for the programs back in the fall of 1997, I realized that the talent I secured to discuss the topic of an outlook on the market required a discussion into the areas that impacted the market. Instinctively, the areas were the obvious ones—the economy and the markets—but in time, it became apparent that the political dynamic also was key to the market's performance. I did not know it at the time, but I was creating the seeds for a research methodology that most professional investors already employed but in an often fragmented way: GEM. For example, most professional investors have access to experts on economic and industry matters. Some have access to (and, importantly, care about) the political dynamic. But, to my knowledge, no one had attempted to pull it all together into a unified investment strategy.

What was obvious to me but not so obvious to many others was the interplay between and among the three components. This was vividly the case as I prepared for and conducted the events as moderator. Researching the three disciplines and interconnecting them at the events made it clear to me that it was to my and the attendees' benefit if we could connect the dots. Couple this with the fact that cause and effect can and do flow between and among groups that are interrelated. Therefore, when it came time to strike out on my own and create my own research and consulting business, GEM became an obvious investment strategy process I would follow.

The next three chapters explore each segment of GEM. Whether you choose such a comprehensive approach or follow one or two areas and not all three, I hope you will find value in the words and process.

CHAPTER 4

The Investment Importance of Politics and Government

The central theme of this chapter is how political power begets economic power. Let me explain.

After love and war, nothing is more fascinating, confusing, and frustrating than politics. Given government's scale and scope and the role it plays, the impact on all facets of life is profound. However, in the minds of the vast majority of investors, the investment importance of government to the markets tends to be restricted to its more traditional roles—regulatory and legislative. From my perspective, these are important and necessary areas of understanding and analysis, but there is another area of equal if not greater importance—the economic power of political power.

Let me clear: Rules and laws are important, as they do impact business. They can tilt the balance of competitive power in one company or industry's favor over another. For example, regulation is often a significant barrier to entry because the rules and the costs to comply with them can be insurmountable burdens for would-be competitors. Additionally, the laws on the books can have the same impact—tilt the balance of competitive power—not to mention the pork that spews out of government (federal, state, and local) that ends up in the pockets of the power brokers.

These points are all true and important, but there is another dynamic that is underappreciated by most investors: the power dynamic, specifically how political power connects to economic power.

Political power begets economic power. Those who control the levers of political power have the greatest potential to set the agenda on and control the economic policy of the single most important player in the economic arena: government. Control the levers of power, and the goods will be delivered to those who helped get officials elected.

Now, for most professional investors (and I assume most readers of this book), what I have written is logical and obvious but hard to quantify. As in the discussion on behavioral finance in Chapter 6, there is no formula like the capital asset pricing model (CAPM) that we can plug into our valuation models and help us determine the intrinsic value of a stock. Yet, the markets do move according to the ebb and flow of political power. In fact, consider the U.S. stock market's performance during the Watergate scandal. Does any knowledgeable investor really doubt that the investing public's confidence was shaken during that period and thereby had an impact on the market? Given the expectational nature of investors, it is the future that concerns us. If policies change, so too will the expectations of the future. And that moves markets.

Economic and social factors provide a dynamic scenario for investors—if only they had a way of evaluating the behemoths called government. I propose that, as difficult as it may be to quantify, investors try to incorporate the political power dynamic, because it does play a significant role—more significant than many give it credit for doing. Accordingly, this chapter presents a few ideas about how to gauge the impact of the political on the economic.

Given the fact that this is a very subjective area, the best way I can describe the central theme of political power begetting economic power is to illustrate it with a few examples beginning with the hot-button item of the past several decades: the culture wars in the United States.

CULTURE WARS AND POLITICAL POWER

They say that watching politics in action is a lot like watching sausages being made—it's better left unseen. But for our purposes we are going to dig into this process and perhaps make a tasty (as in useful to investing) sausage. And we will begin with a few recent real-world examples that I wrote about in my weekly research commentaries, beginning with the so-called culture wars that have been raging between liberals and conservatives in the United States for the past several decades.

Building over time and a major factor in deciding the outcomes of several key U.S. elections, the culture wars between conservatives and liberals have had an indirect impact on the economy and the markets. This is not a mainstream view, however, since cultural issues are not traditionally viewed as having a meaningful impact on the economy and markets. I take a distinctively different perspective.

The significance of the culture wars with regard to the economy and markets lies in their impact on the other element of my GEM (government, economy, and the markets) approach: government—specifically, the levers of power. An example of this was seen in the seemingly unrelated tragedy that occurred in the spring of 2005 when a brain-damaged woman became the focal point of a power struggle between those advocating the right to die and those who champion the pro-life cause. It was the case of Terri Schiavo, and if one could see a bit more deeply into the matter, the issue of who gets and keeps the power controls the economic agenda.

The Political Trinity:
The Economic and Investment Significance of Terri Schiavo[1]

On the surface, it might appear that the tragedy and pain of a brain-damaged young woman and the political and social drama surrounding the situation would have little significance to the economy and the markets. But looks can be deceiving.

The economic and investment significance of Terri Schiavo rests in the attempt of one faction of what I will call the Political Trinity to exercise extraordinary political influence. And in that attempt, it may have seriously damaged the most powerful force in American politics today.

The Political Trinity is the Republican coalition of the strongly religious, the wealthy, and corporate America. It is by far the most formidable force in politics today. It is the epicenter of socioeconomic change in the United States. It is the driving force of economic and political policy. And anything that damages that coalition threatens the Trinity and its ability to maintain power.

The economic and investment implications concerning the struggle over the life of Terri Schiavo reside in the fact that for the first time the Trinity has suffered a serious loss—the consequences of which are yet to be fully understood.

For several decades, a coalition of the strongly religious, the wealthy, and corporate America has been evolving. And, despite a brief flirtation with the triangulation strategy of Bill Clinton, it has found its home primarily within the Republican Party. It is a broad and powerful coalition that will be highly influential for many years, possibly decades to come. This is a point that is little known to the vast majority of Americans who are not clued in to the broad grassroots base and the sophisticated strategy and communications machinery, not to mention money. And it is a point that most investors fail to fully appreciate. As Thomas Frank so accurately points out in his book, What's the Matter with Kansas? *(Henry Holt, 2004), the persistent (and seemingly never-ending) rage of the one class of Americans against some oppressor (which today is the so-called liberal elite) has pro-duced a mutually beneficial coalition between the religious (rep-resenting the oppressed), the wealthy, and corporate America. And while it is beyond the scope of this report to get into all the details and nuances of this major force, it is best to think of the Trinity this way: The religious win elections, and the wealthy (moderate, country club Republicans) and corporate America win the benefits.*

While Frank and others puzzle over why Kansans and other lower- and middle-class Americans would be willing to "vote against their economic interests," the economic and investment implications are clear: Wealthy Americans and corporate America reap the benefits in the form of lower taxes and more laissez-faire economics. This is what market fundamentalism is all about. But all power bases must be very careful not to overreach. And yet that is precisely what appears to have happened with the U.S. Congress. The bold attempt on the part of the religious wing of the Trinity to exercise its power by pressuring the U.S. Congress into enacting a law designed to produce a different result in the Schiavo case has failed.

And in the process, it has damaged the standing of the entire religious segment of the Republican Party among the general American population, as evidenced by the overwhelmingly nega-tive response to the congressional action in nearly every poll taken—including many within the conservative religious commu-nity. It is interesting to note, however, that, thanks to the inepti-tude of the congressional Democrats, neither the Democratic Party nor any one Democrat seems to have directly benefited from this overreaching of power. Given the pathetic state of affairs within the Democratic Party, this is not surprising.

What Does This All Mean?

The economic and investment importance of this is fairly straight-forward: Anything that disrupts the power base of market funda-mentalism threatens its continuing in power. And market fundamentalism draws its power from the Trinity, for without the political power, the viability of market fundamentalism to be the dominant economic view diminishes substantially.

To be clear, however, I firmly believe that when the equity markets are ready to roll over and enter their bear phase, it will be because of economic and not political matters. Nevertheless, cracks in the power base that basically runs the United States, both economically and politically, are always important to note. And that, in my opinion, is the economic and investment significance of the Schiavo story.

INVESTMENT IMPLICATIONS

The issue of political power and the potential damage to the Republican Party and its economic agenda has played out in the months after the Schiavo tragedy. Since the spring of 2005 when this sad saga hit the nation's consciousness, the Republican Party and President Bush have seen their standing among Americans sink to record lows. For example, in the fall of 2005, President Bush's approval rating was below 40 percent. And the Republicans are now sweating the 2006 midterm elections and their potential loss of both houses of Congress. Such an event would be a disaster for the party whose goal is to be in power for a generation, as presidential adviser Karl Rove has sought to construct for the Republicans.

The investment implications of such a shift are broad and potentially damaging to a market that favors Mr. Bush and the Republicans. In fact, it is not at all unlikely that the stock market malaise that has hung over the U.S. equity markets for nearly all of 2005 is attributable to this potential shift in power. Consider the following few facts:

As of November 2005:

- Corporate profits have climbed to record levels.
- Corporate cash levels are approaching $2 trillion.
- Interest rates, while rising some, are still at relatively modest levels.
- Valuations for stocks are very attractive.

In fact, according to the Fed Model,[2] the S&P 500, which stood around the 1200 level in early November, could and should easily have been trading over 1300. (See Table 4.1.)

I have little doubt that a major contributing factor to why the market is so far below its own intrinsic value is the real and potential worsening of political power for the Republicans.

In the next commentary (written on Halloween day, hence the title), the outcome of President Bush's Supreme Court nomination of Judge Samuel Alito is not known. Nor, most importantly, is whether the Democrats will mount a filibuster, thereby triggering the so-called nuclear option

TABLE 4.1 Fed Model as of October 31, 2005

	S&P 500 Earnings							P/E Conversion	
Adjusted 10-Year Treasury	2005		2006						
	$66	$68	$70	$72	$74	$76	$78	10-Year Treasury	P/E
4.00%	1650	1700	1750	1800	1850	1900	1950	4.00%	25.00
4.20	1571	1619	1667	1714	1762	1810	1857	4.20	23.81
4.40	1500	1545	1591	1636	1682	1727	1773	4.40	22.73
4.60	1435	1478	1522	1565	1609	1652	1696	4.60	21.74
4.80	1375	1417	1458	1500	1542	1583	1625	4.80	20.83
5.00	1320	1360	1400	1440	1480	1520	1560	5.00	20.00
5.20	1269	1308	1346	1385	1423	1462	1500	5.20	19.23
5.40	1222	1259	1296	1333	1370	1407	1444	5.40	18.52
5.60	1179	1214	1250	1286	1321	1357	1393	5.60	17.86
5.80	1138	1172	1207	1241	1276	1310	1345	5.80	17.24
6.00	1100	1133	1167	1200	1233	1267	1300	6.00	16.67

S&P 1205
10-Year Treasury 4.55%

Source: Thomson Financial.

by the Republicans. Nevertheless, the potential for such a battle and the consequential gridlock existed and was the topic of the report.

A Ghoulish Decision

With the announcement of Mr. Bush's choice for the Supreme Court, the longer-term picture for the market just got a whole lot worse.

At a time when politics should be a back burner issue for the markets, the present time is the exception to the rule, for the year after a presidential reelection is usually a time of legacy thinking. And it started out that way with Mr. Bush's attempts at addressing the looming Social Security crisis. However, with the exceptions of Ben Bernanke and John Roberts, misstep after misstep has marked this year. And the situation in Iraq gets no better. Which brings us to this morning's announcement of Judge Alito.

Regardless of one's political views, it is fairly clear that Bush is caving in to the radical right. And in doing so, he is virtually guaranteeing a filibuster in the Senate and gridlock in Washington for the foreseeable future. Having been an adviser to the Kerry campaign in 2004, I can assure you that there is no way that the announcement of a staunch conservative as the replacement for the key swing vote on the Supreme Court (Sandra Day O'Connor) will not result in an all-out war that will likely manifest itself in a government divided. And a government divided cannot stand.

For investors, the issue of pro-choice or right-to-life is beside the point. It's all about an effective government and the smooth administration of the economy. Anything that impedes that objective virtually guarantees mediocrity, at best, and disaster, in the extreme.

The U.S. Congress has much work to do. There are far too many extremely important issues that must be dealt with, many of a direct economic nature (deficits, for example) and many of an indirect kind (geopolitical). There is very little margin for error.

Over the near term, the markets may pooh-pooh the implications of the past weeks (Harriet Miers fiasco, I. Lewis "Scooter" Libby indictment), culminating in this morning's announcement. And, yes, we have not completed the topping process, and higher highs could and should happen. But in my humble opinion, the announcement of Judge Alito for the Supreme Court will impact the markets once it becomes apparent that gridlock is just around the corner. This has the potential of a worst-case scenario—the

U.S. government bitterly fragmented at a time when the ante gets higher. The longer-term picture for the market just got a whole lot worse this morning.

Comment

As I noted, at the time of this writing, we don't know if the Alito nomination will lead to gridlock in Washington. However, should that turn out to be the outcome, then the danger to the Republicans in 2006 has been ramped up.

There are times when the economic and the political intersect. One such time was in early 2005, when after years of pressure, the Chinese government made a small but symbolic step toward floating its currency. The consequence as I saw it was a rise in interest rates in the United States for the following reasons.

The End of Cheap Money:
Reverberations of the Chinese Currency Change[3]

After spending several days digesting the opinions of nearly every worthwhile (and some not so worthwhile) analyst and their perspectives regarding last week's surprise announcement of the Chinese currency revaluation, the dominant conclusion I have come to is that the era of cheap money and extraordinarily low interest rates is coming to an end. In other words, medium-term and long-term rates now seem destined to rise, with the 10-year U.S. Treasury likely to top 5 percent before the year is over.

The combination of sustained (albeit slowing) economic growth and the probable reduced appetite for U.S. financial assets (U.S. Treasuries), not to mention the anticipation of moderately higher inflation, strongly suggests that longer-term rates (10-year Treasury, specifically) will be higher by the end of this year.

When unexpected events occur, even seemingly small ones, it takes a few days/weeks/months for the market to adjust. Positions get realigned, and that realignment shows up in the marketplace in the form of changed relationships between and among various market segments. In other words, the potential for divergences and for leadership rotation is high, and bears close watching.

I have attempted to share with you my thinking and provide a macro market perspective. Last week's Chinese currency revaluation and the very solid 2Q05 earnings reports warrant an upward adjustment in both earnings and the discount factor.

Bottom line: Rates are headed higher, and earnings are as well.

INVESTMENT IMPLICATIONS

Rising interest rates impact the valuation model and financial assets across the board. When rates rise, the discount factor does as well. Moreover, higher interest rates mean higher borrowing costs for businesses, thereby creating the potential of a reduction in profit margins.

As a major buyer of U.S. government obligations, if the Chinese were inclined to cut back their subsidization of U.S. consumer spending through the purchase of U.S. Treasuries,[4] a chain reaction of negative proportions could easily develop. Interestingly, rates have risen since this report was issued. Although many attribute it to the Federal Reserve's policy to raise rates and to high energy prices, another factor is that the Chinese have begun a modest reduction in U.S. Treasury obligations. I suspect there is a connection.

SUMMARY

Modern bases of power are more complex than just the sociological or the economic. They are intertwined with each other. And they complement each other. In this first decade of the twenty-first century, the juggernaut that President Bush and his senior adviser, Karl Rove, have so brilliantly constructed interconnects the social with the economic in ways that are unprecedented. Accordingly, anything that threatens that initiative threatens the economic policies of the Bush administration. That may be for the good or for ill and it may be hard to quantify, but it is undeniable that political power is very much connected to economic power. The uncertainty factor has gone way up over the past several years. And all investors know just how much the stock market detests uncertainty.

This chapter is not an especially lengthy one, as the central topic is somewhat narrow: Political power begets economic power. Nevertheless, the topic is a very powerful one, perhaps the most powerful force impacting the market. It's not an obvious point, nor is it a quantifiable one. It's one of those hard-to-quantify aspects that play an important role in moving markets. In fact, this is precisely the dynamic that impacts the market most in the major election years: presidential and midterm.

CHAPTER 5

It's the Global Economy, Stupid

When it comes to making investment decisions, understanding the economic climate is essential. Until recently, it was the domestic economy that mattered most. The global economy was sort of "out there." Trade between countries did take place, of course. And empires were built on it. But, for the most part, the domestic economy was the dominant consideration for investors. That, however, has changed dramatically as the era of the closed domestic economy has ended and a new, more open global economy has emerged. Globalization rules!

Increasingly, understanding the economic climate means understanding the *global* economic climate. For as complicated as a domestic-oriented analysis can be, including the world's economies and the interplay between and among them, not to mention the geopolitical dynamic, can be a very daunting task. However, as with all elements of investing, it is absolutely essential that we do not get lost in the forest for the trees. Here, perhaps more so than in any other area, the ability to determine the critical variables and exercise sound judgment will make the difference between understanding and confusion. Appropriately, the global macro story takes center stage in our efforts to understand the role that the economy plays in investment decision making.

This is also the place where the Funnel described in Chapter 1 begins to kick into action. If you recall, the Funnel starts with the macro environment. The macro environment does include the political and the role that government plays, but it is the macro*economic* environment that we want to gain the necessary insight into so that we can work our way downward toward our valuation model and its inputs. Given its scale and scope, the global macro can easily overwhelm an investor. However, always seek to find the critical variables through the decomposition process, breaking the big pieces into the more manageable ones and then finding the right elements that will help make the Funnel work for you.

Therefore, we must begin to gain a good understanding of some of the standard macroeconomic principles and processes before we can determine what to focus on. And that is where we begin, with a rather quick survey of the vast global economic landscape. Given its immensity and complexity, I will be selective as to what to include and exclude from consideration. Considering the scale and scope of economic matters, it is no wonder that economics is known as the dismal science. The sheer volume of information and the complex interrelationships can numb the mind. Let's see if we can make it a bit less dismal and a lot more insightful.

ALL THINGS ARE GLOBAL

The late Speaker of the House, Tip O'Neill, may have been correct when he stated, "All politics is local," but when it comes to the twenty-first-century economy the observation that "all things are global" is closer to the truth.

The world we live in today is an interactive, interdependent, interconnected environment, one in which what happens here affects what happens there and vice versa. Thanks to information and communications technology (most notable of which is the Internet) and an increasing community of countries adopting a market economy within their domestic economies, the global economy is the domestic economy. And with that adoption most businesses, especially the publicly traded kind, are now truly global enterprises in some manner or other.

For most businesses, the production process is a global undertaking. Manufacture in one country, assemble in another, sell in a third. Go where the costs are lowest and the talent can be had for cents on the dollar and you have business as we know it—globalization on the ascent.

Globalization has gone from a buzzword to an everyday reality. Globalization has taken hold so strongly that countries that were heretofore reliant on state-run economies have opened their doors to the free flow of capital and labor on an unprecedented scale. And nothing punctuates this fact more than China. Granted, there are still many state-run aspects to the way China does business. It is not a true open market economy. But Rome wasn't built in a day. And China, which some believe is poised to succeed the United States as the next Rome, is just the most profound example of the adoption of the market economy and the effects of globalization.

Whole industries are in the throes of change thanks to the global economy. Take a company based in Europe. In the time before globalization, the company might have researched, produced, marketed, sold, and serviced a product to its domestic market. Maybe not 100 percent of companies followed this pattern, but this was predominantly the case. Today, that same European-based manufacturing firm might outsource much of its research and development to India; have most of its basic manufacturing done in China; assemble its products in Southeast Asia; market them via the world's network, the Internet; sell its goods in the United States; and service the sale back where we started—in India. Such is the state of business—world business in the early twenty-first century.

IS THIS NIRVANA?

The economic benefit that globalization has brought to consumers has been a low-price bonanza. Due to the forces of globalization, consumers today have more choices at lower prices. Choice has exploded and with it the products that once were offered by a small number of local firms in the closed domestic economies of the past have been replaced by a veritable plethora of providers, each eager to sell its wares at prices that would be impossible to provide in a closed economy. However, with that choice comes the competitive pressures on the companies competing to maintain and gain market share in a globally competitive environment.

As wonderful as the low-price consumer bonanza has been for consumers, the increased ease of the global production process has created a need for companies to be more productive. As a result, the increased competitive climate in which companies from around the globe compete for the big consumer bucks has motivated enlightened senior managers to seek the benefits of a global enterprise. Therefore, many of them have cobbled together the global corporation whose ability to produce, market, sell, and service its goods in a manner described earlier is becoming the operating standard. In other words, to effectively compete and maintain its competitive edge, a business must utilize the power of globalization to produce products at the lowest cost and of the highest quality possible while, at the same time, seeking to take advantage of the opportunities that the global marketplace has to offer—that is to say, penetrate other world markets.

Lest you think that this globalization juggernaut is restricted to only the big, think again. Thanks to the Internet, this global marketplace is not restricted to the big boys on the block. Everyone can join the party. Just as the Internet and technology have democratized the investment research process (the premise for this book), so, too, have the Net and tech made the world a sales bazaar for all—a place where anyone can set up a booth and pitch their wares.

A grasp of the global economy is a grasp of the forces at work within most domestic economies. It is a little-understood area for most investors, including the professional kind. And it is an area of great interest and concern for policy makers. Consider what then Federal Reserve chairman Alan Greenspan had to say in a speech he gave in Jackson Hole, Wyoming, in August 2003:

> *Despite the extensive efforts to capture and quantify these key macroeconomic relationships, our knowledge about many of the important linkages is far from complete and in all likelihood will always remain so. Every model, no matter how detailed or how well designed conceptually and empirically, is a vastly simplified representation of the world that we experience with all its intricacies on a day-to-day basis. Consequently, even with large advances in computational capabilities and greater comprehension of economic linkages, our knowledge base is barely able to keep pace with the ever-increasing complexity of our global economy.*

Understanding the global economy is a task that screams for identifying the critical variables and exercising the best possible judgment we can muster to determine where we will focus the majority of our limited time and energy. Therefore, let's highlight several key issues, using the political dynamic as our point of departure.

WHAT'S WRONG WITH KANSAS?

The dynamics of globalization are not just economic. They are also affecting the political dynamic within the United States. Take, for example, the issue of voting against your economic interests, as described best by author and Kansan Thomas Frank.

The political and the economic come together very clearly in Tom Frank's book, *What's the Matter with Kansas?*, in which Frank poses the question, "Why are Kansans voting against their economic interests?" when they vote for Republicans who are probusiness and, presumably, antilabor. It is not Tom Frank's politics that is of value to investors, nor is it the solutions he and other like-minded individuals have offered. Rather, it is the conflict among the worker, the consumer, and the voter that needs a word or two.

Since most American workers are a much higher cost factor than, say, a Chinese worker,[1] it behooves the global enterprise to fire the higher-cost U.S. worker and hire the lower-cost Chinese worker. In doing so, the company is better able to compete more effectively by offering higher-quality products at a (necessarily) competitive price. Therefore, one has to wonder why a Kansas voter would elect a probusiness politician, for example, when that same politician is likely to support legislation and regulation that would benefit business to the detriment of the worker, the very same (or is it insane?) person who elected the official in the first place!

The answers can be found in the brilliance of the Republican Party juggernaut that emerged in the mid-1990s[2] and what I call the Political Trinity (introduced in the previous chapter on government). But for our current purposes, the personal trinity—worker, consumer, voter—presents the dilemma of the day for your average American citizen: "What matters to me more—having high-quality, low-cost goods or having a higher-paying job?" And, "Who should I vote for who will serve my needs best?" The answer is—you guessed it—it all depends.

This is a fluid and complex issue and not the central theme of this book. But it does highlight an important dichotomy that globalization has wrought: The benefits of globalization are not without issues. In the United States, for example:

- Consumers benefit from the low costs and high quality that can result from globalization.
- Workers lose as real wage and benefit gains are minimized.
- Companies benefit as lower-cost production results in better profit margins.
- Companies also benefit from the opportunity that access to other countries' markets affords.
- Companies struggle, however, with global competitors.

Another example of the challenges posed by globalization is its impact on those countries (mostly European) that have remained firmly in the grip of a social compact with their citizen workers. Consider the following excerpts from what the economics editor for the *Financial Times*, Martin Wolf, had to say in his October 19, 2005, lead article of the four-part series, "Globalization and the European Union." In his segment titled, "A Bigger Playing Field Needs New Goal Posts," Wolf states:

> *What is called globalization describes the parallel emergence of three new forces. The first is the information and communication revolution. The second is the worldwide movement from planned economies to market economies and from self-reliance to integration within the global economy. The third—closely connected to the first two—is the entry into the world economy of vast new sources of hard-working and highly motivated, but cheap, labor.*

To this we add the following excerpts from the 2004 annual report of the International Monetary Fund:

Euro area authorities faced many policy challenges, Directors noted. In particular, economic growth had come to a virtual stand-still since the last quarter of 2002, with net exports and investment declining, and unemployment on the rise. Moreover, challenges loomed, with the aging of the population and slowing of labor force growth becoming an increasing drag on potential output growth, fiscal sustainability, and old-age income security. EU en-largement, while of benefit to all concerned, would also be a source of new challenges. Directors advised that meeting these challenges successfully would require a sustained shift toward more forward-looking national policies and the vigorous imple-mentation of structural reforms. While adversity had begun to in-duce such forward-looking policies, notably on the structural side, the Board noted that it was essential that these potentially promis-ing steps be sustained once difficulties recede.

Directors considered that the weakness of area-wide activity reflected a number of shocks as well as structural rigidities and policy lapses. The shocks included the bursting equity bubble, low business and consumer confidence, reduced external demand, the correction of the euro to longer-run equilibrium levels, and geopo-litical uncertainties. Rigidities in labor markets and lesser reliance on market-based financing had, in some measure, contained the ef-fects of the shocks, but they had also slowed both the post-bubble and intra-area adjustments. As a result, the area-wide stagnation was expected to be overcome only gradually, with growth remain-ing subpar well into 2004.

Lastly, in addressing the euro area, the Organization for Economic Co-operation and Development (OECD) *Economic Outlook* No. 77 of May 2005 stated:

The recovery has lost momentum since mid-2004, but it should resume in 2006. Growth is projected to drop from just below 2 percent in 2004 to $1^1/_4$ percent in 2005 before recovering to around 2 percent in 2006, with final domestic demand firming. The output gap will remain negative and the unemployment rate high at over $8^1/_2$ percent. Once the impact of the oil price hike pe-ters out, headline inflation should fall to $1^1/_4$ percent. Another hike in oil prices or a further appreciation of the euro could sap *the recovery further. With inflation declining and a large output gap prevailing in 2006, there is room to ease monetary policy, even though liquidity will have to be withdrawn again once the recovery is firming towards the end of the projection period. The euro area lacks resilience against adverse shocks amid slow trend growth—less than 2 percent per annum. Both are shaped by structural factors. Structural policies should aim at completing the European internal market, boosting labor market performance, and encouraging innovation. Fiscal policy should be rooted in long-term sustainability goals. [See Table 5.1.]*

When compared to the United States, the differences are significant. (See Table 5.2.)

No matter how you slice it, the data strongly suggests that those countries (that's you, Europe) that have "structural rigidities" (code for a high social compact) are likely to experience an erosion in their gross domestic product (GDP) performance. This is not to say that one style of capitalism is better than the other. Nor is it to suggest that the two major competing versions (American versus Social Democrat) are the only ones. Moreover, the euro area is a vast and complex mix of countries

TABLE 5.1 Euro Area Demand and Output

	Current Prices (Billions of Euros)	Percentage Changes, Volume (1999 Prices)				
	2001	2002	2003	2004	2005	2006
Private Consumption	3,928.3	0.7	1.1	1.2	1.3	1.7
Government Consumption	1,372.5	3.1	1.7	1.7	1.0	2.0
Gross Fixed Investment	1,442.0	−2.2	−0.4	1.9	2.0	3.0
Public	181.2	2.3	0.4	1.5	2.4	2.2
Residential	372.4	−0.9	0.9	1.6	1.0	1.7
Nonresidential	888.5	−3.7	−1.1	2.2	2.3	3.8
Final Domestic Demand	6,742.8	0.6	0.9	1.4	1.4	2.0
Stockbuilding	−14.6	−0.1	0.3	0.3	0.1	0.0
Total Domestic Demand	6,728.2	0.5	1.3	1.8	1.5	2.1
Net Exports	122.1	0.5	−0.6	0.1	−0.3	0.0
GDP at Market Prices	6,850.3	0.9	0.6	1.8	1.2	2.0

Source: Organization for Economic Cooperation and Development.

TABLE 5.2 Nominal Gross Domestic Product (GDP) in the 1990s (Percentage Change from Previous Year)

	Average 1980–1990	1991	1992	1993	1994	1995	1996	1997	1998	1999
United States	7.6%	3.3%	5.7%	5.0%	6.2%	4.6%	5.7%	6.2%	5.3%	6.0%
Euro Area	8.7	7.4	5.6	2.7	5.2	5.2	3.5	4.0	4.6	3.9
European Union	8.8	7.0	5.2	3.1	5.4	5.3	4.0	4.4	4.8	4.2
Total OECD	10.7	7.0	6.3	5.5	7.6	7.5	7.3	7.2	5.8	5.7

	2000	2001	2002	2003	2004	2005	2006	Fourth Quarter		
								2004	2005	2006
United States	5.9%	3.2%	3.5%	4.9%	6.6%	6.1%	5.7%	6.4%	5.9%	5.7%
Euro Area	5.1	4.1	3.4	2.6	3.8	2.8	3.7	3.4	3.1	4.1
European Union	5.2	4.2	3.7	3.1	4.0	3.0	3.9	3.6	3.3	4.2
Total OECD	6.7	4.0	4.2	4.3	5.5	4.6	4.8	5.2	4.6	4.9

Source: Organization for Economic Cooperation and Development.

and cultures that require a more detailed investigation into the inter-country factors at work. Nevertheless, the overriding conclusion is that those countries that do not adapt to the forces wrought by globalization will suffer the consequences of lower growth and a greater burden on their citizens. And that will not lead to any good.

A FEW KEY MACROECONOMIC INDICATORS

I think you get the picture: In the globalization era, the global economy matters most. Understanding it to the best of our ability is a "need to know," not a "nice to know." And while there are many sources of data on the global economy, I believe that investors are best served if they grasp the forces on a global macro scale and, keeping them firmly in mind, look at the domestic economy and see how it is performing. Put simply, the global economy and the forces of globalization help to frame, to put into context, the domestic economy. With that noted, let's look at a few important domestic macroeconomic indicators.

Gross Domestic Product

The gross domestic product (GDP) of a country is defined as the total market value of all final goods and services produced in a country in a given year. It is used by most investors as a leading indicator of an economy's health and well-being. Produced by the Bureau of Economic Analysis (BEA), the quarterly GDP report for the United States is a front-page news item. For investors seriously interested in understanding the rich content produced by the BEA, gaining a good working knowledge of the approximately 15-page report is time well spent.

Most investors rely on economists to review such data, so reading the GDP report is not at the top of the investor list. But I beg to differ. I believe that in order to gain that deeper sense of the global economy, an investor should find the time to read what amounts to a fairly understandable report. For example, the following excerpts will hopefully pique your interest.

Gross Domestic Product: Second Quarter 2005 (Final)

Real gross domestic product—the output of goods and services produced by labor and property located in the United States—increased at an annual rate of 3.3 percent in the second quarter of 2005, according to final estimates released by the Bureau of Economic Analysis. In the first quarter, real GDP increased 3.8 percent.

The major contributors to the increase in real GDP in the second quarter were personal consumption expenditures, exports, equipment and software, residential fixed investment, and government spending. The contributions of these components were partly offset by a negative contribution from private inventory investment. Imports, which are a subtraction in the calculation of GDP, decreased.

The deceleration in real GDP growth in the second quarter primarily reflected a downturn in private inventory investment that was partly offset by a downturn in imports and an acceleration in exports.

The price index for gross domestic purchases, which measures prices paid by U.S. residents, increased 3.3 percent in the second quarter, 0.2 percentage point more than the preliminary estimate; this index increased 2.9 percent in the first quarter. Excluding food and energy prices, the price index for gross domestic purchases increased 2.1 percent in the second quarter, compared with an increase of 3.0 percent in the first.

Real exports of goods and services increased 10.7 percent in the second quarter, compared with an increase of 7.5 percent in the first. Real imports of goods and services decreased 0.3 percent, in contrast to an increase of 7.4 percent.

What I find of particular value is the BEA data on corporate profits:

Corporate Profits: Second Quarter 2005 (Final)

Profits from current production (corporate profits with inventory valuation and capital consumption adjustments) increased $59.3 billion in the second quarter. In the first quarter, profits increased $68.7 billion. Current-production cash flow (net cash flow with inventory valuation and capital consumption adjustments)—the internal funds available to corporations for investment—increased $41.7 billion in the second quarter, compared with an increase of $95.4 billion in the first.

Taxes on corporate income increased $9.9 billion in the second quarter, compared with an increase of $69.6 billion in the first. Profits after tax with inventory valuation and capital consumption adjustments increased $49.4 billion in the second quarter, in contrast to a decrease of $0.8 billion in the first. Dividends increased $11.4 billion, in contrast to a decrease of $94.4 billion; current-production undistributed profits increased $38.0 billion, *compared with an increase of $93.5 billion. Domestic profits of financial corporations decreased $26.9 billion in the second quarter, in contrast to an increase of $36.0 billion in the first.*

Domestic profits of nonfinancial corporations increased $82.5 billion in the second quarter, compared with an increase of $17.8 billion in the first. In the second quarter, real gross value added of nonfinancial corporations increased, and profits per unit of real product increased. The increase in unit profits reflected an increase in unit prices and decreases in both unit labor and nonlabor costs corporations incurred.

The rest-of-the-world component of profits increased $3.7 billion in the second quarter, compared with an increase of $14.9 billion in the first. This measure is calculated as (1) receipts by U.S. residents of earnings from their foreign affiliates plus dividends received by U.S. residents from unaffiliated foreign corporations minus (2) payments by U.S. affiliates of earnings to their foreign parents plus dividends paid by U.S. corporations to unaffiliated foreign residents. The second-quarter increase was accounted for by a larger increase in receipts than in payments.

Now, no one is trying to turn you into an economist. Heaven forbid! But the data presented does help an investor to understand the forces at work within the economy at a given point in time. And, unlike many of Alan Greenspan's speeches, the GDP report is not written in some arcane, hard-to-decipher language.

The preceding data paint a picture of an economy on fairly solid ground. Growth remains strong and inflation is fairly muted. Corporate profits are doing exceptionally well, notwithstanding how long the economic expansion has been under way and the impact of higher energy prices.

Public sources of economic data such as the BEA report are abundant, with many of high-quality nature. All are free and easy to access. Some of them are listed in Appendix A, including those produced by private organizations. One such important private organization report that moves markets is produced by the Institute for Supply Management (ISM).

Institute for Supply Management Reports

"Founded in 1915, the Institute for Supply Management™ (ISM) is the largest supply management association in the world. . . ." So states the opening text on the web site of the private organization that produces two of the most important monthly reports on the state of economic activity:

the ISM *Report On Business*®, one for manufacturing and the other on nonmanufacturing (known as the services report). Tracking the pace of economic activity, the reports provide a comprehensive survey of businesses and their perspectives and intentions in the coming months and years.

For example, "the Manufacturing ISM *Report On Business*® is based on data compiled from monthly replies to questions asked of purchasing executives in over 400 industrial companies." Data on such areas as new orders, production, employment, supplier deliveries, and inventories are compiled and disseminated.

The Purchasing Managers Index (PMI) is the headline number that investors eagerly await. It provides a composite picture of the trend of the manufacturing sector, expressed in the form of a diffusion index. To illustrate, let's look at the PMI for October 2005 from the ISM:[3]

The PMI indicates that the manufacturing economy grew in October for the 29th consecutive month. The PMI for October registered 59.1 percent, a decrease of 0.3 percentage point when compared to September's reading of 59.4 percent. A reading above 50 percent indicates that the manufacturing economy is generally expanding; below 50 percent indicates that it is generally contracting.

A PMI in excess of 42.7 percent, over a period of time, generally indicates an expansion of the overall economy. The October PMI indicates that both the overall economy and the manufacturing sector are growing. The past relationship between the PMI and the overall economy indicates that the average PMI for January through October (55.4 percent) corresponds to a 4.6 percent increase in gross domestic product (GDP) on an annual basis. In addition, if the PMI for October (59.1 percent) is annualized, it corresponds to a 5.9 percent increase in GDP annually.

The Last 12 Months

Month	PMI	Month	PMI
Oct 2005	59.1	Apr 2005	53.3
Sep 2005	59.4	Mar 2005	55.2
Aug 2005	53.6	Feb 2005	55.3
Jul 2005	56.6	Jan 2005	56.4
Jun 2005	53.8	Dec 2004	57.3
May 2005	51.4	Nov 2004	57.6

Average for 12 months—55.8
High—59.4
Low—51.4

Note the connection between the report and a potential GDP projection as stated in the last line: ". . . if the PMI for October (59.1 percent) is annualized, it corresponds to a 5.9 percent increase in GDP annually." Here an investor has a valuable piece of information made freely available to all and one that we can use to help determine the state of the aggregate economy. Moreover, when you explore each of the aforementioned segments (new orders, production, employment, etc.) you can gain a depth of understanding of the strength and trends in the economy. Take for example that all-important subject of pricing power.

From the same report,[4] here is the segment on prices:

Prices grew significantly again in October as the Prices Index rose to 84 percent, up six percentage points from 78 percent in September. In October, 70 percent of supply executives reported paying higher prices and 2 percent reported paying lower prices, while 28 percent reported that prices were unchanged from the preceding month.

A Prices Index above 47.1 percent, over time, is generally consistent with an increase in the Bureau of Labor Statistics (BLS) Index of Manufacturers Prices. In October, 18 industries reported paying higher prices: Textiles; Furniture; Petroleum; Rubber & Plastic Products; Glass, Stone & Aggregate; Chemicals; Primary Metals; Paper; Fabricated Metals; Transportation & Equipment; Food; Apparel; Instruments & Photographic Equipment; Miscellaneous*; Industrial & Commercial Equipment & Computers; Printing & Publishing; Electronic Components & Equipment; and Wood & Wood Products.

Prices	% Higher	% Same	% Lower	Net	Index
Oct 2005	70	28	2	+68	84.0
Sep 2005	60	36	4	+56	78.0
Aug 2005	36	53	11	+25	62.5
Jul 2005	24	49	27	-3	48.5

In a global economy, the threat to the bottom line due to an inability to raise prices when warranted is real. Remember that competitive forces that are strong can shift the value produced to the buyer. If companies and industries are engaged in a highly competitive atmosphere, their ability to keep the value produced is diminished. Therefore, the ability to raise prices is vital to the bottom line of most businesses. The preceding data suggest that the ability to sustain price increases has improved dramatically over the past four months. Whether this trend holds remains to be seen, as a global economy is a very dynamic place.

The Non-Manufacturing *Report On Business®* provides similar information, this time on the state of business in the services area of the economy. For example, Table 5.3 provides a clear composite picture of the areas surveyed and their data. One can easily get a good picture of where the economy is headed, at least over the near term.

TABLE 5.3   ISM Non-Manufacturing Report

	Non-Manufacturing					
Index	Series Index October	Series Index September	Percentage Point Change	Direction	Rate of Change	Trend (Months)
Business Activity/ Production	60.0	53.3	6.7%	Increasing	Faster	31
New Orders	58.2	56.6	1.6	Increasing	Faster	31
Employment	52.9	54.9	–2.0	Increasing	Slower	25
Supplier Deliveries	58.5	56.0	2.5	Slowing	Faster	50
Inventories	50.0	50.0	0.0	Unchanged	N/A	2
Prices	78.0	81.4	–3.4	Increasing	Slower	29
Backlog of Orders	55.0	52.0	3.0	Increasing	Faster	9
New Export Orders	54.5	55.0	–0.5	Increasing	Slower	4
Imports	53.5	58.5	–5.0	Increasing	Slower	30
Inventory Sentiment	55.0	64.0	–9.0	Too High	Lesser	101
Customers' Inventories	N/A	N/A				

Source: Reprinted with permission from the publisher, the Institute for Supply Management™.

Demographics

The study of socioeconomic groups characterized by age, income, gender, education, occupation, and so on is known as demographics.

In his well-written call to arms, *Running on Empty: How the Democratic and Republican Parties Are Bankrupting Our Future and What Americans Can Do About It*, Peter G. Peterson, former chairman of the Federal Reserve Bank of New York and former United States Secretary of Commerce, discusses the issue of the aging of America. The book helps described the interrelationship (and the consequences) of an aging population and government policy and how they can affect the economic vitality of the United States. Here are a few excerpts that I think will help illustrate the point:

> *For nearly all of human history, until the industrial revolution, people aged sixty-five and over never amounted to more than 2 or 3 percent of the population. In America today, they amount to 12 percent. By the year 2040 they will be reaching 20 percent and may be closing in on 25 percent. . . .*
>
> *For the moment, America is still enjoying the last few years of what has been called a "demographic Indian summer." With the large postwar boom generation in the workforce and a small Depression-era generation retiring, the elder share of the U.S. population has been flat since the mid-1980s. But when boomers start turning sixty-five less than a decade from now, the demographic climate will change abruptly. . . .*
>
> *This explosion in the number of elderly Americans will place an unprecedented economic burden on working-age adults. As recently as 1960 there were 5.1 taxpaying workers for every Social Security beneficiary. This ratio, now 3.3, is officially projected to fall to 2.2 by 2030. By then each two-earner working-age couple will have to support at least one anonymous retiree. . . .*
>
> *The graying of America therefore translates into a huge and growing bill to taxpayers for senior entitlements. Between now and 2040, Social Security outlays as a share of worker payroll are officially projected to rise from 11.1 to 17.8 percent. Both parts of Medicare will rise from 5.6 to 18.2 percent.[5]*

In a segment titled "The 'Grow the Economy' Fantasy," Peterson criticizes the very popular political solution (and I might add one that is also very popular among many Wall Street types) that growth will save the day:

> *The projections are stark. America will have to undertake fundamental reform of senior benefits or else experience a fiscal meltdown*

*within a few decades. Given this choice, it's not surprising that
many leaders of both political parties prefer denial.*

*The magic bullet most often extolled by Republicans (as well
as some Democrats) is faster economic growth. If the economy
grows faster than projected, say these GOP optimists, today's benefit promises will become affordable.*[6]

Leaving aside the conclusion reached by Pete Peterson, the important
takeaway for readers is the process of linking a demographic trend, the aging
of America, with its political and economic consequences. These excerpts
help point out that linkages do exist and insight can be gained if one can see
the bigger picture by examining the segments of the economy. And that brings
us to a very important concept and a poem by a nineteenth-century American
poet, John Godfrey Saxe, based on a fable told in India many years ago.

The Elephant and the Blind Man[7]

*It was six men of Indostan
To learning much inclined,
Who went to see the Elephant
(Though all of them were blind),
That each by observation
Might satisfy his mind.*

*The First approached the Elephant,
And happening to fall
Against his broad and sturdy side,
At once began to bawl:
"God bless me! but the Elephant
Is very like a wall!"*

*The Second, feeling of the tusk,
Cried, "Ho! what have we here
So very round and smooth and sharp?
To me 'tis mighty clear
This wonder of an Elephant
Is very like a spear!"*

*The Third approached the animal,
And happening to take
The squirming trunk within his hands,
Thus boldly up and spake:
"I see," quoth he, "the Elephant
Is very like a snake!"*

The Fourth reached out an eager hand,
And felt about the knee.
"What most this wondrous beast is like
Is mighty plain," quoth he;
" 'Tis clear enough the Elephant
Is very like a tree!"

The Fifth, who chanced to touch the ear,
Said: "E'en the blindest man
Can tell what this resembles most;
Deny the fact who can
This marvel of an Elephant
Is very like a fan!"

The Sixth no sooner had begun
About the beast to grope,
Than, seizing on the swinging tail
That fell within his scope,
"I see," quoth he, "the Elephant
Is very like a rope!"

And so these men of Indostan
Disputed loud and long,
Each in his own opinion
Exceeding stiff and strong,
Though each was partly in the right,
And all were in the wrong!

Moral:
So oft in theologic wars,
The disputants, I ween,
Rail on in utter ignorance
Of what each other mean,
And prate about an Elephant
Not one of them has seen!

Whole textbooks are written about the economy. It is therefore impossible to cover all that needs to be known about the U.S. economy, let alone the world economy, in one chapter. Moreover, important areas such as personal income and consumer spending provide valuable information on their respective segments and on the economy (domestic and global) as a whole. To endeavor to grasp the big picture from the trunks and legs and ears of the global elephant is a fool's errand if an investor does not place the information in context and take a step back to see how it all interrelates.

So, here are a few points that I offer to those seeking to grasp the big picture:

- Become a student of the global economy and globalization.
- Identify and monitor a few key economic indicators.
- Determine how each economic indicator you are analyzing impacts the valuation model inputs.

By keeping the bottom line in sight and stepping back to see how the segments of the big picture can and do interrelate, the seemingly impossible task of understanding the global economy can become surmountable.

We now need to move from the really big picture to just the big picture. And in doing so, we are entering the world of economic sectors and subsectors.

THE MICROECONOMIC ENVIRONMENT

The microeconomic environment is the residence of the economic sectors and subsectors of the economy. Economic sectors are the broad groupings of companies that comprise a given industry classification. For example, the Energy sector is comprised of subsectors that provide energy-related goods and services. As defined by Standard & Poor's, the subsectors of the Energy sector are:

- Oil & Gas Drilling
- Oil & Gas Equipment & Services
- Integrated Oil & Gas
- Oil & Gas Exploration & Production
- Oil & Gas Refining & Marketing
- Oil & Gas Storage & Transportation
- Coal & Consumable Fuels

Each subsector is considered an industry within the larger context of the Energy sector. This study and analysis of economic sectors and subsectors is the study of the microeconomic environment. And, as with the economy as a whole through the study of key trends and indicators, so, too, can we gain insight into the economy through the study of the microeconomic environment.

The economies of the developed nations are a large and complex animal to get one's arms around. They are, therefore, best seen broken down into more manageable pieces. These pieces are the 10 economic sectors. This is especially true for the world's largest economy, that of the United States. So, how does one take on the large and complex? By breaking it down into its component pieces and studying each to gain insight into the whole. There are many ways to break the U.S. economy down into bite-size pieces. The preferred method for most investors, however, is on an economic sector basis.

Economic Sectors

We begin by decomposing the economy into 10 economic sectors:

1. Consumer Discretionary
2. Consumer Staples
3. Energy
4. Health Care
5. Financials
6. Industrials
7. Basic Materials
8. Information Technology
9. Telecommunications
10. Utilities

This is the way Standard & Poor's classifies the economy. This is also the de facto standard used by the vast majority of professional investors. Accordingly, for us, when in Rome, do as the Romans do.

Therefore, here are the definitions of each economic sector as defined by S&P:

Global Industry Classification Standard (GICS)[8]

- *Consumer Discretionary Sector—The GICS Consumer Discretionary Sector encompasses those industries that tend to be most sensitive to economic cycles. Its manufacturing segment includes automotive, household durable goods, textiles & apparel, and leisure equipment. The services segment includes hotels, restaurants and other leisure facilities, media production and services, and consumer retailing and services.*
- *Consumer Staples Sector—The GICS Consumer Staples Sector comprises companies whose businesses are less sensitive to economic cycles: manufacturers and distributors of food, beverages, and tobacco and producers of nondurable household goods and personal products. It also includes food & drug retailing companies as well as hypermarkets and consumer super centers.*
- *Energy Sector—The GICS Energy Sector comprises companies dominated by either of the following activities: the construction*

or provision of oil rigs, drilling equipment, and other energy-related service and equipment, including seismic data collection; companies engaged in the exploration, production, marketing, refining, and/or transportation of oil and gas products, coal, and other consumable fuels.

- **Health Care Sector**—The GICS Health Care Sector encompasses two main industry groups. The first includes companies that manufacture health care equipment and supplies or provide health care–related services, including distributors of health care products, providers of basic health care services, and owners and operators of health care facilities and organizations. The second regroups companies primarily involved in the research, development, production, and marketing of pharmaceuticals and biotechnology products.

- **Financials Sector**—The GICS Financial Sector contains companies involved in activities such as banking, mortgage finance, consumer finance, specialized finance, investment banking and brokerage, asset management and custody, corporate lending, insurance, financial investment, and real estate, including REITs.

- **Industrials Sector**—The GICS Industrials Sector includes companies whose businesses are dominated by one of the following activities: the manufacture and distribution of capital goods, including aerospace and defense, construction, commercial services and supplies, engineering and building products, electrical equipment, and industrial machinery; the provision of commercial services and supplies, including printing, employment, environmental, and office services; the provision of transportation services, including airlines, couriers, marine, road and rail, and transportation infrastructure.

- **Materials Sector**—The GICS Materials Sector encompasses a wide range of commodity-related manufacturing industries. Included in this sector are companies that manufacture chemicals, construction materials, glass, paper, forest products and related packaging products, and metals, minerals, and mining companies, including producers of steel.

- **Information Technology Sector**—The GICS Information Technology Sector covers the following general areas: firstly, Technology Software & Services, including companies that primarily develop software in various fields such as the Internet, applications, systems, databases management and/or home entertainment, and companies that provide information technology consulting and services, as well as data processing

and outsourced services; secondly, *Technology Hardware &
Equipment, including data manufacturers and distributors of
communications equipment, computers and peripheral electronic equipment and related instruments; and thirdly, Semi-
conductors & Semiconductor Equipment Manufacturers.*
- *Telecommunications Services Sector—The GICS Telecommunications Services Sector contains companies that provide communications services primarily through a fixed-line, cellular,
  wireless, high-bandwidth, and/or fiber-optic cable network.*
- *Utilities Sector—The GICS Utilities Sector encompasses those
  companies considered electric, gas, or water utilities, or companies that operate as independent producers and/or distributors of power.*

For investors, the beauty of this segmenting of the economy is twofold:

1. By analyzing the individual economic sectors, we are able to better understand the economy as a whole by understanding the pieces—where
   the growth is and isn't, where the financial strength is rising or falling,
   where the risk is increasing or decreasing.
2. Since most professional investors manage their funds by ensuring that
   they have a balanced exposure to the economy's 10 economic sectors,
   we are better able to understand their portfolio construction and management process.

And this is where exchange-traded funds (ETFs) come into play.

Because there are ETFs for each of the 10 economic sectors, once an investor has determined that a given economic sector looks attractive, he/she
can make that sector bet (which is in effect exactly what professional money
mangers do, only by buying large numbers of stocks). A sector ETF accom-
plishes this with one investment—the ETF. For example, say you determine
that energy prices are in a long-term uptrend; you might consider owning
the Energy sector through the Energy ETF. Conversely, let's say you believe
that consumer spending on discretionary items is about to experience a
yearlong decline; you might avoid that sector by either not owning any
shares of the Consumer Discretionary ETF or by underowning the sector by
underweighting the percentage of your portfolio vis-à-vis the S&P weighting for that sector.[9] And here you have the staple of professional investing:
weighting a portfolio according to economic sectors.

Many professional investors whose investment style is called "generalist" or "balanced" construct their portfolios based on the relative
weighting of each economic sector. Specifically, if a portfolio manager's

performance is benchmarked against the S&P 500, he/she would make his/her portfolio's composition sensitive to the S&P 500's composition. For example, consider the hypothetical weightings of a portfolio manager who is positive on Energy, Health Care, and Industrials; negative on Consumer Discretionary, Financials, and Telecommunications; and neutral on all the remaining four sectors. (See Table 5.4.)

What this table describes is the essence of Core Plus: An investor tilts or biases a portfolio according to his/her opinion of which sectors look attractive and which do not. This is what most generalist and balanced portfolio managers do explicitly or implicitly. It is what they do by investing in hundreds of stocks. It is something that every investor can do by investing in just 10 ETFs!

Two Birds with One Stone

The dual benefit of understanding the growth and profitability prospects for the 10 economic sectors enables us to understand the economy on a more sector-specific basis (thereby helping our understanding of the overall economy) and, at the same time, enables us to determine what our potential equity portfolio mix might be. Now it's time to dig a bit deeper into each sector by gaining a sense of a key metric of sector performance: profitability.

TABLE 5.4 Economic Sector Weightings: S&P 500 versus Hypothetical Weightings

Sectors	S&P 500 Weighting	Hypothetical Weighting	ETF	Relative Weighting
Consumer Discretionary	10.80%	8.00%	XLY	−2.80%
Consumer Staples	9.80	9.80	XLP	0.00
Energy	9.50	14.00	XLE	4.50
Financials	20.90	15.00	XLF	−5.90
Health Care	13.10	18.00	XLV	4.90
Industrials	11.20	14.80	XLI	3.60
Basic Materials	3.00	3.00	XLB	0.00
Information Technology	15.30	12.00	IYW	−3.30
Telecommunications	3.10	2.00	IYZ	−1.10
Utilities	3.40	3.40	XLU	0.00
Total	100.00%	100.00%		0.00%

Source: Compustat, iViewResearch.

Sector Profitability

We begin by putting the sector profitability within the context of the over-all profitability of the economy. Using the S&P 500 and its economic sectors as proxies for the overall economy, my good friend and frequent panelist at my Market Forecast events, Subodh Kumar, chief investment strategist for CIBC World Markets, produced the data found in Table 5.5.

With this data we can see the revenue and operating margin performance of the S&P 500. From this an investor can get a fairly good gauge as to what is the normal level of revenue growth and operating margins for the overall economy. We can also compare one sector to another and to the economy overall.

Another layer of knowledge can be gained by capturing the data produced every quarter during "earnings season." (See Table 5.6.) Although the categorization here is slightly different (different source), the bottom-line content is almost identical. From this we can get some sense of which sectors are most profitable, which are currently above their average, how they compare to their high and low points, and which are above or below the economy. We also have the performance context to evaluate individual industries.

Economic Sectors, Subsectors, and the Industries Within

One more step down the economic curve brings us to the industry groupings and subgroupings. Here, once again, we will stick with the de facto

TABLE 5.5 Operating Margin Data

S&P 500 Data	Q2/2005	High (1996–2004)	Low (1996–2004)	Average
Consumer Discretionary	5.6%	5.6%	2.0%	4.0%
Consumer Staples	6.3	6.6	5.0	5.9
Energy	10.7	10.9	2.7	6.5
Financials	14.6	15.6	8.9	11.7
Health Care	9.6	12.4	7.8	10.5
Industrials	8.3	8.3	4.1	6.6
Information Technology	11.6	11.9	−10.4	7.3
Materials	10.1	10.1	1.7	5.6
Telecommunications	9.8	14.5	2.9	9.9
Utilities	6.3	11.9	2.0	7.1
S&P 500	9.4	9.4	5.1	7.2

Source: Adapted from Compustat, CIBC World Markets.

TABLE 5.6 3Q05 Economic Sector Earnings Results

	Number of Companies	Net on Continuing Operations			Net Income		
		3Q05	3Q04	Percent Change	3Q05	3Q04	Percent Change
Basic Materials	59	$ 4,875	$ 4,852	0.48%	$ 5,160	$ 4,343	18.82%
Consumer Services	183	18,302	12,169	50.40	18,690	11,356	64.57
Consumer Goods	107	14,215	16,661	-14.68	14,219	16,931	-16.02
Oil and Gas	62	29,247	16,398	78.36	29,992	16,585	80.84
Financial	230	34,540	34,732	-0.55	36,062	35,293	2.18
Health Care	132	11,599	10,776	7.65	11,584	11,752	-1.43
Industrial	194	22,307	18,326	21.72	22,433	18,341	22.31
Technology	190	15,058	9,467	59.06	14,946	9,981	49.74
Telecom	11	4,140	-10,505	N/A	4,162	-9,688	N/A
Utilities	49	5,830	5,594	4.22	5,139	4,711	9.09
Grand Total	1,217	$160,114	$118,469	35.15%	$162,387	$119,605	35.77%

Net on Continuing Operations and Net Income figures are in the millions.
Companies reporting as of November 3, 2005.
Source: Wall Street Journal.

standard of S&P. Considering the fact that the list of subsectors and industries is a rather long one (65 subsectors and 145 industries, to be exact), I will use one, Health Care,[10] to illustrate the point:

Sector	Subsector	Industry and Description
Health Care	*Health Care Equipment & Supplies*	*Health Care Equipment* *Manufacturers of health care equipment and devices. Includes medical electronic precision instruments. Includes drug delivery systems.* *Health Care Supplies* *Manufacturers of health care supplies and medical products not classified elsewhere. Includes eye care products.*
	Health Care Providers & Services	*Health Care Distributors* *Distributors and wholesalers of health care products not classified elsewhere.* *Health Care Services* *Providers of health care services not classified elsewhere. Includes dialysis centers and lab testing services.* *Health Care Facilities* *Owners and operators of health care facilities, including hospitals, nursing homes, rehabilitation and retirement centers, and animal hospitals.* *Managed Health Care* *Owners and operators of health maintenance organizations (HMOs) and other managed plans.*
	Biotechnology	*Biotechnology* *Companies primarily involved in the development, manufacturing, or marketing of products based on advanced biotechnology research.*
	Pharmaceuticals	*Pharmaceuticals* *Companies engaged in the research, development, or production of pharmaceuticals. Includes veterinary drugs.*

The breakdown of the Health Care sector provides the categorization of the subsectors and industries and helps an investor to take the next step: measuring the performance. Table 5.7 presents a useful picture.

A more expanded version and one that incorporates several key operating and market metrics for the Health Care sector and industries within is listed on Table 5.8.

With this data, we can see within the Health Care sector which industries are outperforming on a net profit margin basis and which ones are underperforming on a return on equity basis, for instance. Moreover, when we combine this data with the sector operating margin, we can get an inkling as to the sources of performance strength and weakness for the sector as a whole.

Industry Analysis

Next we concentrate on one of the more important aspects of industry analysis: the life cycle of an industry. When we add this information to the sector operating margin and industry performance data, we take a step closer to having a very good context for understanding the dynamics that are at work within an industry, and therefrom a better understanding of the trends and directions in the larger economic sectors.

Note: There are many aspects to industry analysis, including company-specific analysis, particularly study of the leaders within an industry. Understanding the pacesetting actions of an industry leader is vital to the industry analysis process. The field of industry analysis, like the macroeconomy and microeconomy, is broad and warrants a full exploration to the best of one's ability. With that said and given the limitations of a book designed to introduce the core concepts of investment strategy and portfolio construction, we will move on. As noted earlier, the pursuit of a GEM-based investment strategy approach is a rigorous one.

Life Cycle of an Industry

As mightily as we may try to work against the forces of nature, all things must come to an end. This is the case with people and nations, and it is also true for companies and industries. Infinity is a concept that is left for the philosophers. For investors, however, accepting the inevitable would serve us better. Therefore, consider industries (and companies) as progressing like a person through the different stages of life—birth, growth, maturity, and decline, as illustrated in Figure 5.1.

TABLE 5.7 Health Care Industry Earnings Results, Third Quarter of 2005

	Number of Companies	Net on Continuing Operations			Net Income		
		3Q05	3Q04	Percent Change	3Q05	3Q04	Percent Change
Health Care Providers	38	$ 3,745,311	$ 3,278,673	12%	$ 3,711,398	$ 4,298,265	−16%
Medical Equipment	26	970,620	1,494,582	−54	970,620	1,487,482	−53
Medical Supplies	19	1,554,491	1,870,861	−20	1,572,357	1,773,953	−13
Biotechnology	45	958,370	−10,685	101	49,804	1,824	96
Pharmaceuticals	22	4,886,444	4,574,106	6	4,887,567	4,569,741	7
Total	150	$12,115,236	$11,207,537	7%	$12,100,309	$12,179,245	−1%

Source: Wall Street Journal.

TABLE 5.8 Health Care Industry Breakdown

Industry	Market Cap (Billions)	P/E	ROE	Dividend Yield	Debt to Equity	Price to Book	Net Profit Margin (mrg)	Price to Free Cash Flow (mrg)
Health Care	$2,337.41	23.6	13.76%	1.523%	0.005	10.094	9.636	148.238
Biotechnology	332.01	0	1.6	0.015	0.004	11.33	2.7	337.3
Diagnostic Substances	19.65	0	0	0.413	0.002	6.77	-18.9	-47.9
Drug Delivery	23.00	0	0	0	0.054	9.6	-7.9	-1,421.1
Drug Manufacturers—Major	1,059.78	21.3	20.9	2.883	0.005	7.26	16.2	114
Drug Manufacturers—Other	135.56	0	0	0.968	0.002	67.67	-1.2	145
Drug-Related Products	6.66	0	0	0.75	0.007	8.41	-3.7	127.8
Drugs—Generic	24.04	31.7	11.9	0.387	0.005	6.64	10.9	134
Health Care Plans	224.89	20.7	16	0.021	0.003	14.69	5	54.2
Home Health Care	4.54	29.1	9.8	1.231	0.002	11.45	3.9	-28
Hospitals	45.57	0	1.1	1.019	0.013	5.99	0.4	60.6
Long-Term Care Facilities	11.64	18.9	16.8	1.157	0.008	3.84	3.9	-234.5
Medical Appliances and Equipment	164.46	43.9	12.7	0.589	0.002	10.63	11.2	489
Medical Instruments and Supplies	200.91	84.9	10.9	0.836	0.004	11.74	7.4	121.7
Medical Laboratories and Research	24.82	33.9	11.9	0.369	0.001	17.25	7.4	132.3
Medical Practitioners	3.02	76.8	11.2	0.498	0.004	7.73	4.2	-54.4
Specialized Health Services	56.88	26	12.1	0.004	0.003	-102.59	3.6	61.6

Source: Yahoo! Finance.

Industry Growth Stages

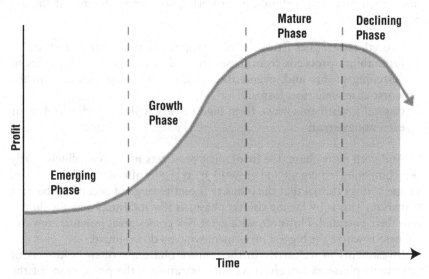

FIGURE 5.1 Industry Growth Stages

Each stage has its own unique characteristics that are of importance to investors.

- The Emerging Phase is marked by earnings losses, moderate growth, and (usually) large capital investments as companies seek to establish the emergent industry as a financially viable one.
- In the Growth Phase, sales growth is rapid, earnings shift from losses in the early part of the growth phase to rapidly rising profitability, and capital investments tend to be large and growing as the industry becomes sustainable.
- The Mature Phase bears witness to a slowing in the year-over-year growth in sales; profitability, however, continues to rise in the early phase as capital investments slow (due to a lessened need to support the top-line sales growth) but then levels off in the latter phase of the cycle.
- The Declining Phase is when growth opportunities are severely limited, profitability begins to decline, and capital investments are not needed beyond the maintenance level.

In this condensed and rather broad generalization of the factors at play during each phase, you should get a fairly good sense of some of the dynamics at work:

- Growth (sales) goes from modest to rapid to leveling off to decline.
- Profitability proceeds from losses to modest profits to high profits to flattening profits and, eventually, back to modest profits and, in the worst-case scenarios, losses.
- Capital investments move from high to very high to modest to low or even nonexistent.

And with each phase, the investment prospects move accordingly. Early stage companies (emergent and growth) are typically afforded high valuations as hope springs eternal that the industry is on the verge of becoming the next PC market. This is by far the riskiest phase, as few industries actually do live up to their potential. However, with great risk comes great potential reward. And here is where the biggest investment winners do originate.

Investments in industries in the mature phase are often holdovers of the growth phase as hopeful investors extrapolate the great years of the past into the future. This is typically the phase of great disappointment for many investors because extrapolating the past is often an exercise in failed thinking. In fact, the investment market is strewn with has-beens seeking to remain the spring chickens they once were. To be clear, however, some industries do reinvent themselves and are able to utilize their strong competitive and profitable position to sustain profitability and growth for many more years. But they are the exceptions and not the rule.

In the final act, the decline phase looks a lot like the stock market's version of eBay: used goods at bargain prices. And, as with the latter stages of the maturity phase, this is also the domain of the so-called vulture capitalists. Occupying the tail end of the life cycle, the vulture capitalists act as their mirror-image counterparts from the other end of the life cycle, the venture capitalists, and seek to pick apart the pieces of the once vibrant entity called the going concern and find another home for the assets. This often results in a rapid jump in the price of the stock of the company and, along with high dividend payments and stock buybacks, is the primary reason to be invested in this space.

GOOD SOURCES

I am not an economist, nor do I want to be one. But an understanding of the global economy is a must-have in today's globalized world. I have determined that it is incumbent upon me to do my level best to gain and maintain an understanding of what to pay attention to and what to ignore or at least minimize in all areas of investment strategy, but in particular when it comes to the massive scale and scope of the global economy.

To help me achieve this tall order, I do a considerable amount of reading (books, reports) and independent research. To do this, I have come to identify and rely on those writers whom I have found to be consistently insightful. They are noted throughout this book. And I encourage anyone seriously thinking about taking on this task to do the same: identify who can be of insightful service, and be committed to hours of research work.

ISSUES

The global macro environment is a place where numerous issues are actively in play. The dynamism of globalization combined with the volatile geopolitical condition makes a study of the global landscape a lifelong project.

Here are a few issues that will help round out your knowledge of the topics discussed in this chapter as well as hopefully provide a source of inspiration for those of you seeking to develop your own deep understanding of the forces of a global economy.

THE BATTLE OF THE CAPITALISMS

There is an economic war raging. It is a battle for the hearts and minds of the competing countries' citizens/voters. In one camp is the American-style version of capitalism in which the profit motive dominates and the social compact is a secondary consideration. In the other camp there is the social democracy model in which the social compact with the citizens takes precedence over the profit motive.

In the second installment in the *Financial Times'* "Globalization and the European Union" series, Nicholas Timmins, the public policy editor with the *Financial Times* and author of *The Five Giants: A Biography of the Welfare State* (HarperCollins, 2001), describes some of the aspects of this battle of the capitalisms as they relate to the American style (what he calls the "Anglo-Saxon" model) and social democratic style (the "social model" welfare state).

In a recent commentary to my clients (March 2006), I addressed some of the key issues raised by Nicholas Timmins in his October 21, 2005, article, "EU Set for Clash on 'Anglo-Saxon' versus 'Social' Welfare Models."

Timmins begins his article by outlining the central issue at work: "Does much of mainland Europe need to break up its 'social model' welfare state in favor of an 'Anglo-Saxon' model along UK and US lines?"

Timmins describes how "the fundamental dispute will be at the heart of next week's summit of the European Union at Hampton Court, heated by fears in France, Germany, and other EU countries that their generous jobless and pensions systems, whose benefits are often pegged to wages, could be slashed if replaced by far less beneficial pay-outs in the US and the UK."

Timmins highlights the differences between the more social compact approach of the developed EU countries versus the U.S. and UK market-centric approach by quoting Richard Layard, an employment economist at the London School of Economics, who cautions that "painting a stark contrast between the so-called 'Anglo-Saxon' model and the European 'social model' is to miss the point.

"The real distinction is between those countries that have had effective active labor policies, and those that have not."

To illustrate this point, Timmins points out that "many of the Nordic countries have high levels of public expenditure and social protection but also high levels of employment thanks to policies that ensure those out of work are actively seeking to return to it."

In contrast, the UK's approach, which has been built around a "rights and responsibilities" agenda, helps crystallize the fundamental differences between the social compact approach between government and workers prevalent in many established and developed European countries and the more market-centric approaches of the United Kingdom (and the United States).

In fact, Timmins sees the approach taken by the United Kingdom as "being drawn from the US." In the United States, the market-centric, rights-and-responsibilities approach to worker relations is very strong. It permeates the political climate as well, and has placed American businesses in a strong global competitive position. In the United Kingdom, however, such a market-centric approach is not as deeply rooted.

For example, according to the Timmins article, John Hills, director of the Center for the Analysis of Social Exclusion (CASE) at the London School of Economics, says that "while much of the rhetoric and the jargon match that of the United States, many of the reforms have involved much more carrot and much less stick than in the US."

In reality, many of the UK reforms were partly derived in response to the competitive advantage gained by such EU countries as Denmark and the Netherlands, which, through active labor market policies, began to push ahead of the United Kingdom. According to Timmins, what Layard argues is that similar programs "have helped Ireland and now Spain and others produce dramatic falls in unemployment."

This shift toward a more market-centric approach to labor has put competitive pressures on all EU countries. In fact, Timmins points out that "both France and Germany have taken steps down this road, although rather more dramatically in Germany than France."

Timmins was prescient in his comments as Germany began to experience labor unrest in the late winter of 2006 with strikes by various unions.

Related to this is the disparity in incomes between various worker classes. For an approximately 20-year span, from the mid-1970s to the mid-1990s, Timmins points out that in the United Kingdom "income inequality rose dramatically, further and faster than in almost any country in the world."

However, since the mid-1990s the income inequality trend was halted. And, according to a recent analysis by CASE, thanks to a series of new tax credits (and higher employment), "the UK has made a significant step on the road to bringing child poverty down towards average EU levels." These developments have helped to alleviate some of the child poverty in the UK "at a time when other high poverty countries within Europe have seen child poverty rise."

Timmins also notes that "while it is true that many of the UK's welfare-to-work policies have seen the financial position of childless adults who remain out of work worsen, . . . the improvement in the number of poorer pensioners has been cut by a quarter since 1997." The result has been a decline in the United Kingdom's overall poverty rate, so much so that the country compares favorably with the rest of Europe.

However, despite the United Kingdom's fine progress and while income inequality has ceased to get worse, the government's policies have yet to eliminate the still significant income disparity.

The picture is, as Timmins notes, complex.

In the early years of the twenty-first century, while "the poor have seen their position improve relative to the middle of the income distribution" curve, "some of that improvement having come directly from [UK] welfare-to-work programs," what has not been impacted is the fact that the rich continue to get even richer at a quickening pace—creating a further income disparity between the rich and very rich versus all other classes.

This trend is also true for the United States and is an area of potential populist politics.

What Timmins and others have highlighted are the challenges faced by the "social welfare models" of developed Europe in a globalized world. If part of the purpose of a government is to help those who cannot help themselves or are in temporary need of assistance, then a solution is needed for how countries like France and Germany, with their highly socialized relationships with their citizens, are going to attract and keep the capital necessary for businesses to compete.

With the free flow of capital, money knows no borders. It will gravitate toward those countries that offer the best rates of return.

How the developed EU countries will balance these issues remains to be seen.

GLOBALIZATION

Globalization was covered fairly well at the beginning of this chapter. Added here are some thoughts regarding the free flow of capital and labor and a potentially dangerous impact that the American version of capitalism might have.

As we know, the world's economies are more interlinked today than ever before. The move toward market economies by an increasing number of countries has been facilitated by trade agreements, information and communications technology, the growth and acceptance of the Internet, and what I call advanced management techniques. These forces, and many others, are all working toward a transformation of historic proportions, the consequences of which are hard to determine. We know the good consequences—higher-quality products at lower prices—but the bad consequences are interconnected with the domestic fiscal policies and cultural institutionalization of a social compact, the most notable of which are in the United States and Europe. Let's consider the factors, good and bad.

In today's world economy, there is an unprecedented free flow of capital and labor. The ability to move trillions of dollars around the world in an instant is commonplace. And corporate ability to outsource talent anywhere in the world enables companies to maintain a quality of service while cutting labor costs. Moreover, this free flow of capital and labor is being facilitated by the Internet and technological innovation.

The implications of the aforementioned trends are profound. The pressures from a market-based global economy mean that investors, specifically institutional investors, are demanding that corporate leaders utilize their capital most effectively. That means that rates of return on capital *and* the growth of cash flows generated *must* exceed the cost of that capital. If this does not occur, then a price will be exacted on the deficient company in question in the form of the "Wall Street walk" (money goes elsewhere as the stock is sold, thereby depressing the price) or a more activist role, including the firing and replacing of senior management.

Financier George Soros shares the following thoughts on globalization:

> I have adopted a rather narrow definition of globalization: I equate it with the free movement of capital and the increasing domination of national economies by global financial markets and multinational corporations. This approach has the advantage of narrowing the focus of discussion. I contend that globalization has been lopsided. The development of our international institutions has not kept pace with the development of international financial markets and our political arrangements have lagged behind the globalization of the economy.
>
> . . . the prevailing view continues to be based on a fundamentally flawed market fundamentalist interpretation of how financial markets operate. That view is now endangering the stability of global financial markets. Instead of moving toward equilibrium, financial markets, left to their own devices, are liable to go to extremes and eventually break down.[11]

The issue of the unfettered free market model, which is in essence what the American-style model is, and the dangers of a reliance upon it to manage itself is expressed by Soros. I am neither advocating for his opinion (which I believe to be true) nor opposing it. But it is a subject area worth understanding, at a minimum.

DEFICITS AND DEBT

Another major issue that the early twenty-first century is struggling with is the profligacy of the United States, both its citizens and its government. This has evolved into a major area of concern for several very bright thinkers.

Living within one's means is always a more stable way to conduct one's financial affairs. The same can be said for governments, which, according to Keynesian economics, do have to run deficits from time to time to offset economic weakness. The problem develops when deficits become too large in both absolute and relative terms and lead to rising interest rates and inflationary pressures. Rising deficits of the fiscal kind are a fact today, and by themselves are manageable—if the economy in question is a closed economy. However, we don't live in a closed economy anymore. In fact, several economists and other notables (including the previously quoted Pete Peterson) are deeply concerned over the growing global imbalances of savings, debt, and deficits. To them, the world is upside down. They believe, and I fully agree with them, that the present situation of big deficits as far as the eye can see and the world's largest economy being the world's largest net debtor is unsustainable and a prescription for disaster if left unchecked.

The world economy cannot sustain the imbalances of deficits and debts, nor can the world's largest economy continue to be the world's largest debtor indefinitely. In fact, the issue of an upside-down economic world was expressed quite clearly by *Financial Times* contributing economist Martin Wolf, when he wrote in April 2005:

> ... *current trends are unsustainable and undesirable. If the trends in imports and exports of the past 15 years were to continue, US net liabilities could jump from roughly a quarter of gross domestic product at the end of 2003 to 120 per cent of GDP by 2014. Even if the current account deficit were to stabilize as a share of GDP, the ratio would reach 80 per cent of GDP. It is hard to believe that the foreign private sector would willingly hold such huge claims, denominated in the dollar, at current US asset prices.*
>
> *Yet it is also hard to imagine that the foreign official sector would, or should, provide resources to the US on so vast a scale. Between 2002 and 2004, inclusive, the foreign official sector's direct financing of the US current account deficit amounted to $718 billion. Between December 2001 and December 2004, global foreign exchange reserves increased by $1,680 billion, to reach $3,730 billion. . . . Goldman Sachs has recently argued that foreign exchange bank reserves exceed the optimal level by $1,400 billion. The precise calculations are questionable. But the point is not.*
>
> *China, for example, had accumulated $600 billion by the end of last year. A 30 per cent appreciation of the renminbi would inflict a loss of 10 per cent of GDP. As Morris Goldstein and Nicholas Lardy of the Washington-based Institute for International Economics argue, this policy cannot make sense. Growing by giving resources away cannot be a sensible strategy.*[12]

In the aforementioned book, *Running on Empty*, Peter Peterson, former Commerce Secretary and lifelong Republican, addressed the issue of deficits in this way: "Deficits have become like aspirin, a sort of fiscal wonder drug. We should take them regularly just to stay healthy and take lots of them whenever we're feeling out of sorts." The former chairman of the Federal Reserve Bank of New York goes on to write:

> *Most economists who study this issue conclude, in general, that the strongest connection is between long-term real interest rates and long-term deficit expectations. A single deficit year doesn't matter much; indeed, a deficit during a recession is usually good policy. What matters is what markets believe about the deficit trend over the next decade or more.*
>
> *So does that mean large long-term deficits always translate into a predictably high real interest rate? Not always—economists always have their provisos. In the near term, interest rates can be hugely influenced by temporary swings in the demand for investment and in the supply of savings. Such swings explain why the interest rates have remained very low over the last few years despite the dramatic shift in deficit projections.*[13]

And Stephen Roach, chief economist with Morgan Stanley, adds the following on September 16, 2005:

> *The disparity between current account deficits and surpluses is now closing in on a record 5 percent of world GDP. Behind this imbalance lurks an important and potentially dangerous asymmetry: Deficits are heavily concentrated in one economy whereas surpluses are spread out widely over a large number of nations. This mismatch could well exert a very destabilizing influence on the coming rebalancing of the global economy.*
>
> *There are no guarantees that there will be a synchronous rebalancing in the mix of global saving—that a US saving increase will be accompanied by declining saving rates elsewhere in the world. To the contrary, there is good reason to fear a further widening of the disparity in global saving and current account positions over the next couple of years. While there is a growing and welcome possibility of some saving reduction in the major surplus economies, that constructive trend could well be more than offset by a sharp deterioration on the US saving front.*
>
> *America's national saving outlook is in the process of going from bad to worse.*
>
> *Today's unbalanced world is in an extremely delicate state of equilibrium. The asymmetrical distribution of current account*

deficits and surpluses around the world means global rebalancing will involve an equally asymmetrical realignment in the mix of global saving. This is potentially a "hair-trigger" result for an already unbalanced world. America is having a highly disproportionate impact on the state of imbalance in today's global economy. As such, there is much greater urgency for the US to raise its record low domestic saving rate than there is for any one country—or group of countries—to draw down surplus saving. Yet a US-centric rebalancing is very much a double-edged sword for a lopsided world: An increase in US saving would also crimp the major engine on the demand side of the global economy. Depending on the path of the saving adjustment—gradual or abrupt—the outcomes could range from a sustained shortfall in global growth to a sharp worldwide recession.

This is where the asymmetries in the mix of global saving have the clear potential to become a serious problem. If the world's dominant deficit economy—the United States—goes even deeper into deficit at the same time the world's surplus economies start to absorb their domestic saving, America's ever-mounting external financing pressures are likely to be vented in world financial markets. This, of course, is the stuff of a classic current-account adjustment— the case for a weaker dollar and higher US interest rates. As long as the non-US world was in an excess saving position, a major repricing of dollar-denominated assets could be avoided. But now, with an asymmetrical shift in the mix of global saving increasingly likely, it could well become all the tougher for the United States to avoid this treacherous endgame.

Here is the question that I have: What happens when (not if) the world economy goes into a slump? With deficits already at record levels, how does the world economy recover when only one lever, monetary policy, is at the disposal of the world's leaders? If this sounds familiar, it is. This is the "pushing-on-a-string" environment of the pre-Depression era. If the world economy must hope that monetary policy alone can help the global economy to recover from a recession, then it is pinning its future on something akin to pushing on a string.

The consequences of such a scenario are mind-boggling. The short and very tragic list includes a massive diminution of America's standing in the world, for the blame will most certainly fall on the leading proponent of the most aggressive form of free market capitalism. Perhaps you can understand why the likes of Paul Volcker, Robert Rubin, the three gentlemen quoted earlier, and a raft of others have such concerns. I do. Do you?

TRADE

A hot-button item is the dramatic decline in the balance of trade of goods and services between the United States and its trading partners, most prominent of which is China. The following balance of trade data from a September 2005 Department of Commerce report is another reason why those noted earlier and others are deeply concerned about deficits and debt:

Period	Balance
2003	
Full Year	−$494,814
First 8 Months	−$328,739
2004	
Full Year	−$617,583
First 8 Months	−$396,421
2005	
First 8 Months	−$463,366

The ability to sustain a trade deficit indefinitely is a major area of concern for many mainstream economists. This deficit situation is directly and primarily attributable to one source: the U.S. consumer.

THE OVEREXTENDED U.S. CONSUMER

In late 2005, one area of great vulnerability for the global economy is the U.S. consumer. Accounting for approximately 70 percent of the U.S. GDP and 30 percent of the world economy, the importance of the U.S. consumer cannot be overstated. Think of it this way: If the U.S. consumer catches a cold, the world economy may get pneumonia.

In so many respects, the world economy today is a leveraged play on the U.S. consumer. China, Japan, Europe, and emerging market countries such as the Asian tigers all depend on the shop till we drop American consumer. With little in the way of real domestic demand for consumer goods in their own countries, China et al. must hope that U.S. consumers can and will continue their spending habits. The key word in the prior sentence is *can*. Can, as in able to do, is the $56 trillion question. For that is what is at stake: the ability of the world economy to grow from that number.

Given the fact that so much of that $56 trillion number (30 percent) depends on the U.S. consumer, understanding his/her ability to support global growth is at the top of everyone's list. Or it should be. With that fact in tow, consider the following remarks:

Remarks from David A. Rosenberg, North American economist at Merrill Lynch, in his October 10, 2005, conference call to clients, discussing the current state of consumer spending:

> *Consumer spending momentum is slowing down visibly. Growth has gone from 4 percent in 2004 to 3.5 percent in 2005, and if our forecast is right, 2.5 percent in 2006 as the negative savings rate gets rebuilt.*

Remarks by Federal Reserve Bank Governor Donald L. Kohn at the 2006 Global Economic and Investment Outlook Conference, Carnegie-Mellon University, Pittsburgh, Pennsylvania, on October 19, 2005, discussing the housing market and the wealth effect on consumer spending:

> *Another source of uncertainty is the housing market. It is possible that the rapid increases in house prices could simply be a reflection of fundamental forces such as an increase in land use restrictions and other legal restraints on building, innovations in mortgage finance, changes in tax laws, and low interest rates. But it could also be the case that much of the very rapid increase in prices very recently has been based on the expectation that the pace of past increases will extend into the future. Or perhaps the increases also have been fueled by eased lending standards that could well be tightened in response to slower price appreciation. If expectations have been realistic and lending practices only marginally important, a slowdown in house-price appreciation could be gradual and the consequences for consumption growth could be modest; indeed, as signs of a slowdown are still quite tentative, continued strength in house prices are an upside risk to any easing of demand going forward. But if disappointed expectations or considerably tighter credit foster more severe or more abrupt price adjustments in enough local housing markets, psychology could amplify the effects of diminished wealth to restrain consumer spending. Economists, including those at central banks, simply are not very good at understanding, much less predicting, the dynamics of asset price adjustments; and I would guess that our ignorance is especially profound when those dynamics may be in the process of shifting.*

Vintage "on the one hand, and on the other" remarks by Fed Chairman Alan Greenspan, discussing the mortgage market and consumer debt at America's Community Bankers Annual Convention, Washington, D.C., on October 19, 2004:

> *Although I scarcely wish to downplay the threats to the U.S. economy from increased debt leverage of any type, ratios of household debt to income appear to imply somewhat more stress than is likely to be the case. For at least a half century, household debt has been rising faster than income, as ever-higher levels of discretionary income have increased the proportion of income spent on assets partially financed with debt.*
>
> *The pace has been especially brisk in the past two years as existing home turnover and home price increase, the key determinants of home mortgage debt growth, have been particularly elevated. Most analysts, even those who do not foresee a mounting bubble, anticipate a slowdown in both home sales and the rate of price increase.*
>
> *To be sure, some households are stretched to their limits. The persistently elevated bankruptcy rate remains a concern, as it indicates pockets of distress in the household sector. But the vast majority appear able to calibrate their borrowing and spending to minimize financial difficulties. Thus, short of a significant fall in overall household income or in home prices, debt servicing is unlikely to become destabilizing.*

There's more. Lots more. And I leave to you to explore this subject in great detail. It is without doubt an extremely important topic to understand.

The issue of appreciating the changed economic picture from a closed domestic economy to the globalized one emphasized in this chapter is a subject that I addressed in a report produced several months ago, at a time when the U.S. economy was slumping and many were wondering whether it was merely going through a midcycle correction or was on the verge of a serious decline.

Old School Economic Thinking: Quicksand for the Twenty-First-Century Investor

When does a soft patch become quicksand?

Of late, there appears to be a rising chorus of concern expressed by an increasingly number of traditional economists over yet another soft patch in the economy. However, what underlies the soft patch scenario is not concern over the seriously unsustainable global structural imbalances or that so much of the world works in a hidden, new, and therefore unknown manner. Rather, their view is that soft patches are followed by strong upturns. In other words, "Don't worry. Be happy." However, I am both worried and of the strong belief that there is reason to be unhappy.

In the globalized world of today, soft patches can easily become quicksand far more rapidly than the traditionalists think, because the global economic and financial environment is far more unpredictable, uncertain, and unknown than the traditionalists realize. Consider the comments by John Plender in the Financial Times *on hedge funds and the banking system: "We have a paradox. More risk is being priced in markets today than ever before, which should make for a more efficient financial system. Yet much of this market activity is untransparent, which is worrying for financial stability."*

From my experience in both moderating numerous events involving economists of all stripes and reading their research, I have found that, for the most part, your classically trained economist tends not to be an out-of-the-box thinker. As a result, he/she tends to frame the world in the classical industrial era sense, not in the more dynamic interdependent, technologically driven global sense. And this old school approach to the twenty-first-century world tends to neglect or minimize the new and hard-to-quantify factors such as those that John Plender (and others) have written about. Moreover, there is the question of speed and the importance of confidence and the role they play in our brave new world. In such a world, soft patches can become quicksand faster than you can say "old school economics doctorate."

INFLATION

Given the importance of how inflation impacts our valuation model's discount factor, not to mention the economy overall, gaining a reasonable understanding of this vital area of the economy is worth a word or two. Let's begin with some information from Yahoo! Finance:

CPI: Consumer Price Index
- *Importance (A–F): This release merits a B+.*
- *Source: Bureau of Labor Statistics, U.S. Department of Labor.*
- *Release Time: 8:30 ET, about the 13th of each month for the prior month.*
- *Raw Data Available At: http://stats.bls.gov/news.release/cpi .toc.htm.*

The Consumer Price Index is a measure of the price level of a fixed market basket of goods and services purchased by consumers. CPI is the most widely cited inflation indicator, and it is used to calculate cost of living adjustments for government programs and is the basis of COLAs for many private labor agreements as well. It has been criticized for overstating inflation, because it does not adjust for substitution effects and because the fixed basket does not reflect price changes in new technology goods, which are often declining in price. Despite these criticisms, it remains the benchmark inflation index.

CPI can be greatly influenced in any given month by a movement in volatile food and energy prices. Therefore, it is important to look at CPI excluding food and energy, commonly called the "core rate" of inflation. Within the core rate, some of the more volatile and closely watched components are apparel, tobacco, airfares, and new cars. In addition to tracking the month/month changes in core CPI, the year/year change in core CPI is seen by most economists as the best measure of the underlying inflation rate.

This is Yahoo! Finance's opinion of the importance of the report, its source, the time of its release, and where to go to get the raw data. Speaking of the raw data, familiarizing oneself with U.S. government reports is an art as much as it is a science. It is also a daunting task for a noneconomist to decipher the language and volume of information published. Nevertheless, it is a very useful exercise and one that an independently thinking investor should be capable of doing. Take, for example, the U.S. Labor Department's Consumer Price Index report for September 2005. (See Table 5.9.)

Consumer Price Index: September 2005

The Consumer Price Index for All Urban Consumers (CPI-U) increased 1.2 percent in September, before seasonal adjustment, the Bureau of Labor Statistics of the U.S. Department of Labor reported today. The September level of 198.8 (1982–84 = 100) was 4.7 percent higher than in September 2004. The Consumer Price Index for Urban Wage Earners and Clerical Workers (CPI-W) increased 1.5 percent in September, prior to seasonal adjustment. The September level of 195.0 was 5.2 percent higher than in September 2004.

The Chained Consumer Price Index for All Urban Consumers (C-CPI-U) increased 0.8 percent in September on a not seasonally adjusted basis. The September level of 114.7 (December 1999 = 100) was 3.5 percent higher than in September 2004.

TABLE 5.9 September 2005 CPI Report: Percent Changes in CPI for All Urban Consumers (CPI-U)

Expenditure Category	2005								
	March	April	May	June	July	August	September	September '05[a]	September '05[b]
All Items	0.6	0.5	-0.1	0.0	0.5	0.5	1.2	9.4	4.7
Food and Beverages	0.2	0.6	0.1	0.0	0.2	0.1	0.2	1.9	2.5
Housing	0.5	0.3	0.1	0.1	0.4	0.2	0.4	4.0	3.1
Apparel	0.8	-0.6	0.0	-0.7	-0.9	1.0	-0.1	0.0	-0.6
Transportation	1.9	1.8	-1.0	-0.1	1.5	2.2	5.1	41.5	14.5
Medical Care	0.5	0.2	0.3	0.2	0.4	0.0	0.3	2.8	3.9
Recreation	0.0	0.2	0.3	-0.3	0.1	0.3	0.4	3.0	1.0
Education and Communication	0.2	0.4	0.0	0.1	0.2	-0.1	0.7	3.2	2.1
Other Goods and Services	0.1	0.0	0.4	0.0	0.6	0.2	0.1	3.5	2.8
Special Indexes									
Energy	4.0	4.5	-2.0	-0.5	3.8	5.0	12.0	122.1	34.8
Food	0.2	0.7	0.1	0.1	0.2	0.0	0.3	1.9	2.5
All Items Less Food and Energy	0.4	0.0	0.1	0.1	0.1	0.1	0.1	1.4	2.0

All data: Changes from preceding month; seasonally adjusted.
[a]Compound annual rate three months ended.
[b]Unadjusted 12 months ended.
Source: Bureau of Labor Statistics.

Please note that the indexes for the post-2003 period are subject to revision.

CPI for All Urban Consumers (CPI-U)

On a seasonally adjusted basis, the CPI-U increased 1.2 percent in September. Energy costs increased sharply for the third consecutive month—up 12.0 percent in September—and accounted for more than 90 percent of the advance in the September CPI-U.

Within energy, the index for energy commodities (petroleum-based energy) increased 17.4 percent and the index for energy services rose 4.6 percent. The index for food, which was unchanged in August, rose 0.3 percent in September, largely reflecting an upturn in the index for fruits and vegetables. The index for all items less food and energy registered a 0.1 percent increase for the fifth consecutive month. Shelter costs, which were virtually unchanged in August, declined 0.1 percent in September, largely as a result of a 2.5 percent decrease in the index for lodging away from home. The index for apparel, which increased 1.0 percent in August, declined 0.1 percent in September. These declines were more than offset by upturns in the indexes for new vehicles, for medical care services, and for communication.

Consumer prices increased at a seasonally adjusted annual rate (SAAR) of 9.4 percent in the third quarter of 2005, following increases in the first and second quarters at annual rates of 4.3 and 1.9 percent, respectively. This brings the year-to-date annual rate to 5.1 percent and compares with an increase of 3.3 percent in all of 2004. The index for energy, which advanced at annual rates of 21.1 and 7.5 percent in the first two quarters, increased at a 122.1 percent rate in the third quarter of 2005. Thus far this year, energy costs have risen at a 42.5 percent SAAR after increasing 16.6 percent in all of 2004. In the first nine months of 2005, petroleum-based energy costs increased at a 67.9 percent rate and charges for energy services increased at a 14.6 percent rate. The food index rose at a 2.2 percent SAAR in the first nine months of 2005.

The index for grocery store food prices increased at a 1.3 percent rate. Among the six major grocery store food groups, the index for nonalcoholic beverages registered the largest increase during this span—up at a 4.3 percent rate—while the index for fruits and vegetables recorded the only decline—down at a 1.7 percent annual rate.

The CPI-U excluding food and energy advanced at a 1.4 percent SAAR in the third quarter, following increases at rates of 3.3

and 1.2 percent in the first two quarters of 2005. The advance at a 2.0 percent SAAR for the first nine months of 2005 compares with a 2.2 percent rise in all of 2004. Each of the major groups—including alcoholic beverages and the non-energy portion of the housing and transportation groups—registered a rate of change in the first nine months of 2005 within 1 percent of that for all of 2004. The annual rates for selected groups for the past seven and three-quarters years are shown [see Table 5.10].

The importance of understanding the consumer price index and the value in reading and understanding government reports such as those from the U.S. Department of Labor lies in two areas: an investor's ability to do original research and the link between inflation and interest rates.

If one is to attempt to incorporate a macroeconomic element into his/her investment strategy, that investor should not rely solely on the comments and opinions of economists, no matter how well respected or impressive they are. To think for yourself is a precious commodity. Being capable of reading and interpreting government and private organizations' reports requires a commitment to learning. It is not easy but it is well worth the effort.

As for this specific report and the link to interest rates, it is well known that interest rates are driven primarily by Federal Reserve policy at the short end of the maturity spectrum and by fixed income investors (often called "bond market vigilantes") at the medium and long end of the maturity spectrum. And their behavior is driven by inflation today and expectations of future inflation rates, for the Federal Reserve's mandate is to provide price stability (along with growth in the economy), and the bond investors' mission is to make correct interest rate bets. As a result, both are very interested in what inflationary pressures there are and might be in the months and years ahead that will impact interest rates today. By studying the government report on inflation, an investor goes a long way toward gaining a valuable insight into this very important area of the economy.

As to the specifics of this report, the key item to note is the last line in the chart: all items less food and energy. It is that figure that excludes the very volatile food and energy factors as they are subject to greater monthly fluctuations and thereby tend to present a distorted picture of the true underlying inflation. It is interesting to note the price action of the benchmark 10-year U.S. Treasury, which was trading around the 4¼ percent level at the time of the report. The price action for the next few months in the fall of 2005 is illustrated in Figure 5.2.

It's interesting to note that the rather benign core inflation rate (all items less food and energy) over the past several years did not produce a decline in the 10-year rate, even after the subsequent report on consumer

TABLE 5.10 CPI Data Since 1998

				Percentage Change 12 Months Ended in December				
Expenditure Category	1998	1999	2000	2001	2002	2003	2004	2005[a]
All Items	1.6	2.7	3.4	1.6	2.4	1.9	3.3	5.1
Food and Beverages	2.3	2.0	2.8	2.8	1.5	3.5	2.6	2.1
Housing	2.3	2.2	4.3	2.9	2.4	2.2	3.0	3.2
Apparel	-0.7	-0.5	-1.8	-3.2	-1.8	-2.1	-0.2	-0.7
Transportation	-1.7	5.4	4.1	-3.8	3.8	0.3	6.5	17.1
Medical Care	3.4	3.7	4.2	4.7	5.0	3.7	4.2	4.0
Recreation	1.2	0.8	1.7	1.5	1.1	1.1	0.7	1.1
Education and Communication	0.7	1.6	1.3	3.2	2.2	1.6	1.5	2.5
Other Goods and Services	8.8	5.1	4.2	4.5	3.3	1.5	2.5	2.8
Special Indexes								
Energy	-8.8	13.4	14.2	-13.0	10.7	6.9	16.6	42.5
Energy Commodities	-15.1	29.5	15.7	-24.5	23.7	6.9	26.7	67.9
Energy Services	-3.3	1.2	12.7	-1.5	0.4	6.9	6.8	14.6
All Items Less Energy	2.4	2.0	2.6	2.8	1.8	1.5	2.2	2.0
Food	2.3	1.9	2.8	2.8	1.5	3.6	2.7	2.2
All Items Less Food and Energy	2.4	1.9	2.6	2.7	1.9	1.1	2.2	2.0

[a]Seasonally adjusted annual rate nine months ended September.
Source: Bureau of Labor Statistics.

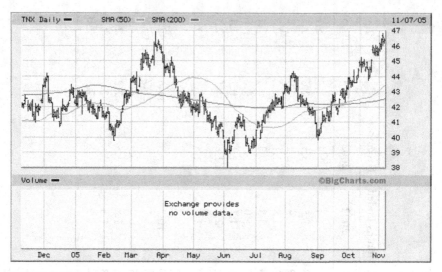

FIGURE 5.2   Ten-Year U.S. Treasury Note
Source: BigCharts.com.

prices was unchanged from the September 2005 report. This strongly suggests that forces other than the rate and trend in inflation are at work. Perhaps the next chapter on the markets might shed some light on the subject.

SUMMARY

Shakespeare wrote, "All the world's a stage." When it comes to twenty-first-century economic matters, it is truly a global stage that businesses and governments are performing on and consumers are affected by—for good or ill.

So, how does an investor digest the scale and scope of so vast a subject as the global macroeconomy? In a word, judgment. Given the scale and scope of the global task at hand, judgment must play a central role in an investor's ability to determine the critical variables at work. Moreover, given the dynamic nature of a globalized world, the shifting areas of investor emphasis are relentless. One day it is the U.S. dollar and its movements, the next it is interest rates, and then the investment emphasis shifts to the trade issues with China, and on and on. If you accept the premise that it is the global economy, stupid, then an investor has little choice but to embrace the task and adhere to the principles of hard work, good sources, critical variables, and judgment to gain the necessary insight that an investment strategy based on incorporating economic matters demands. It is what it is.

TIME TO MEET MR. MARKET

As investors, distilling the coach's room analysis down to an opinion is the work we have predominantly done thus far. We have immersed ourselves in the all-important work of understanding the principles of valuation, the macroeconomy and microeconomy, the political dynamic, and industry analysis—all real-world, real-economy stuff. It's now time to meet Mr. Market.

CHAPTER 6

Say Hello to Mr. Market

Ben Graham, my friend and teacher, long ago described the mental attitude toward market fluctuations that I believe to be most conducive to investment success. He said that you should imagine market quotations as coming from a remarkably accommodating fellow named Mr. Market who is your partner in a private business. Without fail, Mr. Market appears daily and names a price at which he will either buy your interest or sell you his.[1]

So begins the famous story of Mr. Market by legendary investor Warren Buffett and it serves as an excellent transition from the real economy to the financial economy—the markets.

The conclusions an investor draws from the analysis of the real economy—governmental, economic, sectors, and industries—must now be measured against what the market has to say about it. For it is in the field of play of the markets and not in the coach's room of fundamental analysis that the prices are set. It stands to reason, then, that a careful analysis of the game on the field of play is the logical and necessary complement to the fundamental study of the real economy that is done.

Some investors may see the two economies as being mutually exclusive. You believe in either one or the other. There are many astute investors, however, who see the value in utilizing both economies complementarily. One reflects what should be (real-economy-derived intrinsic values) and the other what is (the price of a stock). In my experience, a great many portfolio managers and analysts, perhaps a majority, use both to some degree or another. In fact, every portfolio manager or analyst who uses the comparables method of valuation is, by default, validating the message of the market by considering what other investors think and do in setting the price found in, for example, the price-to-earnings ratio. Therefore, for the reasons that follow, the study of the markets and their role in aiding our quest to determine an investment strategy and build and maintain an effective portfolio is a must-do for investors and our next area of examination.

INTERACTIVE NATURE OF THE MARKETS AND THE ECONOMY

Successful investing doesn't, therefore, depend solely on what *should be* the intrinsic value of a given stock, as most fundamentally oriented investors would insist. Nor is it only about plotting trend lines on stock charts and graphs and looking solely at the market data while ignoring the sectors, industries, and companies that the shares of stock represent. Rather, successful investing begins with an understanding of root causes of investor behavior (investor psychology) and how the interplay between the real economy and the financial economy (the markets) happens.

In my years on Wall Street and in teaching equity analysis classes to prospective and practicing analysts and portfolio managers, I have found that too many investors, professional and non, fail to appreciate the interactive nature of the markets and the economy. They just don't know. Far too many investors rely solely on one discipline—fundamental analysis (intrinsic value, comparables)—or the other—technical analysis. I believe a blend of the two is an extremely effective way to go about formulating an effective investment strategy. For it is the interplay between the two, the real economy (fundamental) and the financial economy (technical), that I have found to be most effective in formulating investment strategy. And the most insightful. Consider the following:

Renowned investor George Soros calls the interactive dynamic between the real and financial economies "reflexivity." Soros describes the interactive nature of the economies in this way: "Each market participant is faced with the task of putting a current value on the future course of events, but that course is contingent upon prevailing valuations in the financial markets."[2] In other words, in the process of predicting the future, today's market value will impact the very outcome it is seeking to predict. Soros goes on the describe the nature of the markets and globalization, the context within which the real economy functions:

> There is a fundamental difference between financial markets and markets for physical goods and services. The latter deal with known quantities, the former with quantities that are not merely unknown but actually unknowable.

Markets do show a tendency toward equilibrium when they deal with known quantities, but financial markets are different. They discount the future, but the future they discount is contingent on how the financial markets discount it at present. Instead of a predictable outcome, the future is genuinely uncertain and is unlikely to correspond to expectations. The bias inherent in market expectations is one of the factors that shape the course of events. There is a two-way interaction between expectations and outcomes that I call "reflexivity."[3]

In his book *Tools of Critical Thinking*, psychologist David A. Levy describes this interactive cause and effect this way:

An effect may be, and usually is, the result of several causes, which are operating concurrently. Virtually every significant behavior has many determinants, and any single explanation is almost inevitably an oversimplification.

Although we typically tend to think of causal relationships as being uni-directional *(Event A causes Event B), frequently they are* bi-directional *(Event A causes Event B, and Event B causes Event A). In other words, variables may, and frequently do, affect each other.*[4]

Many times, when events unfold as "predicted by the market," some investors and many in the financial media refer back to the "wisdom of the market" and the uncanny ability of the market to "make the call" months, even years in advance. What they erroneously attribute to the "wisdom of the market" more likely than not is the result of a self-fulfilling prophecy. The reason that such a self-fulfilling prophecy may come to pass lies in the reality of Soros' reflexivity and Levy's bidirectional cause and effect.

Call it reflexivity, call it interactivity, call it bidirectional cause and effect—call it a banana, if you want—but the bottom line is still the same: The equity markets do two things:

1. They reflect the expectations of investors as determined by the real-economy valuation models (growth prospects and risks of the real economy).
2. They act as an influencing factor upon the real economy.

Given its role as a major influencer of the very environment it is predicting, the study of the market as a *stand-alone entity* should be undertaken. For when we study the market on its own terms and then match up its conclusions with our intrinsic valuation work, we can gain a deeper insight into not just whether the one validates the other but how each influences the outcomes of the other. Before we do, let's consider one more fact.

THE EQUITY MARKETS AS A SOURCE OF COMPETITIVE ADVANTAGE

The interactive importance of the real economy and the markets can also been seen from the perspective of competitive advantage. The equity markets are more than a daily record of opinions and bets. They are also a source of funding.

The market capitalization of a stock is a source of funding for managing the growth of a business, acquiring talent (individuals) and assets (through the acquisition of and merger with other companies). As a result, the equity markets are a source of competitive advantage. If the market cap of Company A is higher than the market cap of Company B, Company A has the advantage to grow the business using equity capital, acquire talent through a more attractive stock option program, and acquire assets and markets through mergers and acquisitions (M&A). In other words, the higher the market cap, the stronger the potential competitive advantage is for a publicly traded company.

While many know this, few make the connection. I rarely hear it mentioned by investors as a part of their investment considerations (the motivation of senior corporate management) when analyzing industries and companies. Yet, every day, some M&A deal goes down or a great talent with outstanding potential is employed with precisely this market cap as a competitive advantage as a major factor.

As with globalization, this may be a hard-to-quantify area and I am sure there are studies about the subject of market cap and competitive advantage that I am not aware of. But there is no denying the logic that a higher market cap begets more strength and, therefore, makes the study of the market all the more important.

WHY WARREN BUFFETT AND BEN GRAHAM ARE WRONG (AT LEAST IN ONE RESPECT) AND GEORGE SOROS AND DAVID LEVY ARE RIGHT

In the opening lines of this chapter, I quoted some of the words of the sage of Omaha. Each year, investors anxiously await the writings of Warren Buffett in his annual report comments to investors in his company, Berkshire Hathaway. In one of his most memorable commentaries, Buffett describes the valuable lessons he learned from famed investor Benjamin Graham, and Graham's analogy of Mr. Market. Buffett's comments highlight several essential points about successful investing. First is the notion that investing is a game of exploitation. The market is prone to excessive mood swings that can be taken advantage of by investors less subject to such bouts of emotionalism. Second, Buffett explodes the folly of market efficiency. For he, like many other astute investors, knows that the market is a pool of investor moods, manias, panics, euphorias, depressions, and so on—all the signs of a social science in action.

Where I believe Buffett gets it wrong is in his conclusions: "In my opinion, investment success will not be produced by arcane formulae, computer programs or signals flashed by the price behavior of stocks and markets."

Now, far be it from me to question a living investment legend, but in one respect I think he may be generalizing just a bit much.

When Buffett discounts the value in the "signals flashed by the price behavior of stocks and markets" as being, in effect, a waste of time for most investors, I believe he is mistaken, as there is a usefulness in such data. Market movements and investor psychology can be a source of valuable information.

To be clear, Warren Buffett and Ben Graham are not alone in their skepticism with regard to the value of measuring the market through technical analysis. A whole slew of like-minded individuals believe that studying the market is a waste of time. One such person, for example, is Burton Malkiel.

"The past history of stock prices cannot be used to predict the future in any meaningful way." So writes the good professor in his well-known book, *A Random Walk Down Wall Street* (W.W. Norton, 1990). Additionally, professional organizations like the CFA Institute relegate technical analysis to a very minor area of study. So, where does this leave us? Are the arguments of Soros and Levy and the members of the Market Technicians Association and those in the emergent behavioral finance field wrong? And are Buffett and Graham and Malkiel and other adherents to the so-called strong form of the efficient markets hypothesis (EMH) right?

The fundamentalists say that they have science on their side. Rooted in the principles of the four-decade-old EMH, fundamentally oriented investors believe that "at any given time, security prices fully reflect all available information." Therefore, the only conceivable way for an investor to outperform the market (earn a return in excess of what one would receive investing in the broad market through an index fund or exchange-traded fund) is by analyzing the real economy, and not by a study of the market itself. But not all versions or forms of the EMH lend themselves to this argument. In fact, the aforementioned Burton Malkiel is a proponent of what is known as the "strong form" of the EMH.

There are three forms of the efficient markets hypothesis:

1. Weak: All past market prices and data are fully reflected in securities prices.
2. Semistrong: All publicly available information is fully reflected in securities prices.
3. Strong: All information is fully reflected in securities prices.

As you can see, no one can beat the market if one believes in the strong form. Everything that exists, known and unknown, is reflected in the prices of stocks. And, according to fundamental believers, since all past market prices and data are fully reflected in securities prices, technical analysts are wasting their time. Only if an investor believes in the weak form of the EMH can he/she stand a chance of achieving a superior rate of return. Now, here's the rub.

The American Heritage Dictionary of the English Language, Fourth Edition, defines a hypothesis as:

> **1.** *A tentative explanation for an observation, phenomenon, or scientific problem that can be tested by further investigation.* **2.** *Something taken to be true for the purpose of argument or investigation; an assumption.* **3.** *The antecedent of a conditional statement.*

In other words, the efficient markets hypothesis is not a fact. It is a multidecade-old area being explored, the outcome of which cannot be assumed. When something has been around for four decades and is still a hypothesis, one has to wonder whether it is really what it claims to be: the complete explainer of market behavior.

WHAT THE TECHNICIANS HAVE TO SAY

The technicians say they have common sense on their side. As one source describes it,

> *According to technical analysts, the fundamental analyst can experience a superior return* only *if they obtain new information before other investors and process it correctly and quickly. Technical ana-*

lysts do not believe that the vast majority of investors can consistently get new information before other investors and consistently process it correctly and quickly.

Technical analysts claim that a major advantage of their method is that it is not heavily dependent on financial accounting statements—the major source of information about the past performance of a firm or industry.[5]

But common sense without science is like a gladiator going into battle without a sword: It's a hard way to win the contest. What technical analysis lacked was the scientific basis for their views. Often besieged and sometimes ridiculed, technical analysis was an investment version of a covered wagon train surrounded by Indians, praying for the cavalry to come over the hilltop.

And then along came behavioral finance.

BEHAVIORAL FINANCE

The study of investor behavior had long been the sole domain of the technical analyst. Market technicians, as they preferred to be called, study the trading patterns of individual stocks and groups of stocks *as well as* the psychology of investors in a quest to predict the future action of stocks, groups of stocks, and the market as a whole. The supposition is that the message of the market is the best indicator of the future direction of the market. It is the manifestation of my field of play versus coach's room analogy in Chapter 2.

To a market technician, an investor is best served by concentrating on what happens on the field of play. All the planning and forecasting on what *should* be the price of a stock, a level of the market derived by using fundamental analysis processes like discounted cash flow (in the coach's room), pales in comparison to what actually happens on the field of play. The message of the market is all that matters.

What behavioral finance has to contribute to the discussion is the science involved. And that science is gaining academic acceptance, as evidenced by the 2002 Nobel Prize in Economics being awarded to two behavioral finance professors: Daniel Kahneman and Vernon L. Smith.

A definition of behavioral finance might be:

- "A theory stating that there are important psychological and behavioral variables involved in investing in the stock market that provide opportunities for smart investors to profit."

- "Behavioral finance as well as behavioral economics applies scientific research on human and social cognitive and emotional biases to better understand economic decisions."
- "A field of finance that proposes psychology-based theories to explain stock market anomalies. Within behavioral finance it is assumed that the information structure and the characteristics of market participants systematically influence individuals' investment decisions as well as market outcomes."

Three definitions, one point: The study of investor behavior and not ivory tower theory better explains stock market behavior. And if the study of investor behavior includes things like market trading patterns and investor psychology, then the cavalry may have just arrived for technical analysis.

PROS AND CONS OF TECHNICAL ANALYSIS

Theories aside, most professional investors use technical analysis to some degree, even if they just glance at a stock chart. Consider this simple fact: If stock trading patterns were not of any value, then why look at a stock chart? If money flows in and out of mutual funds or the sentiment of investors (degree of bullishness or bearishness) were of no value, then why do nearly 100 percent of fundamental investors bother to read the stuff? The answer: Nearly every professional investor is a closet technician. In our case, however, we most definitely have come out in favor of technical analysis.

I like to think of the markets as a giant lab in which the investment rats (that's us investors) run the maze every trading day seeking our tasty morsel of cheese (portfolio performance). We are highly intelligent investment rats. We are rational creatures, most of the time. But we are not pipe-smoking, ivory tower, strictly rational automatons. We are creatures with feelings. We are subject to the whims and wants of the social part of our brains. We experience loss and regret and greed and fear, and they impact our decision making. At times we become euphoric or depressed. We are the market and the market is us. We are Mr. Market.

But we can be understood. We can be studied, and that study can lead to portfolio gains, if we know what to look for and where to look. That is the essence of why technical analysis can and does work—not all the time, but enough of the time that insight can be gained and a point of comparison can be made with the fundamentally derived valuation model.

A FEW GOOD TOOLS

Let's look at a few good technical tools I have found to be worthwhile.

Divergences

Misery loves company. So do investors. If the world is going to hell in a handbasket, then all countries should act uniformly. Conversely, in war, battles are fought to gain ground. But when the generals move out and the infantry doesn't follow, a very bad outcome is likely. Success occurs when all the forces are in sync.

These two simple little analogies describe one of the most effective tools of technical analysis: divergences. When one segment of the market rises past a defined point, say the previous high, and another segment fails to follow suit and does not make a new high, a potentially negative divergence has just occurred. For example, when one index (say, the S&P 500) moves to higher or lower ground (a new recovery high or low, for example) and another index (NASDAQ) does not, trouble may be ahead. Conversely, if the Russell 2000 makes a new low but the S&P MidCap index does not, that is a potentially positive divergence. The granddaddy and best-known example of a tool based on divergences is the Dow Theory.

Dow Theory states that whenever the Dow Jones Industrial Average makes a new recovery (or all-time) high, the Dow Jones Transportation Average must follow suit or confirm that new high or low. The converse is true as well (if Dow Transports make a new high/low, Dow Industrials must confirm). This act of confirmation helps validate the given market move up or down and confirms that the trend is intact.

Dow Theory in Action

Perhaps the most dramatic example of a negative divergence took place at the height of the tech bubble. Beginning in the spring of 1999, the Dow Industrials marched upward to make several all-time highs. However, the Dow Transports went in the opposite direction. The resulting action of a negative divergence was produced. (See Figure 6.1.)

Therefore, when the tragic events of September 11 came to pass, the market was poised for a sustained decline. (See Figure 6.2.) It took until the spring of 2003 for the decline to finally come to an end.[6]

Another example is from an earlier era—the 1970s. At that time, the markets were suffering through a six-year bear market. So, when the

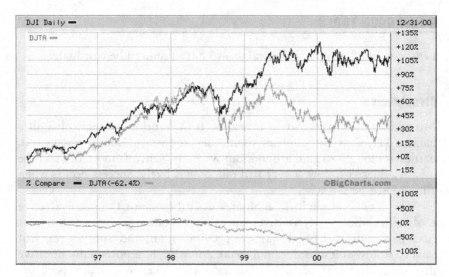

FIGURE 6.1   Negative Divergence
Source: BigCharts.com.

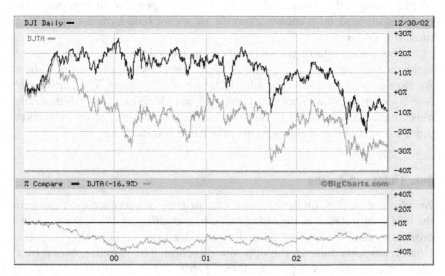

FIGURE 6.2   Market Decline after Negative Divergence
Source: BigCharts.com.

Dow Industrials broke to a new low in the fall of 1974 and the Dow Transports did not, a positive divergence developed. The subsequent market rally brought the bull back to its previous all-time highs, as seen in Figure 6.3.

But when the Dow Transports went on a tear and made successive all-time highs and the Dow Industrials did not, a major negative divergence developed, as pictured in Figure 6.4. This in turn led to a serious correction, as shown in Figure 6.5.

These are but two of numerous examples that show how divergences can be used as a predictive tool. But a rigid interpretation of this rule can lead to an adoption of a dogma and hinder the clearheaded thinking needed for utilizing this helpful tool. In Chapter 9 I show how adherence to one tool, no matter how reliable, can drive an investor to the wrong decisions.

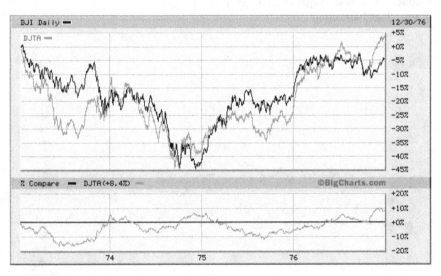

FIGURE 6.3   Positive Divergence
Source: BigCharts.com.

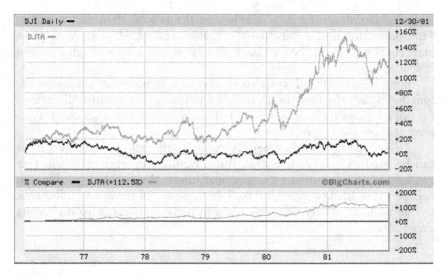

FIGURE 6.4   Major Negative Divergence
Source: BigCharts.com.

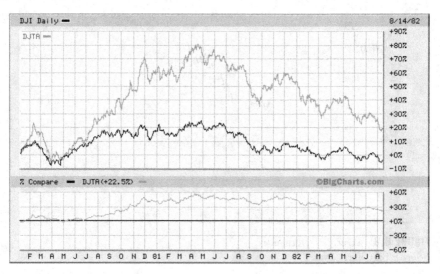

FIGURE 6.5   Serious Correction after Major Negative Divergence
Source: BigCharts.com.

INVESTOR PSYCHOLOGY

Another very important area of technical analysis is the study of investor psychology. Since investing is a social science, understanding the players of the game—their motivations, their desires, their strengths, their weaknesses—is paramount. At present, behavioral finance does this through scientific tests. But behavioral finance is not at the point where tools we can use are available.

While investors await the evolution of behavioral finance, anyone who believes that the psychology of investors is a worthwhile pursuit has to rely on the tools of the trade in technical analysis. And they are very useful tools, indeed, as they do help us understand the state of mind of the market participants.

We begin with one manifestation of investor psychology: the volatility of the market.

Sentiment Indicator #1: The VIX

Using the data it compiles from the puts and calls that trade on its exchange, the Chicago Board Options Exchange calculates the risk appetite of investors. That figure is known as the Volatility Index (VIX), and is a metric that many investors use to gauge market risk, which is interpreted as a reflection of investor sentiment.

Many investors look at the VIX as a longer-term tool, and, like the other sentiment indicators that follow, use it as a contrary indicator: When investors show a greater tolerance for risk, the Volatility Index goes down. Stocks are thereby perceived as less risky. Conversely, when investors are more fearful and have a lower tolerance for risk, volatility goes up. Stocks are then perceived are less attractive. The VIX is the metric that tracks that investor appetite for risk through its measure of put and call buying.

When many investors use the VIX as a longer-term tool, they take the overall lower reading in the VIX to be a sign of investors' comfort with stocks. But what I have learned, thanks to a few of my previous Market Forecast panelists who are market technicians, is that it isn't the level of the VIX that matters most but the near-term movement that has good predictive value.

To illustrate this point, here are two of my recent research commentaries.

In April 2005 the market was in the throes of a serious correction. Doubt was high. On April 18, I produced the following report, which shows the value of the VIX. (See Figure 6.6.)

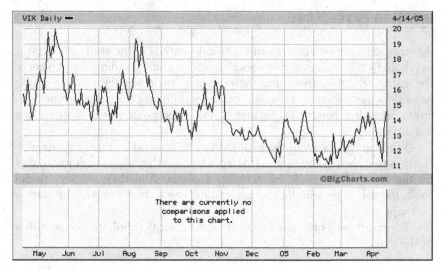

FIGURE 6.6   Volatility Index (VIX), April 2005
Source: BigCharts.com.

Let me state once again—*major market tops do not spring out of thin air. They are the product of many months of a topping process that culminates in a breakdown of the entire market, which leads to a bear market. However, market corrections, sometimes very serious market corrections, can occur seemingly out of the blue, but they are extremely rare and have always led to higher highs and a market top at a much later date. This is what occurred in 1987. It is, however, highly unlikely that this will occur this time around for the reasons noted above and due to the fact that various market metrics, most notable of which is the VIX, are signaling that the decline we are experiencing is nothing more than a shakeout. . . .*

If you have been reading my reports, you know that the kind of increase in fear the VIX has just registered is very bullish for the market. As I wrote last week, "Hopefully, fear and uncertainty will return." Well, they have done so, in spades late last week—and continue to do so today.

This is what shakeouts look like. They test the resolve of the bull by dropping below some important market level, bringing out every worrywart on the planet. I am not one of those worrywarts—at least, not yet.

As the VIX continued to trade around the 16 to 18 level, I followed up this report on May 2 with the following comments: "Oh, how I love the action in the VIX. We have not seen this level of concern and pessimism in a long time."

Three months later, the S&P 500 was up 7 percent, the S&P Mid Cap sector ETF (MDY) was up 14 percent, and the S&P 600 Small Cap sector ETF (IJR) was up 17 percent.

What made the indicator work as a predictive tool was what I learned from my market technician friends: The real value in the VIX is not its level but the power of a rapid rise in fear. In other words, whenever the VIX rises approximately 25 percent from its recent low, the market is poised for a rally. Fear, in the form of a higher volatility reading, has risen sufficiently to support a market rally. But now here is my secret sauce that takes this one valuable point and turns warmed-over ketchup into a delicious pasta sauce: Whenever the VIX rises 25 percent from its recent lows *and* trades at or around that higher level for at least two to three weeks, the odds of a market rally are greatly increased.

This is not to suggest any great investment acumen on my part. Nor is it to imply that what has worked with the VIX time and again in the current market cycle will happen with any degree of consistency in the future. And it is not to suggest that it is the sole tool that made this and other market calls work. But I offer it to you as an example of how a technical tool like the VIX can be a valuable addition to any investor's toolbox.

Sentiment Indicator #2: Flow of Funds

Another measure of investor sentiment is the flow of funds into and out of mutual funds. Investors who believe there is value in such data want to know whether money is flowing into or out of stocks. The answer to this question is of great interest to many professional investors as they seek to determine the flow of funds investors have designated for investment assets, in particular stocks.

Knowing how much money is flowing into what sectors of the market can also provide valuable insights into both the psychology of investors and their preferences. Additionally, it can act as an indicator of future price movements within sectors, because the flow of funds into sectors and industry mutual funds reflects investor sentiment toward one sector over another. Similarly, mutual fund flows between and among country funds show how investors feel about the prospects of one country versus another.

On this last point, CIBC World Markets chief investment strategist Subodh Kumar noted in his report of October 14, 2005:

Global Investor Flows into the United States

As focus shifted to expanding nominal interest rate differentials in 2004, foreign inflows in the U.S. increased 20+%, with inflows in 2005 through July only modestly lower year over year, despite lower long bond yields. Currently, foreign flows into U.S. equities show early stage characteristics. In this cycle, only 5% of total foreign inflows through 2003/2005 have been to equities, versus 20% in 1997–98 and 30+% levels in 1999/2000 (when foreign investors were late buying into growth).

Implicit currency-linked expectations are a potentially important determinant of total return but also can be a disadvantage in prompting laggard activity in markets, after domestic investor patterns are already in transition. In 2004, excessive focus on the U.S. current account deficit led to the prevailing U.S. dollar weakness expectations, while overlooking policy and political weaknesses in Europe—making sustained Asian activity noteworthy. Now, greater pragmatism and the active hunt for yields has led to the U.S. dollar recovery, currently trading at 1.20 versus the euro (nearly 10% higher than the start of 2005 and 4% higher since September) and at 114 versus the yen (near 2005 peak levels and 4.5% higher than September). Sustained U.S. dollar strength (and perceived European economic and political weakness) is likely to support interest in U.S. assets. If interest in growth delivery expands, the incremental increase is likely to be to equities.

At this time and as noted in the previous chapter, the U.S. consumer has a limited capacity to invest. With record U.S. federal budget deficits and the U.S. economy's need to provide equity capital to support growth, the equities markets of this decade have been very dependent on foreign sources to support both low interest rates (or at least lower than they would be without foreign capital) and a good equity market.

Therefore, data such as that provided by Subodh Kumar and various government sources are helpful in telling us the amount of foreign investment that is being made into the U.S. capital markets. The data noted demonstrate that foreign investment into U.S. equities has been below average. Perhaps that helps explain the poor relative performance of U.S. equities vis-à-vis other world markets, developed and developing. (See Figure 6.7.)

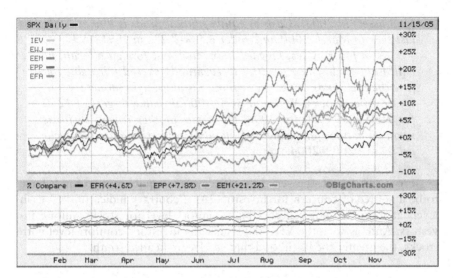

FIGURE 6.7 U.S. Equities versus Other World Markets
Source: BigCharts.com.
ETFs: IEV: Europe 350; EWJ: Japan; EEM: Emerging Markets; EPP: Asia/Pacific
ex Japan; EFA: EAFE; SPX: S&P 500.

As for U.S. mutual fund flows, Subodh notes,

U.S. Mutual Funds

*In his July presentation of monetary conditions, Fed Chairman
Greenspan was balanced in expectations of 3.5% growth and
moderate policy change (albeit cautious on inflation). We have
seen several hawkish comments since the FOMC meeting, but central bankers soft on inflation are rare. The Bank of England and
the Reserve Bank of Australia moderately inverted yield curves
due to strong growth (now weak in the U.K.) and real estate prices
have now switched to abeyance. While we see little incentive for
the Fed to explicitly invert yield curves, such fears have prompted
increasing interest in money market mutual funds in August 2005.
As such fears are expunged, equities will likely recover. However,
fresh inflows will likely be key, in our view. Over 80% of "flight to
safety" money (in money market funds in 1999–2002) is reallo-
cated. Currently money market, at $1.9 trillion, comprises 22.5%
of total assets, much as in 1999 (versus $2.3 trillion and 35.5% of*

total assets in 2002). Cash in equity mutual funds is low at 3.9%
last seen in March 2000 and under 6.5%–7.2% in 1991–1997.

As in prior cycles, laggard individual and foreign allocations
(still low) could cause equities to eventually exceed fair value be-
fore the cycle ends driven by peaking earnings, tight monetary pol-
icy or other shocks. With our S&P 500 fair value targets of 1250
for 2005 and 1300 for 2006, flows are another reason to focus
upon valuation, fair value and quality parameters, over the cycli-
cal bias of 2002–2004.

From this report, the very low cash levels in equity mutual funds have
to be a source of concern for investors. As a contrary indicator, low cash
levels at mutual funds reflect a high comfort level for stocks among investors. And, as with the VIX, the higher the investors' comfort level with
stocks, the greater the likelihood that stocks are headed south.

Sentiment Indicator #3: What the Pros Are Thinking

Professional investor sentiment is our third measure of investor psychology. What professional investors believe the market is going to do is
tracked to gauge the degree of optimism and pessimism among professional investors. Like the funds flow data just noted, professional investor
sentiment is a reverse indicator—when too many bulls are roaming the investment landscape, there are that many fewer potential bulls to convert to
the bullish fold. The implication is, of course, that the current bulls have
most of their money in the market and therefore cannot be a source of future buying strength to take the market higher. To illustrate this point, in
his November 2, 2005, report, Richard Bernstein, Merrill Lynch's chief
quantitative strategist and a frequent panelist at my analysts society's Market Forecast events, wrote,

The Sell Side Indicator remains our most reliable market timing
barometer. It is based on a survey of Wall Street Strategists' recom-
mended asset allocations. We have found, when adding a little
math, that Wall Street's consensus equity allocation has histori-
cally been a reliable contrary indicator. In other words, it has his-
torically been a bullish signal when Wall Street was extremely
bearish, and vice versa.

The latest reading of the indicator (October 31) is 64.6%,
which is up substantially from last month's 61.5%. Within the
current model, any reading at or above 63.1% generates a "sell"
signal, whereas any reading at or below 50.9% generates a

"buy" signal. Thus, the model has given a formal "sell" signal. This is the first time the indicator has moved from "neutral" to "sell" since mid-1998, and its first return to "sell" territory since late-2003/early-2004.[7]

When you combine Rich's research with the several investor sentiment indicators produced each week, the concern, from an investor psychology level, rises even further.

From *Barron's*, November 14, 2005:

High bullish readings in the Consensus stock index or in the Market Vane stock index usually are signs of market tops; low ones, market bottoms:

	Last Week	2 Weeks Ago	3 Weeks Ago
Consensus Index			
Bullish Opinion	*	58%	48%
American Association of Individual Investors' Index			
Bullish	58.6%	43.0%	32.1%
Bearish	23.0	27.6	46.2
Neutral	18.4	29.5	21.8
Market Vane			
Bullish Consensus	63%	61%	60%

UBS Index of Investor Optimism	Oct	Sep	Aug
Overall Index	47	34	61

Putting Investor Psychology in Context

The three indicators of investor sentiment presented earlier provide a good introduction into the discipline of investor psychology. The data contained within each indicator is information that is readily available to most investors, and most of it is free or available for a nominal charge. And all of it is accessible via the Internet. What is not free is the time and experience it takes to acquire a point of view that will enable conclusions, your own conclusions, to be reached. At a minimum, however, you will have been exposed to some of the tools and thinking involved in the investment strategy process.

As with all aspects of formulating an investment strategy and ultimately creating and maintaining an effective portfolio, no one segment, no one area stands alone when reaching the buy, sell, or hold decisions to be made. Each is part of the whole (remember the elephant and the blind men), a piece of the puzzle that must be put together like a mosaic. An understanding of the key concepts and elements of investor psychology is a big piece of the Mr. Market puzzle.

Perception Is Reality

When you boil it down to its essential point, the study of investor psychology is a search for a contrary opinion. An astute investor noticing too much bullish sentiment or a bearish reading that is too high should use that information as a reflection of a market sentiment that may warrant a contrary opinion. For many investors, this is not an easy thing to do—to go against the crowd. And many times, it is advisable to go with the flow and ride the wave of bullish sentiment, for it can take the market to higher levels.

As with all metrics of the market, there is no one magic bullet. One must take a composite approach. In fact, just like all the segments in this book, the psychology of investors as measured by these indicators is a tool to help build an effective investment strategy. They are not *the* tool that contains *all* the answers.

THE QUALITY MIGRATION CYCLE AND MARKET TOPS

Related to investor psychology is the market action of distinct sectors, one versus the other. One use of this information is called rotational investing, in which different sectors are identified to be chosen in the hope that the choice does better than the sector (or industry) that was not chosen. This is the essence of Core Plus, to choose sectors, industries, and styles that will outperform those not chosen, or underweighted. What connects this study of overperforming and underperforming sectors is when the performance data are used to reveal trends in the market overall. Since all bull markets must come to an end, I have discovered an interesting little indicator that helps forecast when that fateful time might occur. I call it the quality migration cycle.

The quality migration cycle is one way of gauging investor sentiment by measuring the stock market performance of various classes of stocks based on one qualitative characteristic—quality. It is also a very effective tool when seeking to predict the end of a major bull market.

Unlike bear markets, which typically end with a dramatic crisis-ridden sell-off, bull markets end typically in a long-drawn-out topping process. And during that process, a leadership change takes place wherein higher-quality stocks outperform their mid- and lower-quality brethren. The logic behind this is simple and elegant. As investors become more bearish due to a potential peaking in the economy and expected subsequent decline, they tend to move money away from lower-quality, higher-growth stocks to higher-quality, lower-risk stocks. This is the stock market's version of the bond market's famous "flight to quality" (the process by which bond investors, being concerned about a pending decline in certainty, move money from lower-quality bonds to higher-quality, less risky bonds). The result in an outperformance of the high-quality stocks, which portends the end of the bull as it signals future trouble ahead. And remembering the interactive nature of the markets and the real economy, the diminution of low- and mid-quality stocks (the main engines of growth for the economy) has the self-fulfilling prophecy prospects of making this "prediction" come true.

I write about this quite a bit in my weekly research reports as the bull market that has been in place since the spring of 2003 is a major bull, the trend of which is the single most important trend we need to get right. For getting the major trend right means getting the asset allocation decision right. And since the asset allocation decision constitutes 85 to 90 percent of investment performance (in diversified portfolios), then we want to use whatever tools we can get our hands on to help us with this critical decision.

Here is one excerpt on the topic that I wrote about in the summer of 2005:

Right on Schedule

The quality migration cycle appears to be well under way as Mid Cap (MDY) is on the verge of making an all-time high and is clearly outperforming the market. What bears watching and why a market top does not appear to be in place is the seemingly unending strength in the Small Cap sector (IJR). What should happen is that IJR should falter on this move and that the S&P 100 (OEX) should develop increasing strength. That's what should happen. But what does happen remains to be seen. In either case, until the OEX rises to the head of the class or the IJR has a blow-off run (highly unlikely), a market top has not been formed.

My concern at that time was with the performance of the Mid Cap sector ETF (MDY). If it begins to falter as the Small Cap has begun to do, and high-quality stocks outperform, then the potential for a rotation from low and mid-quality may be under way. If sustained for several months,

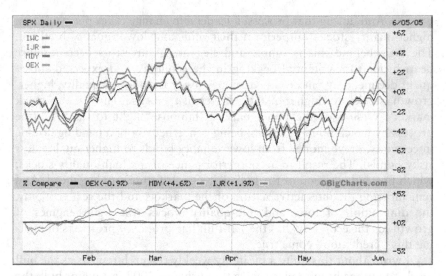

FIGURE 6.8   Mid Cap versus Other Sectors
Source: BigCharts.com.
ETFs: IWC: Micro Cap; IJR: S&P 600 Small Cap; MDY: S&P 400 Mid Cap; OEX: S&P 100; SPX: S&P 500.

this would be a major warning signal that the multiyear cyclical bull may be coming to an end. (See Figure 6.8.)

Note: I use the market size (large, mid, and small cap) as a proxy for quality as the stocks that are the largest have, on average, the highest quality rankings. Conversely, smaller companies (as measured by their market capitalizations) have, on average, the lowest quality, with the mid caps in the middle. Data from other sources using quality rankings (S&P's stock quality rankings), such as Rich Bernstein's quantitative group, show the same performance results.

SUMMARY

I hope I have made the case for the incorporation of a study of the message of the markets in investment strategy decision making. As with the valuation process in the real economy, the political process in government affairs, and economic matters on both a global level and a domestic level, the study of the market is as much art as it is science. Judgment is always required.

It is always necessary to remember that no one area, no one discipline can possibly tell all. Each is an integrated part of the mosaic of investing, the puzzle of which must be put together piece by piece so as to see the whole. The study of the markets is a very essential part of that puzzle.

Three

The Twenty-First-Century Investment Tools

The twenty-first-century investor is witness to a truly liberating point in time. Never before has such an empowerment of investors been created. In effect, a democratization of investing has dawned upon all investors. Successful investing is no longer the sole domain of professional investors with large research budgets and sophisticated access to information. Rather, today's investor can play on a level playing field and compete effectively without having to employ the services of the overpriced and underperforming. But today's investor can do so only if he/she employs two vital things: the principles described in this book and the research tools available. For without the combination of the two, investment results may not be any better than those gotten by following hot stock tips and chasing after rumors. However, if an investor employs the principles learned and the tools to be described, he/she stands a much better chance to eat well *and* sleep well, the investment version of heaven.

Thanks to the triple forces of technology, financial innovation, and regulatory change (primarily Regulation FD—Fair Disclosure), an investor today has the extraordinary ability to research and manage his/her assets in ways that were not possible before. When armed with the effective investment principles described in the earlier chapters, these tools described in the next two chapters are a powerful enabler of effective investment research and management. I am a living example of this. I am walking the walk, so to speak.

The research and investment strategy work that I produce is a product of my utilizing the tools and principles described in this book. This is not some theoretical project but a real-world application that is available to *all* investors. Each day, my research work is conducted primarily from my home office. With a PC and the Net, I employ the principles described in this book to reach my investment strategy conclusions. The results are a matter of record and have been quite good. Since employing the principles and the tools, the strategy results of the recommended investments (the iView Growth Portfolio) have been precisely what I had hoped for: consistency and accuracy. And while past performance is no guarantee of future results, my personal investment skills are all that stand between me and unexceptional strategy and portfolio results. Yours are all that stand between you and the same. So, let's take the time to learn about the tools of the twenty-first-century investment trade and how they can make the difference for you.

Chapter 7 explores the enabling power of exchange-traded funds (ETFs). Chapter 8 describes how the Internet can be used as both an information and a communications resource. The two chapters complete the investment strategy picture and set the stage for the construction of an effective portfolio, the topic of Chapter 9.

An Investment Revolution:
Exchange-Traded Funds

Over the past decade, an investment revolution has taken hold in which investors are now able to invest like investment managers without the cost and supervision of numerous individual positions required of professional investors. Investors can now build portfolios based on:

- Economic sectors
- Industries
- Styles
- Global assets
- Hard assets

Consider these facts:

- Whole sectors can be represented with the purchase of one stock—an economic sector exchange-traded fund (ETF).
- Whole industries can be captured with the purchase of one stock—an industry ETF.
- Whole styles can be captured with the purchase of one stock—a style-oriented ETF.
- Whole countries and regions can be represented with the purchase of one stock—a country or regional ETF.
- Hard assets, like gold, can be captured with the purchase of one stock—a hard asset ETF.

On its own, this would be quite an exhilarating experience. To decide, for example, that the Energy sector or Japan or mid-cap stocks look especially attractive and, therefore, to be able to participate in that decision (right or wrong, up or down) is a power that more and more investors are catching onto with each passing day via the purchase of ETFs.

In the past such a decision to invest in a sector would have required either of the following additional decisions:

- The selection of the individual stocks within that sector, country, or style.
- The placement of money with a money manager specializing in that area.

For those investors with a finite amount of money, time, and resources, not having to decide which one or two stocks within each chosen area to own or which money manager may perform well in the future, ETFs are a fantastic alternative to the choices of the past.

Now, for some investors, having the ability to own whole sectors or styles is a very attractive option. Make the decision, make the bet. But I am aiming for something even more significant. I am aiming for the ability to construct portfolios and produce consistent and reliable investment results using ETFs in a portfolio strategy.

ETFs are more than just an alternative to a great insight on an investor's part. They are a tool that enables the creation of an effective portfolio—an effective portfolio that can produce more consistent results with lower risk than the great-idea-of-the-day investing approach so prevalently advocated by far too many media investment mavens. Great idea investing, like hot tip investing, is just too hit-or-miss to be a reliable longer-term strategy. For most investors, the effective portfolio is a better way to manage one's investment assets.

In the sectors and styles approach that I employ, ETFs are the core investment instrument used. They are the substance of my Core Plus strategy described in Chapter 3. Moreover, with the ability to own sectors, industries, and so on, an investor can construct a portfolio that is suited to his/her needs. Retirement plans can be more effectively met using the Core Plus strategy and ETFs. Growth needs for the future can be more reliably met using Core Plus and ETFs. This list goes on and on. The bottom line is simply this: With ETFs, every investor with a modest sum of money (defined as $25,000) can build a well-diversified portfolio using Core Plus and ETFs and make changes as needed—a true investment revolution for the taking.

TYPES OF ETFs: ECONOMIC SECTORS

The world of ETFs is large and growing. More than 200 ETFs exist to-day and over $300 billion in assets are already invested in ETFs. Take, for example, the Information Technology sector and the primary industries within:

ETF	Symbol
Technology Select Sector SPDR	XLK
iShares Dow Jones U.S. Technology	IYW
iShares Goldman Sachs Technology Index	IGM
streetTRACKS Morgan Stanley Technology	MTK
Vanguard Information Technology VIPERs	VGT
iShares Goldman Sachs Networking	IGN
iShares Goldman Sachs Semiconductor	IGW
iShares Goldman Sachs Software Index	IGV

Or the Health Care sector:

ETF	Symbol
Health Care Select Sector SPDR	XLV
iShares Dow Jones U.S. Healthcare	IYH
Vanguard Health Care VIPERs	VHT
PowerShares Dynamic Pharmaceuticals	PJP
iShares NASDAQ Biotechnology	IBB
PowerShares Dynamic Biotech & Genome	PBE

And in each case, a global ETF on the sector is available.

ETF	Symbol
iShares S&P Global Technology Sector	IXN
iShares S&P Global Healthcare Sector	IXJ

This is but a small sample of the types of sector and industry ETFs one can invest in. To help gain a slightly larger sense of the ETF landscape, here is one way to view what's out there in the world of ETFs.

On a daily basis, I monitor the markets in the manner shown in Table 7.1.

The ETFs, classified by economic sector and selected industry, size and style, global market, and other (hard assets), help me to capture a sense of

TABLE 7.1   Potential ETF Portfolio Mix

Economic Sectors and Selected Industries

Consumer Discretionary	XLY
Consumer Staples	XLP
Energy	XLE
Financials	XLF
Health Care	XLV
Biotech	IBB
Industrials	XLI
Basic Materials	XLB
Information Technology	IYW
Semiconductors	IGW
Software	IGV
Networking	IGN
Telecommunications	IYZ
Utilities	XLU

Size and Styles

Mid Cap	MDY
Mid Cap Value	IJJ
Large Cap—Dow Industrials	DIA
Large Cap—S&P 100	OEF
Small Cap	IJR
Micro Cap	IWC

Global

EAFE	EFA
Europe 350	IEV
Asia Pacific ex Japan	EPP
Japan	EWJ
Emerging Markets	EEM

Other

Gold	GLD

Source: iViewResearch.

the market. This cross-sectionalization of the market provides a quick and deep insight into what areas are performing well and which ones are lagging. There are many more ETFs, but these are the ones that I find to be of greatest use as of the third quarter of 2005. In time, especially as more industry-specific ETFs become available, the list will expand.

Constructing your own market tracking system via ETFs is easy and free. Web sites such as Yahoo! Finance enable the construction you see in Table 7.1—nothing fancy, just effective.

TYPES OF ETFs: SIZES AND STYLES

Investing based on size (market cap) and style (growth, value) is part of the mix, as evidenced by my market tracker in Table 7.1. Here is a small sample of ETFs based on size and style.

Large Cap Growth

ETF	Symbol
iShares S&P 500/BARRA Growth Index	IVW
iShares Morningstar Large Growth Index	JKE
streetTRACKS Dow Jones U.S. Large Cap Growth	ELG
PowerShares Dynamic Large Cap Growth Portfolio	PWB
Vanguard Growth VIPERs	VUG
iShares Russell 1000 Growth Index	IWF
iShares Russell 3000 Growth Index	IWZ
NASDAQ 100 Trust Shares	QQQQ
Fidelity NASDAQ Composite Index Tracking	ONEQ

Mid Cap Value

ETF	Symbol
iShares Dow Jones Select Dividend Index	DVY
PowerShares Dynamic Mid Cap Value Portfolio	PWP
iShares Russell Mid Cap Value Index	IWS
iShares Morningstar Mid Value Index	JKI
PowerShares High Yield Dividend Achievers	PEY
iShares S&P Mid Cap 400/BARRA Value	IJJ

Global (country and regional) and hard assets are also available. And for those investors wishing to satisfying their asset allocation needs, fixed-income-related ETFs are available, as well.

QUICK RECAP

Exchange-traded funds are tailor-made for an investor following a sectors and styles approach to investing. With more than 200 ETFs currently available and over $300 billion (and climbing) in assets, ETFs provide both the liquidity and the diversity needed to build a well-diversified portfolio, and in doing so, they give an investor the best possible chance of earning above-average rates of return. Whether an investor is using ETFs exclusively or as the core of a portfolio around which individual stocks are owned, ETFs, by their very nature, enable the Core Plus investment strategy for consistent and sustainable results.

ADJUSTING FOR WHAT'S INSIDE THE ETF

It's important for an investor to know what is inside an ETF, for while all ETFs are similar they are not identical. Take three of the Health Care sector ETFs noted earlier.

Say, for example, you correctly select the Health Care sector and plan to put some of your funds in a Health Care ETF. It is logical to assume that the return you receive for the ETF selected will match the Health Care index *and* be at least equal to the other available Health Care ETFs. Well, guess what? While the numbers are close, there is sometimes a meaningful enough difference between and among the various Health Care ETFs available. See Table 7.2 for an example.

Now consider the differences in the returns posted by each ETF as shown in Table 7.3.

SUM OF THE PARTS

At the end of the day, all ETFs have one thing in common—they are the sum of their parts. All ETF performance is a product of the composition of the ETF portfolio and, accordingly, the total performance depends on the mix of what is owned. In the case of the Health Care sector ETFs listed in Table 7.2, during the performance period involved XLV clearly lost the comparative race by having a larger proportion of its portfolio in its top 10 positions (61.93 percent versus 54.52 percent for IYH and 53.25 percent for VHT) and, thereby, having a less diverse portfolio and by owning more Pfizer and Johnson & Johnson than IYH and VHT owned. Had Pfizer and Johnson & Johnson outperformed, XLV would likely have outperformed the other two ETFs. However, the three-year performance record does not reflect very well on XLV, suggesting that some further investigation of the portfolio construction policies of XLV would be advisable.

But as sector and style investors and not individual stock pickers, how can we make the decision on which ETF to own? Who is to say that the underperformance of XLV will continue? Is there a solution to this problem? The answer is yes. (After all, I wouldn't pose a question like that in a book like this and not provide an answer.)

The solution is to own all of them. For by allocating the money among

TABLE 7.2 Health Care ETFs

Company	IYH Symbol	IYH Percent of Assets	XLV Symbol	XLV Percent of Assets	VHT Symbol	VHT Percent of Assets
	Top 10 Holdings: 54.52% of Total Assets		Top 10 Holdings: 61.93% of Total Assets		Top 10 Holdings: 53.25% of Total Assets	
Abbott Laboratories	ABT	4.27%	ABT	4.40%	ABT	4.11%
Amgen	AMGN	5.95	AMGN	5.11	AMGN	4.40
Bristol-Myers Squibb	BMY	2.87	BMY	3.35	BMY	2.95
Eli Lilly Co.	LLY	3.20	LLY	4.31	LLY	3.16
Johnson & Johnson	JNJ	11.15	JNJ	13.19	JNJ	11.86
Medtronic Inc.	MDT	3.83	MDT	4.29	MDT	3.67
Merck Co. Inc.	MRK	4.05	MRK	4.64	MRK	4.27
Pfizer Inc.	PFE	11.72	PFE	14.00	PFE	11.77
UnitedHealth Group	UNH	3.89	UNH	4.55	UNH	3.71
Wyeth	WYE	3.59	WYE	4.09	WYE	3.35
Equity Holdings Ratio						
Average Price/Earnings	19.62		Average Price/Earnings	19.50	Average Price/Earnings	18.23
Average Price/Book	2.79		Average Price/Book	2.60	Average Price/Book	2.79
Average Price/Sales	2.31		Average Price/Sales	1.71	Average Price/Sales	1.74
Average Price/Cash Flow	12.99		Average Price/Cash Flow	11.81	Average Price/Cash Flow	8.83

Source: Yahoo! Finance.

TABLE 7.3   Health Care ETF Performance Comparisons

Fund Name	Ticker	YTD Return (Market)	1-Year Return (Market)	3-Year Return (Market)
Vanguard Health Care VIPERs	VHT	7.16%	15.04%	N/A
iShares Dow Jones U.S. Healthcare	IYH	6.97	14.19	9.23
Health Care Select Sector SPDR	XLV	5.78	11.10	6.98

Source: Yahoo! Finance.

the three largest Health Care ETFs, an investor is virtually assured of participation in the bet made on the sector. In fact, this principle can apply to all ETFs. Own the three biggest and rest assured that what you bet on does not suffer for an overowned or underowned individual position.

STYLE ETFs

It is equally important that an investor learn the importance of decomposing a style-oriented ETF into its economic sector classifications (as shown in Table 7.4). For within the style ETF are individual stocks, each belong-

TABLE 7.4   Sector Weightings Adjusted for Style Impact

	iView Sector Weights	Style Impact	Real iView Mix	Market Weight	Difference	Relative Weighting
Consumer Discretionary	6.00%	2.30%	8.30%	10.80%	–2.50%	Underweight
Consumer Staples	6.00	1.52	7.52	9.80	–2.28	Underweight
Energy	4.00	1.23	5.23	9.50	–4.27	Underweight
Financials	10.00	3.03	13.03	20.90	–7.87	Underweight
Health Care	11.00	1.71	12.71	13.10	–0.39	Even
Industrials	12.00	2.67	14.67	11.20	3.47	Overweight
Basic Materials	2.00	0.92	2.92	3.00	–0.08	Even
Information Technology	15.00	2.31	17.31	15.30	2.01	Overweight
Telecommunications	2.00	0.39	2.39	3.10	–0.71	Even
Utilities	2.00	0.89	2.89	3.40	–0.51	Even

Source: iViewResearch; Compustat.

ing to a specific economic sector. It is therefore conceivable that an investor can construct a portfolio that overemphasizes (or underemphasizes) an economic sector, thereby inadvertently making an investment bet that he/she did not intend. For example, say an investor wants to underweight the Consumer Discretionary economic sector because that investor feels that rising interest rates, high consumer indebtedness, and rising energy prices would put a crimp on spending for big ticket or discretionary items. Now let's say that our investor wishes to be fully invested and does not want to place the excess investment funds due to the underweighting of the Consumer Discretionary sector in a money market or longer-term fixed income instrument. Our investor therefore chooses to keep the funds invested in the stock market. Moreover, our investor decides he/she is sufficiently invested in the other economic sectors and wants to take advantage of what he/she perceives as a favorable investment opportunity by investing in the investment style of Mid Cap issues. Our investor then puts the excess funds into a Mid Cap ETF. What our investor must recognize is that 15 percent of the Mid Cap fund chosen may be in the Consumer Discretionary sector. As a result, our investor has inadvertently raised the sector bet above his/her target level.

THE ETF REVOLUTION IS HERE TO STAY

Today's investor has the power to do what only large portfolio managers could do before: create and manage an effective portfolio based on a Core Plus portfolio strategy. Tilting the portfolio to reflect the sectors and styles an investor wants to overweight and away from those areas he/she wishes to minimize has never been so readily available. Moreover, being able to seize the portfolio moment and place a country or hard asset bet has never been so easy and accessible.

Investors can capitalize on the investing revolution for the masses brought on by ETFs in multiple ways. My preference, however, is to build the Core Plus portfolio and put my investment strategy skills to the test. ETFs have made this possible.

CHAPTER 8

Investing's Dynamic Duo: The PC and the Net

Batman and Robin may be crime fighting's dynamic duo, but for investors the investment dynamic duo has to be the personal computer and the Internet. They were made for each other. One serves as a computational and communications device (PC) while the other provides content and the ability to communicate with others (the Net). This is truly a case of one plus one equaling much more than two. How does four or more sound? And when you combine the computational power of the PC with the informational power of the Internet, you truly do have the democratization of investing.

As with the financial innovation of ETFs discussed in the preceding chapter, the power of the PC and the Net has liberated investors and removed yet another barrier to entry for investors who do not have large research budgets or access to high-priced information sources. With the PC and the Net, more than enough is available to help make the best possible investment decisions—provided an investor incorporates sound investment principles into his/her investment strategy and portfolio construction decisions.

Technology has been a transforming agent for business and social life. As is the case with every economic sector, information and communications technology (ICT) has taken the world into the twenty-first century. This is especially true for the world of investing. How to use this technology to your advantage is the focus of this chapter, as the power of the PC and the Net is described.

THE TWENTY-FIRST CENTURY'S INVESTOR TOOLBOX

For the investment professional managing millions (and not billions) of dollars, for the financial adviser, or for your average investor, the Internet is fast becoming the twenty-first century's investor toolbox. With each passing day, the era of expensive analytical investment tools moves more and more into the past. This is clearly a major plus for investors who cannot (or refuse to) pay thousands, even tens of thousands of dollars for high-priced research services.

To say that the Internet provides a plethora of information choices is to understate the issue. For it is easy to drown in the mountain of data available to investors. Yet, while the choices are many, the needs to be satisfied are fairly specific and therefore help in our quest to create the most effective analytical process.

During the dot-com bubble era, the Internet was hyped as the electronic medium that would change everything. And as often happens in bubbles, expectations were raised beyond the means of fulfilling them at that time. In the ensuing years, the Internet may not have "changed everything" but it certainly has impacted nearly every phase of life nearly everywhere in the developed world—and especially for investors.

Information costs are way down, while access to valuable information is way up. Things that were impossible just a decade ago are now fairly commonplace. To Google something has become a verb. And for investors, the capability of research and managing one's assets has never been more diverse, inexpensive, and immediate.

Today's investor has the ability to research the global economy, the powers in government, and the financial markets on an unprecedented scale. The combination of the personal computer and the Internet has literally transformed investing, all for the good. Sources can be readily accessed, information can be customized, data can be downloaded and analyzed, strategy can be formulated, and action can be taken. All this can be done from your desktop, wherever and whenever that may be—at an office, at home, in the morning, late at night. The power of the PC and the Net has made it possible.

The ability to apply the principles described in this book and the ability to create and manage a portfolio can be realized with the power tools of the PC and the Net. So, let's look at a few of these tools in our investor toolbox and see how you can make them work for you.

SOURCES: TRACKING GEM

We begin with some of the information sources needed to track the three aspects of GEM: government, economy, and the markets. However, we will reverse the order and start by checking the markets, as they are the real-time scorecard of the other two. It should be noted that you may decide to use an alternate investment strategy approach. Whatever your strategy, the power of the PC and the Net holds true, regardless of approach or style. So, please consider what you are about to read as one person's guide to the creation of an effective investment strategy and an effective portfolio.

Here are the sources that I go to and what I expect to gain from the content at the web site.

Yahoo! Finance.com

I look to this web site (http://finance.yahoo.com) for:

- General business, economic, and market news.
- Portfolios.
- Charts of stocks, industries, and indexes.
- Company and industry news and data.
- Data and insight.

This web site is my most frequently visited site as it provides nearly all the basic market information that I need to know, quickly and easily. It is my Web browser's home page. The general business, economic, and market news is formatted so that I can quickly scan what is happening in all the vital areas of GEM.

The web site also serves as my portfolio tracker. I can scan the markets (domestic and global, sectors and styles) and see exactly where things stand instantaneously. At the end of every day, I download the portfolio data and dump it into my portfolio monitoring spreadsheet so that I can see exactly how the segments are doing on an intraweek basis. Moreover, I then take that downloaded data and put it into my recommended portfolio mix and immediately know how my portfolio performance is doing intraweek. At the end of every week, the weekly performance data is recorded and the spreadsheet is updated to be ready for the next week.

Wall Street Journal Online

I look to this web site (www.wsj.com) for:

- General market, business, and economic news and data.
- Company and industry news and data.
- Opinions and insight.

The *Wall Street Journal* online edition is the electronic version of the hard copy paper edition. The same stories are covered as in the hard copy versions, although they are not laid out in the same manner. The advantage of the electronic version, which is the advantage of every electronic version from an information resource, is the ability to customize the information according to one's needs. This also includes the ability to search for information previously reported.

What I like most about this web site is the completeness of business, political, and market information. I visit this web site several times a day, usually after hitting my Yahoo! Finance home page to get a more comprehensive picture of the economic, business, and political news of the day. I have found that the *Journal*'s reporters are simply excellent. The articles, often with charts and tables, are informative and often insightful. The opinion pieces written by several contributing reporters provide a perspective that is most helpful.

There are two data-related resources that I reference from the web site. One deals with the economic outlook and the other with corporate earnings. For someone with a limited research budget, the data found on these web pages is very useful.

Financial Times Online

I look to the FT.com web site (www.ft.com) for:

- General market, business, and economic news and data.
- Opinions and insight.

I go to this web site mostly for a different perspective on the news items of interest but, more importantly, for the opinion and insight provided by a variety of outstanding writers. My favorite, by far, is economics expert Martin Wolf. Not only does Wolf provide facts and information, but his insights, written in an educational style, have given me a depth of understanding on a wide range of topics and from both a current and a historical perspective.

BigCharts.com

I look to this web site for charts of stocks, industries, and indexes.

BigCharts.com has a terrific navigational tool for investors. The ability to save a list of favorite charts for easy reference is a plus, as is the ability to do nearly every type of chart analysis one could ask for.

These are my primary publicly available web sites. They are my starting points and often my ending points. But there are lots of other data and insights that I rely on. Here are the private sources I go to and what I expect to gain from the content at each web site.

Morgan Stanley

I look to this web site (www.morganstanley.com/GEFdata/digests/latest-digest.html) for economic analysis and insight.

The blue-chip investment banking firm, Morgan Stanley, must have a Santa Claus gene, as it has made available the excellent work of its chief economist, Stephen Roach, and all the rest of the economics team to everyone at an unbeatable price—*free!* I don't know how long this goodie will remain in Santa's bag, but until it turns to a lump of coal it is one of my favorite economic information web sites.

What has always impressed about Steve and the rest of the Morgan Stanley economics team is their comprehensiveness. Not only do they cover the globe and domestic economic issues, but they do it with strong points of view. Moreover, they each have a very independent style, often disagreeing with another. This is like President Franklin Delano Roosevelt's brain trust on economic strategy.

Merrill Lynch

I look to this web site (www.ml.com) for:

- General market, business, and economic news, data, and insight.
- Portfolios.
- Company and industry news, data, and insight.

Because there are several accounts that I manage and an account of my own, I have access to Merrill's research. The navigational tool that allows access to its research reports based on a keyword search enables me to view the work of, among others, Rich Bernstein (investment strategy, quantitative analysis); David Rosenberg (economy, both domestic and global); David Bowers (investment strategy); Mary Ann Bartels (equity trading, hedge funds); and Dick McCabe (market analysis). I find their work to be very helpful, especially when I disagree with their conclusions. It's always good to know what very talented people think about the same subject you are working on.

The next category is made up of web sites that I visit a bit less frequently, usually several times a month, mostly whenever reports are issued or when I need to research a specific subject area and want data and perspective. They are the governmental web sites and they contain a wealth of unfiltered information. The raw data available is a must-see for my work, and in many cases there is also opinion and insight that is most helpful.

Here are just two of my favorite government sources and what I expect to gain from the content at each web site.

Federal Reserve Board

The web site of the Federal Reserve Board and central bank of the United States (www.federalreserve.gov) is a very useful source of data, information, opinion, and insight. The resources at an investor's disposal provide the Fed's perspective on the economy and monetary policy, a very important subject for all investors to gain as much insight into as possible. The following are two segments of the Fed's web site that I have found quite useful. Both contain links to the information sought.

On its Economic Research and Data web page, the Fed lists the following links:

Statistics: Releases and Historical Data
Daily, weekly, monthly, quarterly, and annual, including commercial paper, loan charge-offs, and medium-term notes.

Surveys and Reports
Includes the senior loan officer survey, the survey on small business finances, and the survey of consumer finances.

Staff Studies
A series of published studies covering a wide range of economic and financial subjects.

Working Papers
Preliminary discussion papers in domestic and international topics, occasional staff studies, and links to other working papers sites.

Federal Reserve Bulletin
Reports and analysis on economic developments, regulatory issues, and new data.

Research Staff and Resources
Staff economists by name, field of interest, and division plus Board resources and career opportunities available to researchers.

Conferences

On the Fed's News and Events web page, an investor can read the thoughts and views of the Fed Governors, among other useful information. What follows is an abbreviated list of the subjects and links on this web page:

Testimony and Speeches
- *Monetary Policy Report to the Congress*
- *Testimony of Federal Reserve Officials*
- *Speeches of Federal Reserve Board Members*

Press Releases
- *Monetary Policy*

Statements by the Federal Open Market Committee and the Board of Governors on the stance of monetary policy and on related procedural matters.

Other press releases, announcements, conferences, and services are listed as well.

FirstGov.gov

A truly invaluable yet less known resource is the FirstGov web site (www .firstgov.gov). On this web site, an investor will find links to all the important statistics and reports from the various governmental bodies and agencies. I go to this web site as a reference source whenever researching any business or economic topic. Here is partial list of what you will find.

Business Data and Statistics
Census Data
- *Domestic Product Tables*
- *Rural America Facts*
- *The U.S. Population Right Now!*
- *U.S. State Population*
- *Welfare Facts*

Earnings Data and Labor Statistics
American Earnings
- *Crop Labor Expenditures by County in U.S. Dollars*
- *Economic Briefing Room*

- *Economic Indicator Release Schedule*
- *Employment and Unemployment, by State*
- *Income, by State and Locality*
- *Labor Statistics*
- *Minimum Federal Wage*
- *Social Security Changes for 2005*
- *Unemployment—by State and Local Areas*
- *Wages, by Area and Occupation*
- *Women in the Labor Force*

Economic Analysis
Reports on the U.S. Economy

- *U.S. Economic Analysis*
- *U.S. Economic Indicators*

Regional Information
County Economics and Demographics

- *Employment Data, by State and Metro Area*
- *National and World Statistics*
- *Regional Data and Statistics*
- *Regional Economic Conditions*
- *State of the Cities Data System*
- *The Economy in Your State*
- *Unemployment Data, by Local Area*
- *Wages, by Area and Occupation*

Statistics Portals
Bureau of Economic Analysis

- *Bureau of Labor Statistics*
- *Census Bureau*
- *Department of Commerce*
- *Department of Labor*
- *Economic Indicators*
- *Economic Research Service*
- *Housing and Economic Research*
- *Searchable Government Databases on Economics, Business and Finance*
- *Stat USA*
- *State of the Nation*

U.S. Businesses

Electronic Commerce Statistics

- *Gross Domestic Product and Other National Accounts Data*
- *Inflation and Consumer Spending*
- Occupational Outlook Handbook
- *Occupational Safety and Health Inspection Data*
- *SEC Requires Sworn Financial Statements*
- *Small Business Statistics*
- *Survey of Current Business*
- *U.S. Businesses by Size*
- *Wages, by Area and Occupation*
- *Workplace Injury, Illness and Fatality Statistics*

Government web sites are not the only sources of information that scan the domestic and global economy. Sites of many private organizations provide very useful data, opinion, and insight and are well worth the time spent visiting them. Most of these organizations are think tanks in which a particular point of view is expressed. In most cases, they should be considered information sources with a point of view, and some might have an ax to grind. So be it. They are still very worthwhile web sites to gain insight into the thinking of some of the leading minds around, regardless of their political agendas.

Here are a four private organization sources that I go to from time to time and a brief featured item from each web site.

Institute for International Economics

On the "Hot Topics" segment of its home page (www.iie.com), the Institute for International Economics (IIE) has the following introduction to the "US Current Account Deficit":

The global current account deficit of the United States is now larger than it has ever been—nearing $800 billion, almost 7 percent of US GDP. To finance both the current account deficit and its own sizable foreign investments, the United States must import about $1 trillion of foreign capital every year or more than $4 billion every working day. The situation is unsustainable in both international financial and domestic political (i.e., trade policy) terms. Correcting it must be the highest priority for US foreign economic policy. The most constructive remedy in the short term *is a three-part package that includes credible, sizable reductions in the US budget deficit, expansion of domestic demand in major economies outside the United States, and a gradual but substantial realignment of exchange rates.*

Cato Institute

In its "What's New" column on its web site (www.cato.org), the Cato Institute provides commentary on recent developments. For example:

Snake Oil: Eliminating the Strategic Petroleum Reserve

Thirty years ago, the Strategic Petroleum Reserve (SPR) was established to guard against disruptions in the nation's oil supply. However, according to a new study by the Cato Institute, there is little evidence to suggest that the SPR is necessary in protecting the U.S. against oil supply emergencies.

In the Policy Analysis "The Case against the Strategic Petroleum Reserve," Cato senior fellows Jerry Taylor and Peter Van Doren argue that the SPR has become costly and counterproductive, claiming that so far the costs of the reserve have greatly exceeded the benefits of the program and will almost certainly continue to do so in the future.

The Heritage Foundation

With George W. Bush in the White House and the Republicans in power, the Heritage Foundation, a very powerful right-wing think tank, is a must-visit web site (www.heritage.org). Here are introductory remarks on one of its favorite subjects, tax reform:

Tax Reform Briefing Room
The Latest

The Panel's Report: A Good Starting Point for Real Reform
November 1, 2005
The President's Advisory Panel on Federal Tax Reform today released its report on reforming the internal revenue code. The report is available on the Panel's website.

"While the Panel's recommendations all point in the right direction, the Panel unfortunately backed away from more sweeping reforms," writes Heritage Foundation tax analyst Dan Mitchell in

his analysis of the Panel's two proposed reform plans. "Lawmakers should use the Panel's report as a starting point on the way to a more simple and fair tax system."

Democratic Leadership Council

When Bill Clinton was in power, the Democratice Leadership Council (DLC) was the must-visit web site of its day (www.dlc.org). As a home for the out-of-power Democratic centrists, this web site, along with its think tank, the Progressive Policy Institute, is worth monitoring. Here is a recent excerpt from the "New Dem Dispatch":

> *DLC | New Dem Dispatch | September 30, 2005*
> *Idea of the Week: What to Do Now in Iraq*
> *While the Bush Administration has committed a long series of mistakes in the aftermath of the removal of Saddam Hussein, America must remain committed to success in Iraq. A failed state in Iraq would destabilize the entire region, hand our jihadist enemies a major victory and result in a devastating blow to our national security credibility and interests. But the right course now is neither to give the terrorists a victory by withdrawing, nor to continue Bush's failed policies. We urge progressives to place maximum pressure on the administration to reverse its mistakes and pursue a new strategy linked to clear benchmarks for success in Iraq and in the broader war on terror.*

Whether it is the political or the economic, private organizational web sites are an invaluable resource for investors. As with the previous section on government sources, the list of private organizations is a very large one. The four just describe form but a tiny sample of what is out there, but they should give you a fairly good idea of what you will find when you make them a resource. The information listed should also provide you with some sense of the content on the web sites of these and other private organizations.

Overall, in the information age that we live in, there are countless other very useful web sites that are well worth adding to an investor's favorites list. Areas such as behavioral finance or developments in Asia or emerging markets can be visited to gain valuable information and insight. The list is endless. It's just a question of finding what works best for you. I have listed those that I have come to depend on. What works for you may lie elsewhere.

NEWSLETTERS AND E-MAIL ALERTS

Another resource that I have come to rely on are e-mail alerts from information sources that I have signed up to receive or get thanks to the relationships that I have built up over the years. Here are those e-mail alerts that I currently receive. I have no doubt that, just like my web sites, this list will evolve and expand over time.

New York Times Online

I get an e-mail alert each morning from the online edition of the *New York Times* (www.nytimes.com) that has been customized to my areas of interest. Titles and a brief synopsis of the key business, market, general news, and opinions are listed. Links to the stories are embedded in the e-mail for easy access to the full story.

What I find particularly useful here is the quick scan of those stories and opinions that may be of interest for me to follow up on.

Wall Street Journal Online

I want to keep my eye on the Asian markets, and I rely on the daily brief updates on them from the online edition of the *Wall Street Journal* (www.wsj.com). Quick links to the full story are embedded in the e-mail—short and to the point.

Financial Times Online

FT.com sends me three alerts: one on Japan, one on China, and one whenever Martin Wolf has published an article. As with the *Journal* newsletter, the Asia region is currently (and for the foreseeable future) a key focus of mine. Therefore, the combination of both the *Journal* and FT.com e-mail alerts helps ensure that I don't miss a story or news item of interest.

CIBC World Markets

My good friend, Subodh Kumar, CFA, chief investment strategist with CIBC World Markets, has me on his e-mail list and sends his reports as they are published. Subodh's reports are about as comprehensive as you will find anywhere in Wall Street research. Adding special value to the reports is the global perspective he brings. A world markets approach to investment strategy helps to broaden my understanding of trends and themes active on the world stage.

Banc of America Securities

Tom McManus, chief investment strategist for Banc of America Securities, produces some of the best market analysis and data around. I find particularly useful Tom's market data—flow of funds, comparative analyses—and his interpretation of the data.

USES: APPLYING THE DATA

Okay. So we have searched the Web, accessed our sources, and downloaded our data. Now what? Well, it's time to put that information to work for us.

The downloaded data that is of informational and analytical value is studied at a more relaxed pace. The reports that are downloaded can be read and studied at a more leisurely, less time-dependent pace, when we want to do so. We thereby avoid delving into a subject at a time when other matters might be more pressing.

As for the raw data downloaded, that is often dumped into a spreadsheet program for analysis. One example of this is the portfolio data that is downloaded from the *Wall Street Journal* online edition and reformatted so that the economic sectors' performance can be seen more cleanly as in Table 8.1.

Table 8.1 shows the earnings performance of the various economic sectors, condensed so that we can see just how each sector has done in the period noted. This data, while directly in the area of our valuation model input of free cash flows, can be used to help gauge that valuation model input. It is also a point of reference to my primary valuation tool for the market overall, the Fed Model (Table 8.2).

The data from the first table show a rate of growth that fully supports a valuation model target of 1333 to 1385 in the S&P 500, as earnings growth was nothing short of spectacular. But what of inflation and the potential for rising interest rates? For that let's use another but very different resource, BigCharts.com. See Figure 8.1 for an example.

Here my technical analysis skills come somewhat into play. The trading pattern of the benchmark 10-year Treasury note suggests that a rise to the previous three-year high of 4.9 percent is possible. But the 10-year is likely to encounter some difficulty moving above that level. If so, then the Fed Model, which factors in not today's 10-year rate but a cushion to the 5.2 to 5.4 percent rate, indicates that the market could rise from its current 1205 level. Moreover, support for a higher market is indicated when one compares the P/E ratio of an average of 19 times

TABLE 8.1 3Q05 Economic Sector Earnings Results

	Number of Companies	Net on Continuing Operations			Net Income		
		3Q05	3Q04	Percent Change	3Q05	3Q04	Percent Change
Basic Materials	66	$ 4,943	$ 4,915	0.55%	$ 5,236	$ 4,407	18.82%
Consumer Services	206	19,058	11,146	70.99	18,448	10,322	78.72
Consumer Goods	114	14,298	16,766	−14.72	14,302	17,033	−16.03
Oil and Gas	76	29,591	16,644	77.79	30,393	16,855	80.33
Financials	240	36,805	36,194	1.69	38,322	36,755	4.26
Health Care	150	12,115	11,208	8.10	12,100	12,179	−0.65
Industrials	212	22,877	18,950	20.73	23,018	19,000	21.15
Technology	206	13,044	9,664	34.98	12,921	10,167	27.09
Telecommunications	15	4,241	−10,423	N/A	4,264	−9,605	N/A
Utilities	69	7,476	7,206	3.75	6,853	6,855	−0.04
Grand Total	1,354	$164,447	$122,268	34.50%	$165,849	$123,967	33.78%

Net on Continuing Operations and Net Income figures are in the millions.
Companies reporting as of November 10, 2005.
Data source: Wall Street Journal online edition.

TABLE 8.2 Fed Model

| Adjusted 10-Year Treasury | S&P 500 Earnings | | | | | | | P/E Conversion | |
	2005 $66	$68	$70	$72	$74	2006 $76	$78	10-Year Treasury	P/E
4.00%	1650	1700	1750	1800	1850	1900	1950	4.00%	25.00
4.20	1571	1619	1667	1714	1762	1810	1857	4.20	23.81
4.40	1500	1545	1591	1636	1682	1727	1773	4.40	22.73
4.60	1435	1478	1522	1565	1609	1652	1696	4.60	21.74
4.80	1375	1417	1458	1500	1542	1583	1625	4.80	20.83
5.00	1320	1360	1400	1440	1480	1520	1560	5.00	20.00
5.20	1269	1308	1346	1385	1423	1462	1500	5.20	19.23
5.40	1222	1259	1296	1333	1370	1407	1444	5.40	18.52
5.60	1179	1214	1250	1286	1321	1357	1393	5.60	17.86
5.80	1138	1172	1207	1241	1276	1310	1345	5.80	17.24
6.00	1100	1133	1167	1200	1233	1267	1300	6.00	16.67

S&P 10-Year Treasury 4.55%

S&P 2005 $66 = 1205

Source: Thomson Financial.

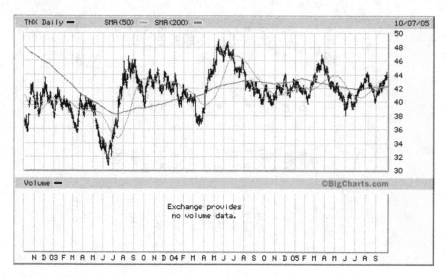

FIGURE 8.1   Ten-Year U.S. Treasury Note
Source: BigCharts.com.

earnings to the admittedly very strong growth rate of 34 percent in the third quarter of 2005.

This is but a very small idea of what can be done utilizing the power of the PC and the Net. I am sure you can be just as creative now that you have the opportunity to do so.

WHY I LOVE THE NET

The great thing about web sites is that you have the ability to search for what you are specifically looking for going back over time. If you missed a report or comment, no problem. Just do a search at the web site.

Another great feature of web sites is the ability to customize the pages you visit. For example, the first four web sites discussed—Yahoo! Finance.com, *Wall Street Journal* online edition, FT.com, and BigCharts .com—provide me with data customized to my needs. The web page opens and what I have designated as my areas of interest are formatted into the view that I see. This saves valuable time and keeps the focus on what I am most interested in, which is provided to me in a clear and concise manner.

TRADITIONAL MEDIA SOURCES

Everything described in this chapter thus far pertains to the new media world of the PC and the Net. There are, however, several other important and/or useful sources of information, data, opinion, and insight that I turn to on a regular basis. Cable news services like CNBC, Bloomberg TV, and EuroNews help keep me informed. And a steady diet of insightful books is always a part of my work, as are selected investment-related publications such as *Institutional Investor* magazine.

WHAT CAN WE EXPECT TOMORROW?

The trend in technology is headed in only one way—up! Resources will get easier to use, less expensive, and more pervasive. Web sites will get more robust, and content services will become more available. Costs may rise, but are likely to remain well within the range of just about everyone.

Mobility is becoming ubiquitous and more robust. BlackBerry devices and cell phones may be everywhere as text and voice devices. But the future lies in even greater capabilities for content delivery to you at all times wherever you are.

The technological and financial innovations of recent decades have enabled more investors to do what previously was reserved for the members of the portfolio manager's club. Today, just about anyone can do this, and do this well. But just as with any tool, technology is not a substitute for human skill and capability. The valuation principles, an effective investment strategy, and a portfolio strategy rooted in the Core Plus principles enable an investor to use the tools described in these two chapters of Part Three to great advantage.

Now, let's look at how it can all come together.

Four

Putting It All Together: Creating and Maintaining an Effective Portfolio

"**W**hat you see depends on where you stand" is one of my favorite expressions. It's a telling statement about how the reality of the world depends on one's perception of it. The statement applies to all aspects of life but it has a dual meaning for investors. On one level, it describes the analytical process and its biases and pitfalls as we humans do our very best to be as objective as we can be. Often, that effort falls short and the human qualities of fear and greed overwhelm our more rational, dispassionate side. This was discussed in some detail in the preceding eight chapters and the Introduction.

On another level, our perception of the world is a necessary component of portfolio construction as our personal wants, needs, and obligations are incorporated into our tolerance and preferences for risk. Investor tolerances of and preferences for risk are the subjects of the next chapter. For it is in the construction of an effective portfolio that investors bring to bear their personal wants, needs, and obligations to modify the model portfolio derived by the analytical process. In other words, we create a model portfolio that is a reflection of our best judgment as to the asset allocation decision made. And then we create the specific sectors and style allocations according to our best judgment. The two steps to the process are: determine what is the appropriate asset allocation mix (stocks, bonds, and cash), and determine what sectors and styles we will invest in.

The essence of creating and maintaining an effective portfolio is, therefore, centered on taking the recommended investment approach of the model portfolio and integrating the personal circumstances of an investor. Some categorization occurs as investors with like wants and needs fall neatly into predetermined boxes (capital preservation, income, income and growth, growth, and aggressive growth). But an investor should always be mindful of not generalizing too much and adhering too strictly to what the category says. In other words, use the categorization as a guideline, just as you would with the model portfolio.

Another important point to remember is the need to manage risk. Some wise advisers say that managing a successful portfolio is all about managing risk. These are words from the wise to the wise and I fully endorse them. Manage your assets by being ever mindful of minimizing your risks. In this way, the hard work done analyzing the macroeconomy, microeconomy, and the markets will be put to good use in the most productive manner.

CHAPTER 9

Building the Effective Portfolio

We've analyzed. We've planned. Now, it's time to put it all together.

Putting it all together means building an effective portfolio. I use the term *effective portfolio* because a portfolio's goal should be to meet the needs of the client and not some arbitrary market benchmark. Issues like risk tolerance and personal preferences all come to bear in the final step, the end goal of our work.

Building an effective portfolio is a three-step process. It begins with the asset allocation decision, moves on to the portfolio construction process, and continues with the ongoing adjustments into the future. So, let's start with step one.

THE ASSET ALLOCATION DECISION

"You gotta be in it to win it" is the New York Lottery slogan. And while I don't want to equate investing with gambling (yes, there *is* a difference), the slogan does apply when it comes to the single most important factor that determines the rate of return of a portfolio: the asset allocation decision. For the asset allocation is by far the most important investment decision an investor can make. It is more important than what you buy or when you buy it. In short, it's more important than any other investment decision you will ever make.

Study after study has shown that the asset allocation decision determines 85 to 90 percent of the investment performance of a well-diversified portfolio. It is for this purpose—to make the best possible asset allocation decision—that so much of this book is focused on that subject: to get this point as right as possible. It is why 85 to 90 percent of my work is dedicated to the 85 to 90 percent of what constitutes the bulk of investment performance.

It is important to note that concentrated portfolios, such as industry-specific or style-specific portfolios, are in a different class from diversified portfolios. For example, the investment performance of a technology portfolio or a small-cap portfolio or a short-only portfolio is most often radically different from that of a well-diversified portfolio. The risk factors are also dramatically different. For most investors, a diversified portfolio is most appropriate. The question becomes, therefore, what constitutes a *well-diversified* portfolio. The advice rendered in this book is that every sector be represented in an investor's portfolio, but that value is added in the tilting or biasing of the portfolio in favor of or against specific economic sectors. This is the essence of the Core Plus approach to managing a well-diversified portfolio.

Interestingly, however, this focus on what matters most is not the case for most investors. In fact, far too many investors, professional and non, spend the bulk of their time (85 to 90 percent) on what to buy and when to buy it—analyzing individual stocks, studying companies to gain some kernel of an idea that other investors have not discovered, chasing some hot tip, or trying to time the market using whatever tools work for the moment. The list goes on and on. Why is this so? Who knows?

Now, to be fair, some investors have no choice in the matter. They must search out the best individual ideas they can find because that's their job—finding the best ideas and building a portfolio around the best of the best. Specifically, this is the circumstance of many mutual fund managers. Their primary job is not to determine whether or not to be in the market, nor is it to determine what their asset allocation should be. Rather, they are constrained by the rules of the assets they manage. Accordingly, their mandate is to earn the highest rate of return for the amount of risk allowed within the parameters of the assets managed. As a result, nearly all mutual fund portfolio managers *must* put their assets to work in their defined area.

What this means is that, in most cases, a mutual fund manager cannot go below a certain level invested in stocks. For example, the mutual fund's prospectus might say that no less than 60 percent of the fund's assets must be invested in stocks. The asset allocation decision is, therefore, then left to the investor (that's you), while the mutual fund manager must do his/her best to earn a rate of return in excess of the designated benchmark (the technology index or the health care index, for instance).

For most average investors, however, no such contractual constraints exist. An investor is free to choose how much or how little to commit to a given asset class, thereby enabling that investor to avoid bear markets, if possible. And this is a huge source of competitive advantage: the ability to commit to focusing on the asset allocation decision above all else. And, in the process, this tilts the odds of investment success in your favor.

Since we investors are in the business of devising our own investment strategies and constructing and managing our own effective portfolios, we can invest as much or as little as we wish in the stock market in our portfolios. We can overweight or underweight sectors and styles according to our investment strategy. We do not have to go before an investment committee and ask for approval to buy or sell a position. We are liberated in our ability to construct our effective portfolio to the best of our ability.

But a word of caution: With that liberty comes the responsibility of performance. There are no excuses. And thanks to ETFs, an investor no longer can claim that he/she was unable to capitalize on the investment strategy arrived upon.

Now that we know that our primary portfolio goal is to determine the appropriate asset allocation decision and that we can approach the construction of our portfolio completely unfettered, we are now ready to tackle some of the mitigating factors necessary for a customized, effective portfolio.

Mitigating Factor 1: Eat Well or Sleep Well

An investor needs to determine the level of risk he/she is comfortable with. The level of risk (a/k/a risk tolerance) that an investor is comfortable with is a defining characteristic of what will eventually become the portfolio. This is an important but highly subjective decision. For example, individuals who experienced the bad times of the Depression of the 1930s are far more inclined to avoid taking risks as opposed to a baby boomer who had no such traumatic experience.

There are many basic and several reasonably sophisticated portfolio analysis tools that will help an investor determine what his/her risk tolerance is. What they seek to achieve can, in effect, be encapsulated in the following question: "If all you had was $100,000 to invest, what matters more to you—making or losing $10,000 of your money?" If the answer is making $10,000, then the thought of losing 10 percent of one's investible assets is a lesser concern than missing the opportunity of making 10 percent, and that takes an investor one step closer to determining just how much to put into stocks.

But a risk preference is just that: a preference or choice of a highly subjective and personal nature. There are other factors that must weigh into the decision of how much to invest in risky assets like stocks. For example, let's say an investor says that he/she is willing to lose 50 percent of his/her money for the chance to make 50 percent. Is that the prudent thing to do? If all that investor has to be concerned with is himself or herself and there are no others involved, then that investor is better able to choose this highly dubious direction. But that is not the norm. Most investors have others to be concerned about, including themselves when time works against them. In other words, the older you needs the younger you to take care of him/her. This is just another way of introducing the second mitigating factor: obligations.

Mitigating Factor 2: Obligations

To help determine an investor's risk tolerance, another factor to bear in mind is the scale and scope of an investor's obligations. An investor's age, assets, income, lifestyle, and the like must be considered in deciding on the risk to be accepted. The two most common examples are the investor who has a current obligation to provide for and the investor who has a future obligation to tend to. Depending on the specifics of the circumstances, the degree to which the investible assets must be made available now (to care for an elderly parent) or in the future (to provide for retirement) will influence the asset allocation and portfolio construction decisions to be made.

Mitigating Factor 3: Future Assets to Consider

A number of investors are likely to receive money at some point in the future, some through inheritances and others in the form of receipt of deferred assets, like retirement funds. These assets must be considered when making asset allocation and portfolio construction decisions. In the case of retirement funds to be received, an investor should manage all the investible funds as though they were part of one account. In other words, the investible assets I have access to today and the assets I will have access to tomorrow need to be treated as though I have them all in one account. Moreover, the timing of the funds and amount of the total along with the current and future lifestyle are all factors that impact the investment choices made today. When it comes to the subject of assets to be inherited, however, this issue gets a tad more complicated.

Future assets that will be inherited have certain issues at work:

- How to manage the assets for the current owner.
- How to plan for the inevitable day when money is inherited.

This is not to mention the uncertainty and timing of the receipt of the funds. The question of when death will occur and the potential of changing circumstances of the parties involved make planning on these funds a difficult consideration. Nevertheless, let's assume that the funds are certain to be passed on thanks to a irrevocable living trust, for example. Then the managing of the assets for the benefit of the benefactor who is still alive must be taken into consideration should the recipient be the fiduciary of the assets.

The combinations are many and they could (and do) easily fill an entire book. The main point, however, is that funds that will be received sometime in the future can and will influence the decisions to be made today.

Mitigating Factor 4: Changing Circumstances

The one constant in life is change. Lifestyles change, jobs change, relationships do as well, great opportunities arise, and unforeseen problems pop up when we least want them. Life is full of surprises, and some of them can be quite nasty. Preparing for the unknown is always advisable. And nothing speaks more loudly than the age-old expression, "You don't know what you don't know." Changing circumstances, especially the unexpected kind, should be prepared for.

With these four mitigating factors taken into consideration, let's understand some of the important basics of making the asset allocation decision with three easy examples.

THE ASSET ALLOCATION MIX: FACTORING IN RISK

Take for example an investor who is comfortable investing 100 percent of his/her money in stocks and who has few or no mitigating factors that would lower that risk exposure, and that same investor expects the stock market to rise by 12 percent over the next 12 months. Add to this the expectation that bonds are expected to produce a total return of 6 percent and that cash (money market) will generate a 3 percent return. Finally, let's assume that the volatility of the three asset classes relative to the market (with the S&P 500 as our proxy for the market) is 100 percent for stocks, 40 percent for bonds, and 0 percent for cash (or a beta of 1, .4, and 0, respectively). The asset allocation mix that might be considered is shown in Table 9.1.

TABLE 9.1   Asset Allocation Mix

	Expected Return	Percent of Portfolio	Portfolio Adjusted Expected Return	Beta	Risk-Adjusted Expected Return
Stocks	12.00%	60.00%	7.20%	1.00	7.20%
Bonds	6.00	30.00	1.80	0.40	4.50
Cash	3.00	10.00	0.30	0.00	0.30
Total		100.00%	9.30%	0.72	12.00%

Source: iViewResearch.

Here an investor can invest 60 percent in stocks, 30 percent in bonds, and 10 percent in cash and still generate a rate of return (adjusted for risk) equal to putting 100 percent of the money into stocks *but* with less volatility (only 72 percent as volatile). Therefore, an investor with a risk tolerance that warrants putting 100 percent of his/her money into stocks may decide that putting less than that amount will generate a return equal to the more risky 100 percent in stocks level.

Now let's say another investor is a less risky investor and needs more ready cash available. The asset mix and associated returns might resemble Table 9.2.

Lastly, let's assume that our original risk-taking investor expects stocks to generate a 15 percent return. The original asset mix might look like Table 9.3. The trade-off between the higher return (15 percent) with higher risk in stocks (beta of 1) versus the lower portfolio return (13.8 percent) but much lower level of risk (beta of .72) presents a dilemma for our investor: whether to go with the higher return and higher risk or

TABLE 9.2   Asset Allocation Adjusted for Less Risk

	Expected Return	Percent of Portfolio	Adjusted Expected Return	Beta	Risk-Adjusted Expected Return
Stocks	12.00%	50.00%	6.00%	1.00	6.00%
Bonds	6.00	30.00	1.80	0.40	4.50
Cash	3.00	20.00	0.60	0.00	0.30
Total		100.00%	8.40%	0.62	10.80%

Source: iViewResearch.

TABLE 9.3 Asset Allocation with Higher Return Expectations

	Expected Return	Percent of Portfolio	Portfolio Adjusted Expected Return	Beta	Risk-Adjusted Expected Return
Stocks	15.00%	60.00%	9.00%	1.00	9.00%
Bonds	6.00	30.00	1.80	0.40	4.50
Cash	3.00	10.00	0.30	0.00	0.30
Total		100.00%	11.10%	0.72	13.80%

Source: iViewResearch.

go with the slightly lower return (1.2 percent lower) and much lower risk (30 percent less volatile). Decisions, decisions. No easy answers. Judgment and choice.

PORTFOLIO CONSTRUCTION: CORE PLUS

Once investors have determined what their risk tolerance is and, therefrom, what their appropriate asset allocation mix should be, the next step involves the building of the equity portion of the portfolio.

Sound portfolio construction begins with a core of economic sectors underweighted, even, or overweighted according to your investment strategy call. From this base, an investor can tilt or bias the portfolio to whatever economic sector, industry, or individual stock he/she wishes. This is what I call the Core Plus approach to money management. You start with the economic sectors as your core and tilt or bias the portfolio according to the investment strategy decisions made for each sector.

There are two benefits to the Core Plus approach. First, it places the portfolio emphasis where it belongs—on what matters most, the sectors and styles owned. Second, it puts the portfolio in alignment with the way nearly all professional money managers do their work. Except for those professional investors who focus exclusively on one sector or industry or who have a defined limited strategy (a hedge fund manager focusing on Emerging Markets or Health Care), most portfolio managers weight their portfolios according to the economic sectors of the economy. A basic Core Plus portfolio might look like the one in Table 9.4.

TABLE 9.4 Portfolio Weightings Relative to Economic Sector Weightings

Economic Sectors	Market Weight	Portfolio Weight	Relative Weight	ETF
Consumer Discretionary	10.80%	8.50%	−2.30%	XLY
Consumer Staples	9.80	11.00	1.20	XLP
Energy	9.50	12.00	2.50	XLE
Financials	20.90	17.00	−3.90	XLF
Health Care	13.10	11.00	−2.10	XLV
Industrials	11.20	14.00	2.80	XLI
Basic Materials	3.00	3.00	0.00	XLB
Information Technology	15.30	17.00	1.70	IYW
Telecommunications	3.10	3.10	0.00	IYZ
Utilities	3.40	3.40	0.00	XLU
Total	100.00%	100.00%	0.00%	

Source: iViewResearch; Compustat.

In this example, our investor is:

- Bullish on Energy, Information Technology, Industrials, and Consumer Staples.
- Neutral on Telecommunications, Utilities, and Basic Materials.
- Bearish on Consumer Discretionary, Financials, and Health Care.

And, as you can see, an ETF reflecting each economic sector is listed.

This is a basic Core Plus portfolio in action. If our investor is right, he/she benefits; if wrong, he/she loses. But because the weightings are just a few percentage points apart, when one is wrong the pain is not that great. Conversely, if our investor gets it right, he/she makes money in a consistent but decidedly unflashy fashion. If it's fun and glamour you want, then Core Plus is not for you. If, however, the potential of consistent results is what you seek, then you may want to go a little further and consider the following more elaborate mix involving sectors, styles, global assets, and other assets (Gold). See Table 9.5 for an example.

This equity portfolio example depicts a severe underweighting in the economic sectors overall and in certain specific sectors like Financials and Energy. Counterbalancing that strong underweighting are bets in style, global, and other categories, which are designed to produce an above-average return at the same or lower risk. Moreover, some money is allocated to a few industries within certain sectors, such as Biotech and Networking.

TABLE 9.5 Potential Portfolio Mix

Sectors and Industries	Market Weight	Portfolio Weight	ETF
Consumer Discretionary	10.80%	6.00%	XLY
Consumer Staples	9.80	6.00	XLP
Energy	9.50	4.00	XLE
Financials	20.90	10.00	XLF
Health Care	13.10	8.00	XLV
Biotech		3.00	IBB
Industrials	11.20	12.00	XLI
Basic Materials	3.00	2.00	XLB
Information Technology	15.30	12.00	IYW
Networking		3.00	IGN
Telecommunications	3.10	2.00	IYZ
Utilities	3.40	2.00	XLU
Subtotal	100.00%	70.00%	
Size and Styles			
Mid Cap		5.00%	MDY
Mid Cap—Value		4.00	IJJ
Large Cap—Dow Industrials		4.00	DIA
Large Cap—S&P 100		7.00	OEF
Global			
Emerging Markets		3.00%	EEM
Japan		3.00	EWJ
Other			
Gold		4.00	GLD
Subtotal		30.00%	
Total		100.00%	

Source: iViewResearch; Compustat.

INCORPORATING RISK

Going back to the economic sector example, the issue of risk in the form of a volatility metric like beta should be examined to see if the recommended sector mix is above, equal to, or below the risk of the market weighting. Table 9.6 shows the individual betas for each economic sector ETF, the weight-adjusted portfolio beta for the market (which you would expect to

TABLE 9.6 Portfolio Weightings with Risk Factors

Economic Sectors	Market Weight	Portfolio Weight	Relative Weight	ETF	Beta	Market Weight Beta	Portfolio Weight Beta
Consumer Discretionary	10.80%	8.50%	–2.30%	XLY	1.30	0.14	0.11
Consumer Staples	9.80	11.00	1.20	XLP	0.44	0.04	0.05
Energy	9.50	12.00	2.50	XLE	0.62	0.06	0.07
Financials	20.90	17.00	–3.90	XLF	0.97	0.20	0.16
Health Care	13.10	11.00	–2.10	XLV	0.54	0.07	0.06
Industrials	11.20	14.00	2.80	XLI	1.09	0.12	0.15
Basic Materials	3.00	3.00	0.00	XLB	1.37	0.04	0.04
Information Technology	15.30	17.00	1.70	IYW	1.72	0.26	0.29
Telecommunications	3.10	3.10	0.00	IYZ	1.13	0.04	0.04
Utilities	3.40	3.40	0.00	XLU	0.51	0.02	0.02
Total	100.00%	100.00%	0.00%			0.99	1.00

Source: iViewResearch; Compustat; Yahoo! Finance.

be 1.00 as the collective economic sectors equal the S&P 500 in terms of beta since it is in effect the market), and the portfolio weight-adjusted beta. In this example, the overweighting in the high-volatility Information Technology and Industrials sectors is offset by the overweighting in the low-volatility Energy and Consumer Staples sectors and the underweighting in the high-volatility Consumer Discretionary sector. The net effect is a portfolio that is no more volatile than the market overall.

As you can easily imagine, the asset allocation and equity portfolio combinations can be endless. And with the introduction of more industry, global, style, and other ETFs, no investor will be left wanting more choices.

This now brings us to the third and final step in our portfolio construction process: ongoing adjustments.

MAKING ADJUSTMENTS

The one constant in life is change. And for portfolios, change means making adjustments. If we have established our asset allocation mix and our equity portfolio has been put together, we must now consider how, when, and why we will need to make changes to what we own. The first consideration is a personal one: our changing personal circumstances.

Changing Personal Circumstances

Life happens. Things change. And with change comes the need to adjust our risk tolerance levels upward or downward. For example, if the risk tolerance goes down as one gets closer to retirement, so, too, must the exposure to stocks and the specific equity sector mixes.

Changing Market Expectations

If our investment strategy work leads to the conclusion that stocks are more or less attractive and a change in return expectations is the result, then adjustments to the asset allocation mix must be made. Here is where judgment really shows its worth. For there are no easy answers, no easy rules. As circumstances change, so, too, must the mix between and among asset classes, if warranted.

Changing Sector and Style Expectations

If growth prospects or risk factors increase or decrease, so, too, must the equity portfolio mix. For example, if Energy goes from attractive to neutral, then an even weighting is most likely warranted.

Adjusting for the Style Bets

One more adjustment should be noted.

If the portfolio you construct includes style investments, you must not forget the fact that each style ETF is comprised of economic sectors and it is very easy to inadvertently overweight (or underweight) an economic sector you did not intend to overweight (or underweight). For example, the Mid Cap Value ETF, IJJ, currently has more than 20 percent of its portfolio in the Financials sector. Therefore, if your investment strategy recommended an underweighting in Financials, owning IJJ could expose your portfolio to more Financials issues than you intended.

THE TIP OF THE INVESTMENT ICEBERG

The examples noted in this chapter are just the tip of the investment iceberg. Asset allocation and equity portfolio combinations enable an investor to choose from a wide range of mixes. Starting with our investment strategy conclusions and a recommended portfolio, we then move on to incorporate some of our personal preferences and risk tolerance factors to reach an appropriate asset allocation and portfolio mix suited to our needs. As time passes, our personal and the markets' circumstances will change. With that change, we need to make adjustments to our mixes. This is the essence of creating and maintaining an effective portfolio, one that will enable us to utilize the power of ETFs and draw our own investment strategy conclusions.

What is left is to take the personalization aspect of creating and managing an effective portfolio to the next level. That is the subject of the next and final chapter: "Let's Get Personal."

CHAPTER 10

Let's Get Personal

I once asked a good friend why the movie *The Shawshank Redemption* held such a strong appeal to viewers. His answer was, "We all have our personal prisons to break out of." Well, with a little luck and lots of hard work, all investors can break out of the prison of conventional thinking and the media-obsessed instant investment decision making and enter the world of sound investment principles and the enabling power offered by the technology and financial innovation described in this book. The investment prison break has begun!

FROM THE GENERAL TO THE SPECIFIC

In Chapter 9, I presented several generalized portfolio strategies. They will now serve as a foundation that should be used as guidelines to the more specific personal needs of most investors. What we now need to do is add that personal element in the form of portfolio strategy groupings.

Granted, everyone's personal circumstances are unique, but there are enough similarities that we can categorize most typical investor profiles into five primary groupings:

1. Capital preservation
2. Income
3. Income and growth
4. Growth
5. Aggressive growth

Each group represents the primary focus of the money being managed and a given level of risk tolerances and personal preferences. With a finely developed investment strategy, the portfolio profiles of each can now be examined. Let's start with the investment strategy assumptions for our five profiles.

INVESTMENT STRATEGY ASSUMPTIONS

All growth-oriented assets *always* sell at a discount to some expected future value. Let me say that again: All growth-oriented assets, every single one of them, *always* sell at a discount to some expected future value. Accordingly, today's price *always* trades at a discount to next year's expected price. I emphasize the word *always* simply because it's a fact: growth-oriented assets like stocks offer the potential for an investment payoff primarily in the form of a capital gain. Whether next year's price turns out to be higher than today's price is the work of investment strategy and remains to be seen. Moreover, next year's price may turn out to be higher than this year's price but at such a small increment that it ends up producing a rate of return that is below what we should earn given the level of risk taken. Therefore, the primary mission of investment strategy is to:

- Determine what level the market should trade at one year from today.
- Determine what level each economic sector should trade at one year from today.
- Determine how certain we are of our projections.

In determining our asset allocation and equity portfolio mixes, we must first have a forecasted return for the three asset classes: stocks, bonds, and cash. When it comes to bonds and cash, much of the same analytical work that we do to determine the macro and micro outlooks is used to help determine the expected level of interest rates over a reasonable investment time horizon. The standard time horizon that I use is one year. I am aware of longer time horizons, but in today's hyperactive world of investing, one year is a good time frame to work with.

Therefore, the same analytical processes and principles employed in our macro and micro work combined with the historical returns on the asset classes and the market metrics of technical analysis might lead us to the following expected return assumptions:

Stocks	12%
Bonds	6%
Cash	3%

If we add a little extra risk for the lower-quality, higher-risk small market cap stocks, we can assume that they might generate a return of 15 percent.

The last step is to determine our expectations for the next 12 months for each economic sector. To do this, we refer to a number of published sources on the consensus expectations of analysts to arrive at the numbers found in Table 10.1.

TABLE 10.1 Economic Sector Estimated Growth Rates, P/E Ratio, and PEG Ratio

Economic Sectors	2005 Est. Growth	2006 Est. Growth	P/E	PEG
Consumer Discretionary	−4.50%	22.00%	20	0.91
Consumer Staples	6.00	10.00	18	1.80
Energy	46.00	8.00	13	1.63
Financials	9.00	11.00	12	1.09
Health Care	7.00	11.00	18	1.64
Industrials	16.00	16.00	16	1.00
Basic Materials	16.00	8.00	16	2.00
Information Technology	13.00	18.00	21	1.17
Telecommunications	2.00	4.00	19	4.75
Utilities	19.00	11.00	17	1.55
S&P 500	11.00%	9.00%	16	1.78

Source: Thomson Financial.

Standing at this specific point in time (the end of 2005) and looking one year out, we can note the listed earnings growth. We then take the current price-earnings (P/E) ratio for each sector and compare that P/E to the expected growth rate to determine the price-earnings/growth (PEG) ratio. The PEG ratio is an excellent shorthand tool to determine the market's take on valuation (remember that the P in the P/E ratio is the market's judgment on value). There are several issues to note from the data, and this is where our opinion and judgment come into play:

- The Consumer Discretionary growth expectation is extraordinarily high, in my opinion. High growth levels can result from a depressed current year level thereby producing a higher than normal year-over-year growth rate. This is the case when it comes to the Consumer Discretionary sector. However (here comes the judgment), concerns over the ability of consumers to sustain their spending habits, especially in the area of big ticket items (the bread and butter of the Consumer Discretionary sector), strongly suggest that this number may actually come in under expectations and, therefore, disappoint those more optimistic investors. Accordingly, the P/E and 2006 estimated growth rate may turn out to be on the high side.
- A slowing is expected in Energy, Utilities, and Basic Materials as the boom years are producing hard year-over-year comparisons.

Nevertheless, the market is affording both the Utilities and Basic Materials sectors a PEG ratio that is comparable to the market. Their PEG ratios are not so egregious, however, and investing in these sectors at an even weighting should not be a problem.

■ When it comes to valuation metrics like the P/E and PEG ratios, Telecommunications is a severely depressed sector in which the numbers are almost meaningless. A more appropriate way to evaluate the merits of this sector would involve a normalizing or averaging of the earnings part of the equation to produce a less cyclically distorted number. Alternatively, looking several years down the road might produce a more normal earnings number.

This data and commentary should provide an investor with a good sample of the process and thinking when it comes to deciding where the fair value of the moment lies. Armed with these assumptions, let's see how five different investors, each at a distinct level of want and need, might build their portfolios.

Capital Preservation

Primary Objective	Preservation of investment capital
Expected Rate of Return	Low
Risk Tolerance	Low

Possible Asset Allocation Mix

Stocks	10%
Bonds	60
Cash	30

Now, using the same S&P weightings as in Chapter 9 for each economic sector, considering their level of risk (in the form of beta), and adding their current dividend yield (an important element of a very low-risk investor), we might construct an equity portfolio that looks like the ones in Tables 10.2 and 10.3.

Possible Equity Portfolio Mix   *Comment:* With this mix, the portfolio is below average in risk (portfolio beta of .84 versus market beta of .99) and above average in yield (2.04 percent versus 1.6 percent). A key point to remember is that a balance needs to be struck between higher risk (beta) and a higher dividend yield. That is why the higher-risk reading in Basic Materials (1.37) results in a suggested slightly above-average portfolio exposure

TABLE 10.2 Capital Preservation Portfolio: Beta

Economic Sectors	Market Weight	Portfolio Weight	Beta	ETF	Market Weight Beta	Portfolio Weight Beta
Consumer Discretionary	10.80%	5.00%	1.30	XLY	0.14	0.07
Consumer Staples	9.80	10.00	0.44	XLP	0.04	0.04
Energy	9.50	5.00	0.62	XLE	0.06	0.03
Financials	20.90	15.00	0.97	XLF	0.20	0.15
Health Care	13.10	10.00	0.54	XLV	0.07	0.05
Industrials	11.20	10.00	1.09	XLI	0.12	0.11
Basic Materials	3.00	5.00	1.37	XLB	0.04	0.07
Information Technology	15.30	5.00	1.72	IYW	0.26	0.09
Telecommunications	3.10	10.00	1.13	IYZ	0.04	0.11
Utilities	3.40	25.00	0.51	XLU	0.02	0.13
Total	100.00%	100.00%	0.00		0.99	0.84

Source: Compustat; Yahoo! Finance; iViewResearch.

TABLE 10.3 Capital Preservation Portfolio: Yield

Economic Sectors	Market Weight	Portfolio Weight	Dividend Yield	ETF	Market Weight Dividend Yield	Portfolio Weight Dividend Yield
Consumer Discretionary	10.80%	5.00%	0.79%	XLY	0.09%	0.04%
Consumer Staples	9.80	10.00	1.77	XLP	0.17	0.18
Energy	9.50	5.00	1.14	XLE	0.11	0.06
Financials	20.90	15.00	2.13	XLF	0.45	0.32
Health Care	13.10	10.00	1.25	XLV	0.16	0.13
Industrials	11.20	10.00	1.45	XLI	0.16	0.15
Basic Materials	3.00	5.00	1.93	XLB	0.06	0.10
Information Technology	15.30	5.00	1.51	IYW	0.23	0.08
Telecommunications	3.10	10.00	2.30	IYZ	0.07	0.23
Utilities	3.40	25.00	3.11	XLU	0.11	0.78
Total	100.00%	100.00%			1.60%	2.04%

Source: Compustat; Yahoo! Finance; iViewResearch.

(5 percent versus 3 percent) despite the above-average yield of 1.93 percent versus 1.6 percent.

Income

Primary Objective	Income with some degree of capital preservation
Expected Rate of Return	Low
Risk Tolerance	Low

Possible Asset Allocation Mix

Stocks	25%
Bonds	60
Cash	15

Possible Equity Portfolio Mix   *Comment:* Here the focus is on current *and* future income. (See Tables 10.4 and 10.5.) Therefore, those sectors that might produce a greater growth potential would be increased over those sectors that are expected to generate a more modest growth potential. That is why I might increase Industrials by 5 percent, Information Technology by 2 percent, and Energy by 3 percent and concurrently decrease Utilities

TABLE 10.4   Income Portfolio: Beta

Economic Sectors	Market Weight	Portfolio Weight	Beta	ETF	Market Weight Beta	Portfolio Weight Beta
Consumer Discretionary	10.80%	5.00%	1.30	XLY	0.14	0.07
Consumer Staples	9.80	10.00	0.44	XLP	0.04	0.04
Energy	9.50	8.00	0.62	XLE	0.06	0.05
Financials	20.90	15.00	0.97	XLF	0.20	0.15
Health Care	13.10	10.00	0.54	XLV	0.07	0.05
Industrials	11.20	15.00	1.09	XLI	0.12	0.16
Basic Materials	3.00	5.00	1.37	XLB	0.04	0.07
Information Technology	15.30	7.00	1.72	IYW	0.26	0.12
Telecommunications	3.10	10.00	1.13	IYZ	0.04	0.11
Utilities	3.40	15.00	0.51	XLU	0.02	0.08
Total	100.00%	100.00%	0.00		0.99	0.90

Source: Compustat; Yahoo! Finance; iViewResearch.

TABLE 10.5   Income Portfolio: Yield

Economic Sectors	Market Weight	Portfolio Weight	Dividend Yield	ETF	Market Weight Dividend Yield	Portfolio Weight Dividend Yield
Consumer Discretionary	10.80%	5.00%	0.79%	XLY	0.09%	0.04%
Consumer Staples	9.80	10.00	1.77	XLP	0.17	0.18
Energy	9.50	8.00	1.14	XLE	0.11	0.09
Financials	20.90	15.00	2.13	XLF	0.45	0.32
Health Care	13.10	10.00	1.25	XLV	0.16	0.13
Industrials	11.20	15.00	1.45	XLI	0.16	0.22
Basic Materials	3.00	5.00	1.93	XLB	0.06	0.10
Information Technology	15.30	7.00	1.51	IYW	0.23	0.11
Telecommunications	3.10	10.00	2.30	IYZ	0.07	0.23
Utilities	3.40	15.00	3.11	XLU	0.11	0.47
Total	100.00%	100.00%			1.60%	1.87%

Source: Compustat; Yahoo! Finance; iViewResearch.

by 10 percent. Also, note that our beta rose from .84 for the capital preservation profile to .90 for this investor type.

Income and Growth

Primary Objective	Income plus some growth
Expected Rate of Return	Average
Risk Tolerance	Average

Possible Asset Allocation Mix
Stocks	40%
Bonds	45
Cash	15

Possible Equity Portfolio Mix   *Comment:* Our income and growth portfolio shown in Tables 10.6 and 10.7 has a further upward tweaking with a touch more Information Technology and Basic Materials and a slight reduction in Consumer Staples and Utilities. This helps provide an increase in the growth potential without sacrificing too much in the way of current

TABLE 10.6 Income and Growth Portfolio: Beta

Economic Sectors	Market Weight	Portfolio Weight	Beta	ETF	Market Weight Beta	Portfolio Weight Beta
Consumer Discretionary	10.80%	5.00%	1.30	XLY	0.14	0.07
Consumer Staples	9.80	8.00	0.44	XLP	0.04	0.04
Energy	9.50	8.00	0.62	XLE	0.06	0.05
Financials	20.90	15.00	0.97	XLF	0.20	0.15
Health Care	13.10	10.00	0.54	XLV	0.07	0.05
Industrials	11.20	15.00	1.09	XLI	0.12	0.16
Basic Materials	3.00	7.00	1.37	XLB	0.04	0.10
Information Technology	15.30	10.00	1.72	IYW	0.26	0.17
Telecommunications	3.10	10.00	1.13	IYZ	0.04	0.11
Utilities	3.40	12.00	0.51	XLU	0.02	0.06
Total	100.00%	100.00%	0.00		0.99	0.95

Source: Compustat; Yahoo! Finance; iViewResearch.

TABLE 10.7 Income and Growth Portfolio: Yield

Economic Sectors	Market Weight	Portfolio Weight	Dividend Yield	ETF	Market Weight Dividend Yield	Portfolio Weight Dividend Yield
Consumer Discretionary	10.80%	5.00%	0.79%	XLY	0.09%	0.04%
Consumer Staples	9.80	8.00	1.77	XLP	0.17	0.14
Energy	9.50	8.00	1.14	XLE	0.11	0.09
Financials	20.90	15.00	2.13	XLF	0.45	0.32
Health Care	13.10	10.00	1.25	XLV	0.16	0.13
Industrials	11.20	15.00	1.45	XLI	0.16	0.22
Basic Materials	3.00	7.00	1.93	XLB	0.06	0.14
Information Technology	15.30	10.00	1.51	IYW	0.23	0.15
Telecommunications	3.10	10.00	2.30	IYZ	0.07	0.23
Utilities	3.40	12.00	3.11	XLU	0.11	0.37
Total	100.00%	100.00%			1.60%	1.82%

Source: Compustat; Yahoo! Finance; iViewResearch.

income. Accordingly, the portfolio yield declines and risk rises slightly over the preceding income profile.

Growth

Primary Objective	Growth
Expected Rate of Return	Average
Risk Tolerance	Average

Possible Asset Allocation Mix

Stocks	60%
Bonds	30
Cash	10

Possible Equity Portfolio Mix *Comment:* One of the focuses in this profile is to get the beta up. (See Table 10.8.) Therefore, the higher-beta sectors (Information Technology, for example) are increased to an overweighting. Interestingly, the dividend yield is little changed despite the greater risk level assumed. (See Table 10.9.) This is clearly attributable to the fact that in a low-interest-rate environment, dividend yields are not as important to most investors.

TABLE 10.8 Growth Portfolio: Beta

Economic Sectors	Market Weight	Portfolio Weight	Beta	ETF	Market Weight Beta	Portfolio Weight Beta
Consumer Discretionary	10.80%	8.00%	1.30	XLY	0.14	0.10
Consumer Staples	9.80	8.00	0.44	XLP	0.04	0.04
Energy	9.50	10.00	0.62	XLE	0.06	0.06
Financials	20.90	15.00	0.97	XLF	0.20	0.15
Health Care	13.10	8.00	0.54	XLV	0.07	0.04
Industrials	11.20	16.00	1.09	XLI	0.12	0.17
Basic Materials	3.00	7.00	1.37	XLB	0.04	0.10
Information Technology	15.30	17.00	1.72	IYW	0.26	0.29
Telecommunications	3.10	6.00	1.13	IYZ	0.04	0.07
Utilities	3.40	5.00	0.51	XLU	0.02	0.03
Total	100.00%	100.00%	0.00		0.99	1.05

Source: Compustat; Yahoo! Finance; iViewResearch.

TABLE 10.9 Growth Portfolio: Yield

Economic Sectors	Market Weight	Portfolio Weight	Dividend Yield	ETF	Market Weight Dividend Yield	Portfolio Weight Dividend Yield
Consumer Discretionary	10.80%	8.00%	0.79%	XLY	0.09%	0.06%
Consumer Staples	9.80	8.00	1.77	XLP	0.17	0.14
Energy	9.50	10.00	1.14	XLE	0.11	0.11
Financials	20.90	15.00	2.13	XLF	0.45	0.32
Health Care	13.10	8.00	1.25	XLV	0.16	0.10
Industrials	11.20	16.00	1.45	XLI	0.16	0.23
Basic Materials	3.00	7.00	1.93	XLB	0.06	0.14
Information Technology	15.30	17.00	1.51	IYW	0.23	0.26
Telecommunications	3.10	6.00	2.30	IYZ	0.07	0.14
Utilities	3.40	5.00	3.11	XLU	0.11	0.16
Total	100.00%	100.00%			1.60%	1.66%

Source: Compustat; Yahoo! Finance; iViewResearch.

Aggressive Growth

Primary Objective	Aggressive growth
Expected Rate of Return	Above average
Risk Tolerance	Above average

Possible Asset Allocation Mix

Stocks	80%
Bonds	10
Cash	10

Possible Equity Portfolio Mix *Comment:* In our aggressive growth portfolio shown in Tables 10.10 and 10.11, the ramping up of Information Technology and Industrials to strong overweights introduces the idea that we need to go beyond the economic sectors in order to satisfy the needs of the aggressive growth investor. Adding individual industries, going global, and adding other assets like Gold are all appropriate to consider. Moreover, the style bets of mid-cap and small-cap issues are also worth pursuing. To help illustrate this point, take a second look at far more diverse portfolio mix from Chapter 9 (Table 10.12).

TABLE 10.10 Aggressive Growth Portfolio: Beta

Economic Sectors	Market Weight	Portfolio Weight	Beta	ETF	Market Weight Beta	Portfolio Weight Beta
Consumer Discretionary	10.80%	8.00%	1.30	XLY	0.14	0.10
Consumer Staples	9.80	6.00	0.44	XLP	0.04	0.03
Energy	9.50	10.00	0.62	XLE	0.06	0.06
Financials	20.90	15.00	0.97	XLF	0.20	0.15
Health Care	13.10	6.00	0.54	XLV	0.07	0.03
Industrials	11.20	18.00	1.09	XLI	0.12	0.20
Basic Materials	3.00	10.00	1.37	XLB	0.04	0.14
Information Technology	15.30	20.00	1.72	IYW	0.26	0.34
Telecommunications	3.10	5.00	1.13	IYZ	0.04	0.06
Utilities	3.40	2.00	0.51	XLU	0.02	0.01
Total	100.00%	100.00%	0.00		0.99	1.11

Source: Compustat; Yahoo! Finance; iViewResearch.

TABLE 10.11 Aggressive Growth Portfolio: Yield

Economic Sectors	Market Weight	Portfolio Weight	Dividend Yield	ETF	Market Weight Dividend Yield	Portfolio Weight Dividend Yield
Consumer Discretionary	10.80%	8.00%	0.79%	XLY	0.09%	0.06%
Consumer Staples	9.80	6.00	1.77	XLP	0.17	0.11
Energy	9.50	10.00	1.14	XLE	0.11	0.11
Financials	20.90	15.00	2.13	XLF	0.45	0.32
Health Care	13.10	6.00	1.25	XLV	0.16	0.08
Industrials	11.20	18.00	1.45	XLI	0.16	0.26
Basic Materials	3.00	10.00	1.93	XLB	0.06	0.19
Information Technology	15.30	20.00	1.51	IYW	0.23	0.30
Telecommunications	3.10	5.00	2.30	IYZ	0.07	0.12
Utilities	3.40	2.00	3.11	XLU	0.11	0.06
Total	100.00%	100.00%			1.60%	1.61%

Source: Compustat; Yahoo! Finance; iViewResearch.

TABLE 10.12 Diversified Growth Portfolio

Sectors and Industries	Market Weight	Portfolio Weight	ETF
Consumer Discretionary	10.80%	6.00%	XLY
Consumer Staples	9.80	6.00	XLP
Energy	9.50	4.00	XLE
Financials	20.90	10.00	XLF
Health Care	13.10	8.00	XLV
Biotech		3.00	IBB
Industrials	11.20	12.00	XLI
Basic Materials	3.00	2.00	XLB
Information Technology	15.30	12.00	IYW
Networking		3.00	IGN
Telecommunications	3.10	2.00	IYZ
Utilities	3.40	2.00	XLU
Subtotal	100.00%	70.00%	
Size and Styles			
Mid Cap		5.00%	MDY
Mid Cap—Value		4.00	IJJ
Large Cap—Dow Industrials		4.00	DIA
Large Cap—S&P 100		7.00	OEF
Global			
Emerging Markets		3.00%	EEM
Japan		3.00	EWJ
Other			
Gold		4.00%	GLD
Subtotal		30.00%	
Total		100.00%	

Source: Compustat; iViewResearch.

While the mix shown in Table 10.12 (circa the fourth quarter of 2005) is a model portfolio one (more growth than aggressive growth), it does provide a glimpse into what a more aggressive growth portfolio might include. All one need do is increase such industry bets as Biotech or Networking or add a small-cap growth ETF, just to name a few. And, as noted before, as more industries, global markets, and subsectors are added, the possibilities of properly satisfying our growth and aggressive growth investors increase.

And that brings us to another possibility: adding individual stocks.

TO ADD OR NOT TO ADD, THAT IS THE QUESTION

With the core portfolio constructed of ETFs, an investor can now consider adding individual stocks to the portfolio mix in an appropriate proportion that can, hopefully, add several percentage points of return to the overall portfolio. The key words in the preceding sentence are *appropriate proportion*. Keeping in mind the fact that balance and diversification are keys to investment success, an individual stock should never exceed 5 percent of the total assets being managed. In the Core Plus approach to portfolio construction, adding stocks to the mix is a discretionary call. And one should never get too carried away or fall in love with the next great idea. Nevertheless, adding a modest amount of individual stocks to the overall portfolio is not an inappropriate act, particularly for growth and aggressive growth investors.

Interestingly, adding some individual stocks that have been analyzed using the valuation principles described in Chapter 1 has the added benefit of bringing us closer to the sectors and styles that comprise the bulk of the portfolio. For example, individual stocks can also be a very effective indicator of the trends within the industry and sector they trade in. A company leader in the transportation or biotech field, for instance, might provide meaningful insights into the direction of its respective industry. While not the dominant reason to add stocks to a sectors and styles ETF portfolio, they can serve a dual purpose: potentially earn a greater rate of return and provide insight into key sectors and styles.

. . . AND IN THE STARRING ROLE: YOU

I started off this book with the twin questions, "Why this book? Why now?" I hope that I have answered those questions by illustrating a fairly complex but doable approach to investment independence that technological and financial innovation has empowered all investors with. And, in many respects, that is what this book is really about: the empowerment of investors to do as the big boys and girls do, and create an effective investment strategy and build and maintain an effective portfolio.

But it should be noted that investing is not a one-time event. It should not be treated like a photograph: an in-the-moment, hot-tip, idea-driven snapshot with little or no follow-through on what happens after the idea has been bought. Rather, consistent, successful investing entails an ongoing commitment and involvement by you. It is, in effect, an investment movie, if you will, and you are in a starring role. For the first time in investment history, the ability to analyze and manage the markets is now in your hands. I hope I have been able to point you in the right direction.

To quote the famous nineteenth-century English novelist George Eliot: "It's never too late to be what you might have been."

Conducting Your Own Research

A major premise of this book is encapsulated in one word: empowerment. Today's investor has the unprecedented ability to do what only professional investors with significant resources could do before: build diversified, effective portfolios.

A key component of this empowerment is the ability to find and utilize information, most of which is free or at such a low cost as to make it available to just about every investor. All that is needed is a computer, an Internet connection, and a desire to do original research, to think for oneself, and to come to one's own conclusions. Another key component of investor empowerment is the ability and willingness to conduct original research for oneself. This involves the desire to identify and be comfortable in reading and understanding reports produced by governmental and nongovernmental bodies.

This appendix shows how easy and readily available information to conduct quality research is. Publicly available information from governmental and nongovernmental sources is presented and described, much of which provides not just useful information but also valuable insights. The reports provided here, some in their entirety, are designed to make one primary point: The reports are not as arcane as one might be led to believe. They are often written in very understandable, plain English. Their availability and clearheadedness make them a more than worthwhile exercise for the seriously involved investor to pursue.

But first, a warning! Today's investment environment is a double-edged sword. An investor can utilize the powerful tools described in this book for good or ill. An investor today can take the power of the Internet and make better-informed decisions with a goal of constructing a durable and sustainable effective portfolio that will generate positive results for years to come. Or an investor today can do what far too many investors do: make portfolio decisions based on the hot idea of the day and not construct a balanced portfolio. And in the process of following the fool's gold of the past, some investors make the same fundamental mistakes as were common before electronic trading and information were made available. The choice is there, and no excuses will disguise the fact that an investor can no longer claim that he/she has been denied the opportunity to utilize the tools the pros have used and take for granted.

The danger of poor portfolio choices doesn't stop with the inclusion of exchange-traded funds (ETFs) in a portfolio. For an investor today can take the power of sector and style investing provided by ETFs and build the same kind of unbalanced portfolios that he/she could with individual stocks or mutual funds. Put another way, investors today can ignore the sound investment principles articulated in this book and continue to *do the wrong things with the right tools* and build the same kind of lopsided investment house that they could have in the past. Only by *combining* the new tools *with* sound investment principles can today's empowered investors be assured of the best chances of producing *consistent* investment results that are in their favor.

Empowerment is a good thing. Investors can take it as far and as deep as they want to. Taking the next steps, being actively involved in researching sometimes raw data, will bring you that much closer to self-reliance—and, hopefully, greater and more consistent investment success.

HOW TO CONDUCT YOUR OWN RESEARCH

Being empowered means being an independent thinker: one who is able to do all that is needed to create the foundation for an effective portfolio—an effective investment strategy. Being an independent thinker means being capable of conducting one's own research. For the ability to conduct your own research will enable you to formulate a depth of understanding about a subject that cannot be accomplished by relying on others.

Until the age of the Internet, the ability to conduct quality independent, original research was hampered by cost and access. Today, as outlined in Chapter 8, the power of the PC and the Net is the great enabler of conducting one's own research. Accordingly, the vast majority of the research work I do takes place on my desktop, with my ever-trusty cell phone by my side.

My research sources are many. I rely on government and private sources, not to mention quality media publications like the *Wall Street Journal* and the *Financial Times*. Thanks to the Internet and the ability to download data directly into my computer, this readily available, high-value data eventually finds its way into text and spreadsheet programs for further study and analysis. I also find great value in the events that I produce. However, not everyone gets to moderate events. And as useful as events can be, I am very selective as to which ones I go to, as they can be very time-consuming and produce little in the way of new knowledge—although networking at events can be helpful.

What I Seek to Learn

The primary focus of my research is to obtain raw knowledge, gain insights, and determine the context of the information, all with the goal of identifying how they impact the critical variables of already formed opinions and my valuation drivers, which were noted in the early chapters. Specifically, I seek to understand:

- Does the research match my prevailing opinion?
- Does the research contradict my prevailing opinion?
- Is there a new insight or perspective to be gained?
- Is the information from a source that I want to go back to again and again?
- Are there new sources of data that I have identified?

New Sources and Ideas

I am always on the lookout for new sources of information and ideas. Frequently, I come across some that appear to be very useful. And I am excited when a new point of view, unique perspective, or well-articulated insight is found. But my initial enthusiasm for my newfound research source is always viewed with a skeptical (not cynical) eye and is put to the test. For example, I ask myself:

- How reliable are the opinions expressed in the material that I am researching?
- What are the credentials of those whose data I am evaluating?
- In the case of Washington think tanks, is there a political agenda they are serving?

Many times, I find these new sources and ideas in the course of my daily readings. Other times, they may come from a television program I am watching or be found at an event I attend or conduct. You never know where or when a valuable piece of information may come your way. But if your eyes are not on the lookout and your ears not tuned, that valuable resource may just whisk right by you. I guess the moral of this story is to always be looking and listening, for you never know when that information opportunity will come knocking.

Real-Time Data

Staying current on the economy and the market is very important. While my investment perspective is a more longer-term view, the daily and weekly actions of the economy and the market are very much a part of my research day. In fact, I view the economic reports and market activities as a continuous vote on the state of the economy and the markets. Each week, various sources produce the economic reports due out for the week. These reports are an invaluable real-time tracking tool for investment strategy formulation. They help keep me current and grounded in where the economy and markets are *right now*.

It is important to note, however, that it is easy to get caught up in the action. Many television programs are geared to be very "in the moment." The hot idea and the breaking story drive viewership. The problem with this is the tendency of many investors to lose sight of the forest for the trees because of too much short-term thinking and too much hot idea thinking. And, as a result, the context for investment strategy and the building of an effective portfolio get lost in translation.

Bottom line: Stay current with day-to-day real-time data, but don't get caught up in the frenzy of hot ideas or short-term thinking. Use the information as a daily tracker of your opinion—does it validate or contradict your prevailing view? If you always seek to place the information into the context of the potential change to your prevailing view, your current investment strategy, and how and in what ways it might change your portfolio, you will keep your eye on the ball and your ear tuned to change. Remember: Change is the one constant. When it comes to investing, change is everything.

RESEARCH EXAMPLES

Federal Reserve

For most of his career in public life, former Federal Reserve chairman Alan Greenspan has taken obfuscation to a high art. His language has been quite opaque. His skill at speaking at length and not saying much has been legendary. They even invented a name for it: Greenspanspeak.

However, for some inexplicable reason as he approached the end of his term as Fed chairman, Greenspan was apparently consumed in a bout of clear speaking. In a speech before the National Italian American Foundation, he articulated a very cogent perspective on his 18 years at the Fed. I reproduce his words to show how easily available such very valuable insights into the economic process and the many complex and challenging episodes the United States and the global economy have experienced during his 18-year tenure as head of the Fed can be. (See "Useful Links" at the end of this appendix.)

Alan Greenspan Speaking Before the National Italian American Foundation (Washington, D.C., on October 12, 2005)

It is a pleasure once again to speak before the National Italian American Foundation. I have long since been awarded the status of honorary Italian, for which I am sincerely appreciative.

In my more than eighteen years at the Federal Reserve, much has surprised me, but nothing more than the remarkable ability of our economy to absorb and recover from the shocks of stock market crashes, credit crunches, terrorism, and hurricanes—blows that would have almost certainly precipitated deep recessions in decades past. This resilience, not evident except in retrospect, owes to a remarkable increase in economic flexibility, partly the consequence of deliberate economic policy and partly the consequence of innovations in information technology.

A couple of weeks ago, I outlined to a convention of fellow economists how I believe this all came about. I should like to share some of those views with you this morning.

For this country's first century and a half, government was only peripherally engaged in what we currently term the management of aggregate demand. Any endeavor to alter the path of private economic activity through active intervention would have been deemed inappropriate and, more important, unnecessary. In one of the more notable coincidences of history, our Declaration of Independence was signed the same year in which Adam Smith published his Wealth of Nations. *Smith's prescription of letting markets prevail with minimal governmental interference became the guiding philosophy of American leadership for much of our history.*

With a masterful insight into the workings of the free-market institutions that were then emerging, Smith postulated an "invisible hand" in which competitive behavior drove an economy's resources toward their fullest and most efficient use. Economic growth and prosperity, he argued, would emerge if governments stood aside and allowed markets to work.

Indeed, within a very few decades, free-market capitalism became the prevailing stance of most governments' economic policy, even if it was often implemented imperfectly. This framework withstood the conceptual onslaughts of Robert Owen's utopians, Karl Marx's communists, and later, the Fabian socialists.

The free-market paradigm came under more-vigorous attack after the collapse of the world's major economies in the 1930s. As the global depression deepened, the seeming failure of competitive markets to restore full employment perplexed economists until John Maynard Keynes offered an explanation that was to influence policy practitioners for generations to come. He argued that, contrary to the tenets of Smith and his followers, market systems did not always converge to full employment. They often appeared to settle at an equilibrium in which significant segments of the workforce were unable to find jobs. In the place of Smith's laissez-faire approach arose the view that government action was required to restore full employment and to rectify what were seen as other deficiencies of market-driven outcomes.

A tidal wave of regulation soon swept over much of the American business community. Labor relations, securities markets, banking, agricultural pricing, and many other segments of the U.S. economy became subject to the oversight of government.

The apparent success of the economy during World War II, which operated at full employment in contrast to the earlier frightening developments during the Depression years, led to a considerable reluctance to fully dismantle wartime regulations when the hostilities came to an end.

However, cracks in the facade of government economic management appeared early in the post–World War II years, and those cracks continued to widen as time passed. At the macro level, the system of wage and price controls imposed in the 1970s to deal with the problem of inflation proved unworkable and ineffective. And at the micro level, heavy regulation of many industries was increasingly seen as impeding efficiency and competitiveness. By the early 1980s, the long-prevalent notion that the centrally planned economy of the Soviet Union was catching up with the West had begun to be discredited, though it was not fully discarded until the collapse of the Berlin Wall in 1989 exposed the economic ruin behind the Iron Curtain.

Starting in the 1970s, U.S. Presidents, supported by bipartisan majorities in the Congress, responded to the growing recognition of the distortions created by regulation, by deregulating large segments of the transportation, communications, energy, and financial services industries. The stated purpose of this deregulation was to enhance competition, which had come to be seen as a significant spur to productivity growth and elevated standards of living. Assisting in the dismantling of economic restraints was the persistent, albeit slow, lowering of barriers to cross-border trade and finance.

As a consequence, the United States, then widely seen as a once-great economic power that had lost its way, gradually moved back to the forefront of what Joseph Schumpeter, the renowned Harvard professor, had called "creative destruction"— the continual scrapping of old technologies to make way for the innovative. In that paradigm, standards of living rise because depreciation and other cash flows of industries employing older, increasingly obsolescent technologies are marshaled, along with new savings, to finance the production of capital assets that almost always embody cutting-edge technologies. Workers, of necessity, migrate with the capital.

Through this process, wealth is created, incremental step by incremental step, as high levels of productivity associated with innovative technologies displace less-efficient productive capacity. The model presupposes the continuous churning of a flexible competitive economy in which the new displaces the old.

As the 1980s progressed, the success of that strategy confirmed the earlier views that a loosening of regulatory restraint on business would improve the flexibility of our economy. No specific program encompassed and coordinated initiatives to enhance flexibility, but there was a growing recognition that a market economy could best withstand and recover from shocks when provided maximum flexibility.

Beyond deregulation, innovative technologies, especially information technologies, have contributed critically to enhanced flexibility. A quarter-century ago, for example, companies often required weeks to discover the emergence of inventory imbalances, allowing production to continue to exacerbate the excess. Excessive stockbuilding, in turn, necessitated a deeper decline in output than would have been necessary had the knowledge of the status of inventories been fully current. The advent of innovative information technologies significantly shortened the reporting lag, enabling flexible real-time responses to emerging imbalances.

Deregulation and the newer information technologies have joined, in the United States and elsewhere, to advance flexibility in the financial sector. Financial stability may turn out to have been the most important contributor to the evident significant gains in economic stability over the past two decades.

Historically, banks have been at the forefront of financial intermediation, in part because their ability to leverage offers an efficient source of funding. But in periods of severe financial stress, such leverage too often brought down banking institutions and, in some cases, precipitated financial crises that led to recession or worse. But recent regulatory reform, coupled with innovative technologies, has stimulated the development of financial products, such as asset-backed securities, collateral loan obligations, and credit default swaps, that facilitate the dispersion of risk.

Conceptual advances in pricing options and other complex financial products, along with improvements in computer and telecommunications technologies, have significantly lowered the costs of, and expanded the opportunities for, hedging risks that were not readily deflected in earlier decades. The new instruments of risk dispersal have enabled the largest and most sophisticated banks, in their credit-granting role, to divest themselves of much credit risk by passing it to institutions with far less leverage. Insurance companies, especially those in reinsurance, pension funds, and hedge funds continue to be willing, at a price, to supply credit protection.

These increasingly complex financial instruments have contributed to the development of a far more flexible, efficient, and hence resilient financial system than the one that existed just a quarter-century ago. After the bursting of the stock market bubble in 2000, unlike previous periods following large financial shocks, no major financial institution defaulted, and the economy held up far better than many had anticipated.

If we have attained a degree of flexibility that can mitigate most significant shocks—a proposition as yet not fully tested—the performance of the economy will be improved and the job of macroeconomic policymakers will be made much simpler.

Governments today, although still far more activist than in the nineteenth and early twentieth centuries, are rediscovering the benefits of competition and the resilience to economic shocks that it fosters. We are also beginning to recognize an international version of Smith's invisible hand in the globalization of economic forces.

Whether by intention or by happenstance, many, if not most, governments in recent decades have been relying more and more on the forces of the marketplace and reducing their intervention in market outcomes. We appear to be revisiting Adam Smith's notion that the more flexible an economy, the greater its ability to self-correct after inevitable, often unanticipated disturbances. That greater tendency toward self-correction has made the cyclical stability of the economy less dependent on the actions of macroeconomic policymakers, whose responses often have come too late or have been misguided.

It is important to remember that most adjustment of a market imbalance is well under way before the imbalance becomes widely identified as a problem. Individual prices, exchange rates, and interest rates adjust incrementally in real time to restore balance. In contrast, administrative or policy actions that await clear evidence of imbalance are of necessity late.

Being able to rely on markets to do the heavy lifting of adjustment is an exceptionally valuable policy asset. The impressive performance of the U.S. economy over the past couple of decades, despite shocks that in the past would have surely produced marked economic contraction, offers the clearest evidence of the benefits of increased market flexibility.

We weathered a decline on October 19, 1987, of a fifth of the market value of U.S. equities with little evidence of subsequent macroeconomic stress—an episode that hinted at a change in adjustment dynamics. The credit crunch of the early 1990s and the bursting of the stock market bubble in 2000 were absorbed with the shallowest recessions in the post–World War II period. And the economic fallout from the tragic events of September 11, 2001, was moderated by market forces, with severe economic weakness evident for only a few weeks. Most recently, the flexibility of our market-driven economy has allowed us, thus far, to weather reasonably well the steep rise in spot and futures prices for oil and natural gas that we have experienced over the past two years. The consequence has been a far more stable economy.

Flexibility is most readily achieved by fostering an environment of maximum competition. A key element in creating this environment is flexible labor markets. Many working people, regrettably, equate labor market flexibility with job insecurity.

Despite that perception, flexible labor policies appear to promote job creation, not destroy it. An increased capacity of management to discharge workers without excessive cost, for example, apparently increases companies' willingness to hire without fear of unremediable mistakes. The net effect, to the surprise of most, has been what appears to be a decline in the structural unemployment rate in the United States.

Protectionism in all its guises, both domestic and international, does not contribute to the welfare of American workers. At best, it is a short-term fix at a cost of lower standards of living for the nation as a whole. We need increased education and training for those displaced by creative destruction, not a stifling of competition.

A consequence of our highly competitive, rapidly growing economy is that the average American will hold many different jobs in a lifetime. Accordingly, education is no longer the sole province of the young. Significant numbers of workers continue their education well beyond their twenties. Millions enroll in community colleges in later life, for example, to upgrade their skills or get new ones. It is a measure of the dynamism of the U.S. economy that community colleges are one of the fastest growing segments of our educational system.

Moving forward, I trust that we have learned durable lessons about the benefits of fostering and preserving a flexible economy. That flexibility has been the product of the economic dynamism of our workers and firms that was unleashed, in part, by the efforts of policymakers to remove rigidities and promote competition.

Although the business cycle has not disappeared, flexibility has made the economy more resilient to shocks and more stable overall during the past couple of decades. To be sure, that stability, by fostering speculative excesses, has created some new challenges for policymakers. But more fundamentally, an environment of greater economic stability has been key to the impressive growth in the standards of living and economic welfare so evident in the United States.

Comment   In this speech, Alan Greenspan has provided investors with an invaluable set of insights, expressed with great clarity. In a relatively brief period, he takes the reader over several centuries to articulate several key concepts of economic principles to help put his nearly two decades of service as chair of the Fed in context. What is particularly noteworthy is his description of the "flexible" economy. "Flexibility is most readily achieved by fostering an environment of maximum competition. A key element in creating this environment is flexible labor markets," he writes and thereby helps a reader begin to appreciate a central tenet of global economic success—the ability to adapt to changing circumstances. Greenspan also references the role technology has played, as well as financial innovation—two themes that I have mentioned at several points in this book.

The bottom line is that such insights are readily available. Alan Greenspan has shown how *all* investors can reap the benefits of his knowledge. It's just a click away.

Economic Reports

"To really get a complete sense as to what goes on at the FOMC meetings, you really have to go through the actual transcripts—the scrubbed-down minutes we all focus on every six weeks are very limited in what they offer us in terms of details, insights, and nuances. It's only in the unedited transcripts that we see the real Fed in action." So wrote David Rosenberg, chief North American economist for Merrill Lynch. Dave was referring to specific reports of the Federal Reserve Open Market Committee meetings, but the principles apply to all government reports. To do original research and to gain added insight, it is important that an investor be committed to going the extra mile to become comfortable with reading government reports.

As with the Greenspan speech, there is often a wealth of useful information and insight contained in these reports. And, thanks to the Internet, there are easily and freely available. Here is an example of an important government report, the one on the U.S. gross domestic product (GDP).

Every quarter, economists and investors look forward to the U.S. Department of Commerce's gross domestic product report. Contained within the report is a wealth of information.

Gross Domestic Product: Second Quarter 2005 (Final) and Corporate Profits: Second Quarter 2005 (Final)

Real gross domestic product—the output of goods and services produced by labor and property located in the United States—increased at an annual rate of 3.3 percent in the second quarter of 2005, according to final estimates released by the Bureau of Economic Analysis. In the first quarter, real GDP increased 3.8 percent.

The GDP estimates released today are based on more complete source data than were available for the preliminary estimates issued last month. In the preliminary estimates, the increase in real GDP was also 3.3 percent.

The major contributors to the increase in real GDP in the second quarter were personal consumption expenditures, exports,

*equipment and software, residential fixed investment, and govern-
ment spending. The contributions of these components were
partly offset by a negative contribution from private inventory investment. Imports, which are a subtraction in the calculation of
GDP, decreased.*

*The deceleration in real GDP growth in the second quarter
primarily reflected a downturn in private inventory investment
that was partly offset by a downturn in imports and an acceleration in exports.*

*Final sales of computers contributed 0.32 percentage point to
the second-quarter growth in real GDP after contributing 0.37
percentage point to the first-quarter growth. Motor vehicle output
subtracted 0.01 percentage point from the second-quarter growth
in real GDP after contributing 0.15 percentage point to the first-
quarter growth.*

*The price index for gross domestic purchases, which measures
prices paid by U.S. residents, increased 3.3 percent in the second
quarter, 0.2 percentage point more than the preliminary estimate;
this index increased 2.9 percent in the first quarter. Excluding food
and energy prices, the price index for gross domestic purchases increased 2.1 percent in the second quarter, compared with an increase of 3.0 percent in the first.*

*Real personal consumption expenditures increased 3.4 percent
in the second quarter, compared with an increase of 3.5 percent in
the first. Real nonresidential fixed investment increased 8.8 percent, compared with an increase of 5.7 percent. Nonresidential
structures increased 2.7 percent, in contrast to a decrease of 2.0
percent. Equipment and software increased 10.9 percent, compared with an increase of 8.3 percent. Real residential fixed investment increased 10.8 percent, compared with an increase of 9.5
percent.*

*Real exports of goods and services increased 10.7 percent in
the second quarter, compared with an increase of 7.5 percent in
the first. Real imports of goods and services decreased 0.3 percent,
in contrast to an increase of 7.4 percent.*

*Real federal government consumption expenditures and gross
investment increased 2.4 percent in the second quarter, the same as
in the first quarter.*

*National defense increased 3.7 percent, compared with an in-
crease of 3.0 percent. Nondefense decreased 0.2 percent, in contrast to an increase of 1.1 percent. Real state and local government*

consumption expenditures and gross investment increased 2.6 percent, compared with an increase of 1.6 percent.

The real change in private inventories subtracted 2.14 percentage points from the second-quarter change in real GDP after adding 0.29 percentage point to the first-quarter change. Private businesses reduced inventories $1.7 billion in the second quarter, following increases of $58.2 billion in the first quarter and $50.1 billion in the fourth.

Real final sales of domestic product—GDP less change in private inventories—increased 5.6 percent in the second quarter, compared with an increase of 3.5 percent in the first.

Gross Domestic Purchases

Real gross domestic purchases—purchases by U.S. residents of goods and services wherever produced—increased 2.1 percent in the second quarter, compared with an increase of 4.0 percent in the first.

Gross National Product

Real gross national product—the goods and services produced by the labor and property supplied by U.S. residents—increased 3.2 percent in the second quarter, compared with an increase of 3.9 percent in the first. GNP includes, and GDP excludes, net receipts of income from the rest of the world, which decreased $3.6 billion in the second quarter after increasing $2.4 billion in the first; in the second quarter, receipts increased $21.3 billion, and payments increased $24.9 billion.

NOTE.—Quarterly estimates are expressed at seasonally adjusted annual rates, unless otherwise specified. Quarter-to-quarter dollar changes are differences between these published estimates. Percent changes are calculated from unrounded data and are annualized. "Real" estimates are in chained (2000) dollars. Price indexes are chain-type measures.

This news release is available on BEA's web site at www.bea .gov/bea/rels.htm.

Comment   One benefit to investors who are not familiar with this type of report is the key sources of economic performance. For example, "The major contributors to the increase in real GDP in the second quarter were personal consumption expenditures, exports, equipment and software, residential fixed investment, and government spending. The contributions of these components were partly offset by a negative contribution from private inventory investment. Imports, which are a subtraction in the calculation of GDP, decreased." Other important data include, among others:

- National defense.
- Real final sales.
- Real exports of goods and services.
- Real federal government consumption expenditures.
- Gross investment.
- Real nonresidential fixed investment.
- Nonresidential structures.
- Real imports of goods and services.

Familiarity with the details of the major contributors, as well as other important data, helps an investor to get a better sense of the scale and scope of economic analysis. An investor should not expect, however, much in the way of opinion. The commentary tends to be more descriptive as opposed to opinion based. The opinions are, therefore, left up to the reader and economists. Accordingly, familiarizing oneself with the report itself should enable the investor to gain a deeper insight into the opinions of those who do this for a living—economists.

Bottom line: Despite their reputation as a sleep aid for insomniacs, government reports afford an investor the potential for greater understanding of the drivers of economic performance, as well as a better understanding of economists' take on how the economy is performing.

Market Commentary

Over the past decade, China has burst onto the world economic scene with great force. China has become both a producer of goods to the world economy and a source of capital to the United States in the form of U.S. government bond purchases. Many have commented that China, as the host nation for the 2008 Olympics, is attempting to do what Japan did with the 1964 Olympics: show the world it has arrived.

Much has been written about China, and it is an ideal subject to help show how investors can utilize publicly available information from nongovernmental sources. To be clear, though, there is a wealth of information about China from governmental sources as well. What follows is what one can find from the private sector of the economy.

The global economic environment in 2005 has been a complex and confusing one. As of mid-2005, U.S. economic growth has been consistently strong and inflation and interest rates have remained quite low, helping to facilitate a very solid growth in corporate earnings and cash flows. And for many sectors, it has been a very good stock market. But the dangers of structural imbalances—large current account, trade, fiscal deficits—threaten to tip the world economy into a perilous downward spiral. And when you consider that the ability of the United States to counter such an economic contraction through traditional deficit spending is all but impossible, the dangers of global economic depression are very real, and many believe quite probable.

However, in the midst of this danger sits the potential of a China-led economic boom. The upcoming 2008 Olympics in Beijing are expected to be the worldwide showcase event for China, just as the 1964 Olympics in Tokyo were for Japan. And China is doing everything it can to ensure that its economy is on an upswing in 2008. And as China goes, so goes most of Asia and the world economy.

Here are a few reports on China and globalization. My comments follow each report.

Morgan Stanley's Chief Economist Stephen Roach: China and the Worldview

There's nothing like an 11-day spin around the world—a brief touchdown in London, followed by lengthier stops in India and Australia—to set the global prognosis in context. The world is struggling mightily with putting the theories of globalization into practice. There is broad recognition of ever-mounting imbalances of a US-centric world, but there is deep conviction that the global economy has a new savior—China.

The Chinese economy has a new image in the broader global community. After years of believing that the inevitable China crisis was just around the corner, the world has rushed to the other side of the ship. China's booming economy is now widely expected to keep on booming for the foreseeable future—an impression certainly validated by the latest batch of Chinese economic statistics on GDP, industrial output, and money and credit (see my 21 October dispatch, "Wrong on the China Slowdown"). There is even hope that the Chinese consumer is now positioned to fill any void left by the American consumer. Australians are especially enamored of China—and with understandable reason: Australia has benefited dramatically from a Chinese-induced surge in its export prices. According to Gerard Minack, head of our new Aussie macro team, the rise in commodity prices has boosted Australia's terms of trade enough to have added two percentage points to the country's national income in the 12 months ending June 2005.

India is also quite taken with China—but for very different reasons. Basically, India wants to figure out how it can be the next China. Mindful of the huge gap that has opened up in the past 25 years in terms of infrastructure, foreign direct investment (FDI), saving, and the sheer scale of the Chinese production platform, there is a certain urgency in coping with the "left-behind" syndrome. In my recent conversations with senior Indian government officials, there was considerable focus on the FDI issue. With a 28% national saving rate that is only a little more than half that of China, India's need for external capital can hardly be minimized. India's new government seems especially focused on changing the closed FDI culture that has long hobbled the nation's development. As I noted recently, broad-based movement now seems to be under way on the FDI front—from telecom to retail (see "Here Comes the Indian Consumer," 1 November 2005).

The China fixation also plays a key role in shaping the ongoing debate in India between manufacturing and services. Given an "inclusive" India's new priorities in coping with massive rural unemployment, the country's focus is on labor-intensive manufacturing activities. That's a tough calculus in today's IT-enabled world, where manufacturing prowess has become increasingly capital intensive. That's especially the case in India, which has a strong competitive edge in IT-enabled manufacturing. To be sure, there may be important labor-intensive exceptions for India, such as textiles, auto components, small office accessories, toys, shoes, and some household equipment and appliances. But the real question is whether the potential scale of activity in such small-scale industries is sufficient to make a meaningful dent in India's high rural unemployment.

But the conclusion that hit me hardest from this world spin was the belief that nothing could shake the China boom. Whether it is urbanization, industrialization, or infrastructure imperatives, the world seems increasingly convinced that very rapid Chinese growth in the 8–9% range is here to stay. Implicit in that conclusion is the belief that the Chinese economy has now developed a new immunity to the ups and downs of the global business cycle. That may be wishful thinking. As I pointed out to the groups I spoke with, China's growth dynamic remains heavily skewed toward exports and export-led fixed asset investment. These two sectors now account for more than 85% of Chinese GDP and continue to grow at nearly a 30% y-o-y [year-over-year] rate. By contrast, the Chinese consumption share of GDP seems set to fall further this year [2005] from the record low of 42% hit in 2004.

This structure of the Chinese economy speaks of a stealth vulnerability that the worldview refuses to consider. China's main source of end-market demand is not internal consumption but the American consumer. Fully 35–40% of Chinese exports currently go to the United States. The investment dynamic is also dependent on the need to expand export-producing capacity. Consequently, a lot obviously hangs on the staying power of US consumption. Therein lies the risk—both for China and for an increasingly China-centric Asia-Pacific. Despite negative personal saving rates, record household sector debt burdens, and a lingering shortfall of labor income generation in the US, few in the world believe that a decade of nearly 4% real US consumption growth is at risk. Should that view turn out to be wrong, then Asia-Pacific would be in for a rude awakening. That would be true of Korea, Taiwan, Malaysia, Thailand, and Singapore—all of which have become tightly intertwined in a China-centric supply chain. It would also be true of Japan, whose largest export market is now China. And it would have a major impact on Australia, where Chinese exports have become a major source of growth over the past several years.

Needless to say, a few eyebrows were raised when I conveyed the latest estimates of our US team that growth in real consumer demand was on pace to slow to an anemic 1.2% annualized clip in the current quarter. I stressed that a saving-short, overly indebted, income-deficient US consumer was highly vulnerable to a shock. Sharply higher energy prices and/or a bursting of the US property bubble would undoubtedly be much tougher to digest in that context. In my encounters overseas, most agreed that the American consumer is running flat out and is unlikely to deliver much added impetus to global economic growth. But there seemed to be little fear of a sharper adjustment to the downside. Nor was there much appreciation of what such a possibility could mean to China—the new savior of an unbalanced global economy.

There was one group I encountered on this trip that got it— the Chinese. On the first day of this tour, I stopped off in London. One meeting was with a group of some 30 senior executives from leading Chinese businesses, who were immersed in the China Executive Learning Program (CELP)—an intense 18-day curriculum run by Cambridge University. Mindful of the unbalanced structure of their own economy, they were quick to grasp the significance of a potential slowing of the American consumer. With support from internal Chinese consumption in an embryonic stage at best, the CELP participants did not rule out a slowdown in China's overall GDP growth. The disconnect came on the rest of my trip—with the belief that China was now an autonomous growth story, with little that could get in the way of persistently rapid 8–9% growth over the next several years.

For sure, I don't want to generalize on the basis of a week and a half of global travel. But this year-end trek has just begun—over the next six weeks, it's two more trips to Asia with another dose of Europe and my first trip to the Middle East wedged in between. By then, if I can think straight from the jet lag, I will have a much more comprehensive sense of global sentiment. At that point, I'll be very surprised if the world's China fixation has faded. I'll be even more surprised if I find concern over Chinese growth prospects. And I'll be shocked if the worldview uncovers the link between the seemingly resilient Chinese producer and the increasingly vulnerable American consumer.

There's always the possibility that China could develop a self-sustaining internal consumption dynamic that would shield it from an externally-driven slowing in the United States. Alternatively, other sources of global consumption—such as Japan and Europe—could fill the void. But in my view, these are all long-tailed developments, at best—unlikely to temper the potentially imminent mismatch between the overextended U.S. consumer and an externally-dependent Chinese producer. If such a mismatch comes to pass, global equities could quickly come under pressure and bond markets could be given another boost.

Comment   Never one to shrink from expressing his point of view and always providing a strong insight into the global macroeconomic trends, Steve's opinion pieces are must-reads, in my opinion. I don't have to agree with his conclusions but do appreciate and respect his ability to synthesize the vast scale and scope of the global economy into a very easy-to-understand narrative. Moreover, by providing the personalized stories of his interaction with professional money managers, business leaders, government officials, and fellow economists, Steve takes an investor into his world.

This particular report focuses on the strongly held belief by many that China can continue to grow at an extraordinary rate seemingly indefinitely. Steve obviously begs to differ and expresses his perspective on the issue. Steve also brings his perception of key U.S. trends ("I stressed that a saving-short, overly indebted, income-deficient US consumer was highly vulnerable to a shock.") into the equation and thereby puts the domestic issue into the global context.

There are other highly informative economists available. The Steve Roach example shows how an investor can benefit from the comments and opinions of those very qualified investment professionals via the Internet, and in the process verify one's point of view and potentially gain an insight into key trends.

One cannot discuss China without putting it within the context of globalization. Chapter 5 on the economy devotes a fair amount of attention to several aspects of globalization. Chapter 4 describes several key points of the political dynamic. The convergence of the two—the global economy and the political—is expressed quite well in an October 5, 2005, *Financial Times* article by Anthony Bubalo, a research fellow at the Lowy Institute for International Policy in Sydney, Australia.

As you will read, the article describes the rise of China (and India and other Asia current and emergent powerhouses) and its potential geopolitical impact on the United States. It is an article worth noting, particularly because many investors unfortunately do not connect the dots and therefore they fail to include such hard-to-quantify factors in their valuation models. And that is a major shortcoming of the rigid approach to investment analysis and portfolio strategy. Here is the article.

Asia's Alliance with the Middle East Threatens Us

A new global alignment is emerging that will have profound implications for the shape of the international system. Asia and the Middle East are often acknowledged as the main theatres within which the key themes of contemporary world politics are played out. But frequently overlooked is the growing web of ties between these two regions—ties that have as a common theme resistance to US political, economic, military and even cultural hegemony.

The most prominent strand of this affiliation is energy. While Asia has long depended on the Middle East for oil and gas, the nature of that relationship is changing. Asia has become an even more voracious consumer of oil and gas, while the Middle East's ties to its traditional energy partner, the US, have become increasingly strained. Today Chinese, Indian, Malaysian and Japanese energy companies are winning exploration and co-production contracts in the region. There are undoubtedly sound economic reasons for this. But it no doubt helps that these companies are free of the political baggage—human rights or nuclear proliferation concerns, for example—that constrains their US counterparts.

A second strand of the Middle East–Asia relationship flows from the first: a growing political and, potentially, strategic affinity. Take China's energy investments in Iran and Sudan. They are not meant to be a poke in Washington's eye. Chinese oil companies do better in these countries because US sanctions mean there is less competition from American players. But, given the centrality of energy security to Chinese foreign policy, an economic imperative soon becomes a political one. Thus, China has opposed oil sanctions on Sudan and resisted efforts to take the Iranian nuclear issue to the United Nations Security Council.

China's attractiveness is not, however, limited to the Middle East's rogues. The Sino-Saudi relationship has developed dramatically since Beijing secretly sold medium-range missiles to Riyadh in the mid-1980s. More recently a Chinese company was one of the first foreigners to gain gas exploration rights in the Kingdom. The sole US bidder withdrew, ostensibly for commercial reasons.

Of course, China is not yet a viable strategic alternative to the US in the Middle East. But this will change. It already has the ability to supply states such as Iran with weapons to "deter" US military designs. China is also acutely conscious of the vulnerability of its long sea lines of communication to the Middle East. As it develops its ability to project naval power—it has already helped Pakistan build a deep-water port on its west coast—the potential for Sino-US strategic competition in the Middle East will grow.

Faith and ideology are other emerging axes of the relationship. Washington tends to view Islamic Asia's growing interest in Islamic fundamentalism exported by countries such as Saudi Arabia through the prism of the war on terror. This is simplistic. Instead of being driven solely by an interest in extremism, this complex phenomenon is partly a response to what Asian Muslims see as the penetration of their societies by a decadent and highly commercialised American culture.

This is just one example of efforts in Asia and the Middle East to find alternatives to globalisation's pervasive American themes. There are others. Malaysia has been promoting reform in the Islamic world and will soon host the inaugural World Islamic International Forum—a "Davos for Muslims." Meanwhile, Middle East regimes talk about the "China model" of open economies and closed political systems.

It would, of course, be wrong to see examples of an emerging Asian–Middle Eastern affinity as a formal anti-American alliance. But in many respects it does not matter. Regardless of whether the

*web of ties becomes institutionalised or remains disparate, formed
through government and non-government bodies, the result will
be the gradual erosion of US hard and soft power in both the Middle and Far East.*

*In the Middle East, America's capacity to reward and sanction
will be undercut by regional countries turning eastward for everything from political support in the Security Council to alternative
markets. In Asia, a tendency toward more independent foreign
policy will be reinforced by a growing sense that Asian and US interests in the Middle East do not necessarily coincide. And globally, it could well be conflict in the Strait of Hormuz rather than
the Strait of Taiwan that sparks a much-anticipated Sino-US rivalry, ultimately challenging the unipolarity that has defined the
past 15 years of international politics.*[1]

Comment It has long been my view that the point at which the world
knows when China is ready to assume its place as the second most powerful economic power in the world is when it gains control of the relationships long held by the United States. The article brings to clear light how
such relationships can, and are, changing. The implications are broad and
significant.

At stake are the competitive positions of nations. And while global is
the economic stage upon which all actors perform, domestic considerations, specifically the political, are and always will be a critical factor influencing business and economic matters, not to mention military issues.

Staying attuned to the issues at work and connecting the economic and
political dots is vital toward understanding the interactive dynamics between
and among the three forces impacting stocks—government, economy, and
the markets. The article brings to light key insights into that process.

The primary point of the quotes and articles is to illustrate that today's
investor can easily access and fairly easily understand what was once the
domain of the privileged and the few. By utilizing the power of the Net, an
investor today can tap a wealth of valuable information and then decide
for himself or herself what to do with that information. Hopefully, he/she
will incorporate it into an investment strategy approach that gets plugged
into an effective portfolio. But that is up to today's investor.

The opportunity, the empowerment, is there. What one does with it is
up to each person. It is my hope, and a major goal of this book, that most
investors will turn information into knowledge. And that means building
and maintaining effective portfolios rooted in sound investment principles.

USEFUL LINKS

Examples

Greenspan speech
    www.federalreserve.gov/boarddocs/speeches/2005/20051012/
    default.htm

2Q05 GDP Report
    www.bea.gov/bea/newsrel/gdpnewsrelease.htm

Steve Roach commentary
    www.morganstanley.com/GEFdata/digests/20051104-fri.html

Martin Wolf commentary (requires subscription)
    http://news.ft.com/cms/s/51aa4f28-40bb-11da-b3f9-00000e2511c8
    .html

General Resources

FirstGov at www.firstgov.gov/Business/Business_Data.shtml is an indispensable resource. Other useful web sites include:

American Stock Exchange
    www.amex.com

BigCharts
    www.bigcharts.com

Bureau of Economic Analysis
    www.bea.gov

Cato Institute
    www.cato.org

Democratic Leadership Council
    www.dlc.org

Department of Labor
    www.dol.gov

Federal Reserve Board
    federalreserve.gov

Financial Times
    www.ft.com

Heritage Foundation
    www.heritage.org

Institute for International Economics
    www.iie.com

Institute for Supply Management
www.ism.ws

International Monetary Fund
www.imf.org

Merrill Lynch
www.ml.com

Morgan Stanley Economic Research Team
www.morganstanley.com/GEFdata/digests/latest-digest.html

New York Times
www.nytimes.com

Organization for Economic Cooperation and Development
www.oecd.org

Wall Street Journal
www.wsj.com

World Bank
www.worldbank.org

World Trade Organization
www.wto.org

Yahoo! ETF Center
finance.yahoo.com/etf

Think Tank Lists

College of Liberal Arts
www.libarts.ucok.edu/political/links/think.htm

SIL International
www.sil.org/sildc/ThinkTanks_DC.htm

World Press Organization
www.worldpress.org/library/ngo.cfm

Style Investing and Risk

Throughout this book, I have referenced investing based on styles—investing based on the attributes of the stock and the company. In fact, the title of the book includes the word *styles*. But just what is style-oriented investing? And how does it fit within the effective investment strategy and portfolio construction process proposed by this book?

UNDERSTANDING STYLE INVESTING: THE QUANTITATIVE STRATEGY APPROACH

To begin, style-oriented investing is simply the purchase of stocks based on their attributes. The attributes of a stock could be its size (market capitalization) or market classification such as growth or value. Other attributes include quality ratings, volatility metrics (beta), and dividend yield. Moreover, stocks can be classified by company performance attributes such as return on equity, earnings revisions, and return on capital. And attributes that combine market metrics with company performance, such as the projected price-earnings/growth (PEG) ratio and price to cash flow, among others, are also used.

Anything that can be classified, therefore, can be measured. Accordingly, the market performance of stocks (and sectors, industries, etc.) can be measured to determine their relative performance. With that data, an investor can seek out which style has performed a certain way under certain economic and market conditions and may be likely to perform in the same manner in a given future market environment. For example, if the economy is the an early stages of recovery, higher-risk, lower-quality, lower-priced, more leveraged companies tend to perform best in the stock market. Conversely, at the end of an economic expansion, lower-risk, higher-quality, less leveraged companies tend to outperform. Therefore, an investor standing at the beginning edge of an economic recovery would be more inclined to own a higher-risk, lower-quality stock. Conversely, the same investor standing at the end of an economic recovery (a flattening or slowing of economic growth) would be more inclined to own lower-risk, higher-quality issues. What you see depends on where you stand. Let's consider that period when strong economic growth begins to give way to a natural slowdown. How can an investor use the aforementioned knowledge of prior market action during such periods for investment benefit? One way is to watch how the market, a predictor of future events, acts.

One application that I utilize is what I call the quality migration cycle. Using the ratings of stocks based on quality range (from A+ to the low-quality C and D ratings), I have combined this quantitative ranking based on quality with market performance in an attempt to determine if a bull market is coming to an end. Specifically, if a bull market is topping out (and bull markets tend to top out over time before declining), then high-quality stocks should be outperforming. But rarely does a market led by lower-quality issues simply leap to outperformance by high-quality issues. Rather, there is typically a progression from low to mid to high quality, each taking a turn outperforming the market. The key investment strategy point is that with each stage of outperformance, the market is undergoing what I call its quality migration cycle:

- Low quality outperforms in the early to early mature stage of a bull market.
- Medium quality outperforms from the early mature to early declining stage.
- High quality outperforms from that point until a bear market bottom process gets under way.

In a similar fashion, Liz Ann Sonders, chief investment strategist with Charles Schwab & Co., wrote in an investment commentary on November 14, 2005:

Big Time: Large-Cap Growth's Resurgence?

We believe small-cap's leadership is coming to a close as its duration is getting more extended (even if not yet unprecedented): Over the past 45 years, the median small-cap leadership period lasted about 4¾ years, including a mega leadership period from the mid-1970s through the mid-1980s. The current small-cap leadership period is now more than 6½ years long (in the tooth?). . . .

Liz Ann goes on to explain two key components of her rationale:

One reason for this is the increasing pressure rising interest rates are having on smaller companies, as larger companies tend to be more interest-rate insensitive. Technical conditions still show a prejudice toward small-caps during up-moves in the market overall, but we think we've reached the turning point where large-caps will show more life, even during rising market periods.

While it's not quite my quality migration cycle, the similarities are there. Certainly the reasoning is close. But, more importantly, it points out an investment strategy based on styles. Liz Ann then takes it one step further and links the projected market action to both the real economy (interest rate effects) and technical analysis (technical conditions).

Style Investing in Action

My good friend Rich Bernstein over at Merrill Lynch heads Wall Street's top quantitative research department. In his recent report of July 15, 2005, "Style Allocation Quarterly," Rich describes the difference between value and growth managers in his unique and insightful way:

Value managers are typically defined as low-expectations managers because they tend to search for investments among stocks that are out of favor. The assumption behind value investing is that the consensus view of a company is overly pessimistic, and that the stock's valuation will improve once the consensus changes. Value managers, therefore, usually search for stocks that sell below the worth of a company's assets or below the value of its future growth prospects.

Growth managers are typically defined as high-expectations managers who prefer to search for investments among stocks that have a proven track record of superior earnings growth. Growth stock investors usually pay a high premium to hold such stocks because the market realizes the superior qualities of the company. The assumption behind growth stock investing is that the market will continue to reward the superior grower.

These are the two basic style investing categories, growth and value. But, as you might suspect, there are many other categories of style investing beyond the basic two. Rich has listed some of the following style categories. As you can see, in addition to your basic growth and value categories, there are quite a few additional style categories that an investor can track:

- Dividend growth
- P/E-to-growth
- One-year return on equity
- Five-year return on equity
- One-year ROE (adjusted for debt)
- Five-year ROE (adjusted by debt)
- Return on assets
- Return on capital
- Beta
- Variability of earnings
- Estimate dispersion
- Neglect-institutional ownership
- Neglect-analyst coverage
- Size
- Foreign exposure
- Share repurchase
- Equity duration

Style Investing Recap

Investing based on styles is an alternative way of investing. Investing based on the style of a stock has moved well beyond its early days and the basic growth-versus-value paradigm. Today, there are numerous ways of slicing and dicing the market and constructing portfolios based on a style. Moreover, as described in previous chapters, the ability to blend a style approach with an economic sector approach can add valuable extra returns and, in the process, reduce risk. In other words, style investing takes sector-based investing to another level.

UNDERSTANDING RISK

At the end of the preceding style investing segment and at various points throughout the book, I have used the word *risk*. In the chapter on valuation and in other chapters, the application of risk has been in the form of beta, the volatility of a stock.

Investorwords.com has a very good web page on the definition of risk and the types of risks an investor faces. Investorwords.com defines risk as "The quantifiable likelihood of loss or less-than-expected returns," and goes on to provide the following list of the various types of risk an investor faces:

- Currency risk
- Inflation risk
- Principal risk
- Country risk
- Economic risk
- Mortgage risk
- Liquidity risk
- Market risk
- Opportunity risk
- Income risk
- Interest rate risk
- Prepayment risk
- Credit risk
- Unsystematic risk
- Call risk
- Business risk
- Counterparty risk
- Purchasing-power risk
- Event risk

As noted in earlier chapters, according to the efficient markets hypothesis, all of these risks are incorporated in one figure, beta, and incorporated in a stock's price and its trading action is the "wisdom of the market."

Beta is what is called a "single-factor" measure of risk. It rests on the assumption that the wisdom of the market embeds in beta all that is needed to predict the riskiness of a stock investment. This is problematic on two levels. First, it is a backward look. Second is the issue of whether there is a widely accepted alternative to beta. (The short answer is no.)

There are alternatives (such as arbitrage pricing theory (discussed later), but none of them has taken hold as *the* substitute for beta. Accordingly, as flawed and incomplete as beta is, it, like the capital asset pricing model (CAPM: the cost of equity capital), is the best of a bad lot. Therefore, I believe that one can use beta as a risk metric provided an investor *starts with the current beta* and then adjusts it to reflect one's own view of the *future* beta. In other words, you start with the backward-looking beta and then, exercising your best judgment (based on an analysis of the future outlook for the economy and the markets), adjust the future beta to reflect what you consider to be the likely scenario for the markets. It's not easy to do, and is most definitely fraught with forecasting problems.

Nevertheless, I believe it is better than using the current beta, and my advice is to never use the current beta but rather use one that is adjusted *by you* by taking as many of the 19 risks listed earlier that apply (mortgage risk, for example, may not be applicable) and deriving your own risk metric, your own *future beta*.

To go just a bit deeper into the 19 risks listed, here are the definitions and brief descriptions of three key risks—liquidity, market, and business—as provided by Investorwords.com.

Liquidity Risk

The risk that arises from the difficulty of selling an asset. An investment may sometimes need to be sold quickly. Unfortunately, an insufficient secondary market may prevent the liquidation or limit the funds that can be generated from the asset. Some assets are highly liquid and have low liquidity risk (such as stock of a publicly traded company), while other assets are highly illiquid and have high liquidity risk (such as a house).

Market Risk

Risk which is common to an entire class of assets or liabilities. The value of investments may decline over a given time period simply because of economic changes or other events that impact large portions of the market. Asset allocation and diversification can protect against market risk because different portions of the market tend to underperform at different times.

Business Risk

Risk associated with the unique circumstances of a particular company, as they might affect the price of that company's securities.

Going Beyond Beta

Beta is a very useful and well-established tool. An investor would be ill-advised if he/she ignored such a tool, despite its numerous and apparent shortcomings. Putting it differently, "When in Rome, do as the Romans do." We may want a replacement tool for risk measurement, but, at a minimum, if everyone else is using it, then we must use it as well. That is not to say we should accept beta unaltered. Adjust it to make it work more effectively. But use it because it is the accepted standard.

Having made this point, it is worthwhile to briefly view the primary competing risk tool, the arbitrage pricing theory (APT), a multifactor approach to risk measurement. The APT is also worth studying as it attempts to do exactly what I have suggested in adjusting beta: take several factors into consideration. Here is a quick look at APT.

Arbitrage Pricing Theory

Theeconomist.com (the web site for the *Economist* magazine) provides this definition of the arbitrage pricing theory:

> *This is one of two influential economic theories of how assets are priced in the financial markets. The other is the capital asset pricing model. The arbitrage pricing theory says that the price of a financial asset reflects a few key risk factors, such as the expected rate of interest, and how the price of the asset changes relative to the price of a portfolio of assets. If the price of an asset happens to diverge from what the theory says it should be, arbitrage by investors should bring it back into line.*

APT is a multifactor risk model that attempts to identify and then incorporate into a formula several key risk factors.

APT creator Stephen Ross, along with N. Chen and R. Roll, identified four macroeconomic factors as significant in explaining security returns:

1. Inflation
2. Gross domestic product
3. Investor confidence
4. Shifts in the yield curve

Other practitioners have used these four factors as a point of departure and incorporated other factors that might help measure uncertainty (risk). Whatever the factors used or the model used, however, risk (uncertainty) is so important in valuation models that all investors should spend time understanding risk measurement in the best way possible.

Notes

Introduction

1. Successful investing is defined as generating a rate of return adjusted for risk in excess of the rate of return you would have generated placing your funds in an index fund.

CHAPTER 1   Valuation's Core Concepts

1. Then there is the additional factor of when we sell our stock. What is its present value?
2. Which speaks volumes for the company in question, as the point for most stock investing is to generate growth rates greater than what the market has to offer. More on this point later.
3. Death becomes us when a company cannot find exceptional opportunities and does not distribute the excess capital in the form of either dividends or stock repurchases.
4. Gerald I. White, Ashwinpaul C. Sondhi, and Dov Fried, *The Analysis and Use of Financial Statements* (New York: John Wiley & Sons, 2002).
5. Off-balance-sheet liabilities, stock options, research and development costs, and joint ventures, to name a few.
6. As you will see shortly and as has been suggested thus far, prices and units sold are greatly influenced by the competitive conditions of the industry in which a company operates, its ability to identify the appropriate competitive strategies, and its financial wherewithal to make those competitive strategies work.
7. A practice that also shows up when it comes to making the final investment strategy decision.
8. Moreover, as you will note in Chapters 3 and 9, the Core Plus approach to portfolio management using ETFs minimizes the risk of single-issue surprises.
9. The difficulty also comes from the fact that, when it comes to value, human nature gets in the way. This is discussed in the next chapter under the topics of investing as a social science and behavioral finance.
10. Michael Porter, *Competitive Strategy* (New York: Free Press, 1980).
11. Ibid.
12. Sometimes, the mostly live-and-let-live relationship between the two gets frayed.
13. Porter, *Competitive Strategy*.
14. Ibid.

15. Ibid.
16. A company should seek to excel in only one of the Three Generic Strategies. Few companies can excel in more than one, as the skill sets and resources are quite different for companies seeking to be cost leader or following a differentiation strategy. The danger is being stuck in the middle and excelling in neither area, thereby not gaining a competitive advantage.
17. Leverage declined due to a reduction in the assets-to-liabilities ratio. In this example, the assets remained the same while the equity rose. Remember that the difference between the assets and the equity is the debt owed—the liabilities.
18. While this is a fairly surface description of the sustainable growth rate, the concept is key. The net return to equity owners (in this case, ROE) is multiplied by the amount of funds retained to the business. If, in this example, the company paid no dividends, then ROE would be its sustainable growth rate.
19. Note that I use the phrase "equity cash flows of a business." That is because we are discounting the cash flows to the equity holders of a business. There are other holders of the business, such as debt owners. We need to calculate the cash flows to the firm, as opposed to just the equity owners. Accordingly, the discount factor includes the CAPM cost of equity calculation but it also includes the after-tax cost of debt. This is known as the weighted average cost of capital (WACC).
20. Some use alternative methods to measure risk, such as the arbitrage pricing theory (APT). However, at present CAPM remains king of the hill.
21. The interplay between the real economy and the financial economy (the markets).

CHAPTER 2 Investment Strategy: Concepts and Principles

1. The interplay between the real economy and the financial economy (the markets). Most investors understand that the real economy is the basis upon which the financial economy operates. What is not so well appreciated is the fact that the financial economy has a profound impact on the real economy. More on this later.
2. Kenichi Ohmae, *The Mind of the Strategist* (New York: McGraw-Hill, 1982).
3. Ibid.
4. This is Soros' reflexivity in action.

CHAPTER 3 The Essential Elements of an Effective Portfolio

1. Merrill Lynch, ETF Investor Profile Portfolios, October 5, 2005.
2. Jason Trennert, *New Markets, New Strategies* (New York: McGraw-Hill, 2005).

3. Charles D. Ellis, *Investment Policy* (New York: Dow Jones–Irwin, 1985).
4. Ibid.

CHAPTER 4   The Investment Importance of Politics and Government

1. iView Research, March 28, 2005.
2. The Fed Model is a valuation tool that is purportedly favored by former Fed chairman Alan Greenspan, among others.
3. iView Research, July 25, 2005.
4. Less demand for Treasuries means higher rates, which leads to an increase in the cost of living for U.S. consumers, which has the potential of reducing personal spending.

CHAPTER 5   It's the Global Economy, Stupid

1. Wages plus benefits.
2. With the takeover of both houses of Congress.
3. Reprinted with permission from the publisher, the Institute for Supply Management™.
4. Reprinted with permission from the publisher, the Institute for Supply Management™.
5. Peter G. Peterson, *Running on Empty: How the Democratic and Republican Parties Are Bankrupting Our Future and What Americans Can Do About It* (New York: Farrar, Straus, and Giroux, 2004), 57–59.
6. Ibid., 67–68.
7. www.noogenesis.com/pineapple/blind_man_elephant.html.
8. Copyright © 2006 Standard & Poor's and MSCI. Reproduction of this material in any form is prohibited without prior written permission.
9. This is the essence of Core Plus.
10. Copyright © 2006 Standard & Poor's and MSCI. Reproduction of this material in any form is prohibited without prior written permission.
11. George Soros, *Open Society* (New York: Public Affairs, 2000).
12. Martin Wolf, "Global Imbalances Will Require Global Solutions," *Financial Times*, April 27, 2005.
13. Peterson, *Running on Empty*, 41.

CHAPTER 6   Say Hello to Mr. Market

1. Warren Buffett, Letter to Investors, Berkshire Hathaway, February 29, 1988.
2. George Soros, *Open Society* (New York: Public Affairs, 2000).
3. Ibid.
4. David A. Levy, *Tools of Critical Thinking* (Long Grove, IL: Waveland Press, 2003).
5. Frank K. Reilly and Keith C. Brown, *Investment Analysis and Portfolio Management* (Orlando, FL: Dryden Press, 1997), 775.

6. Although many segments of the market actually reached their lows by mid-October 2002.
7. Reprinted by permission. Copyright © 2005 Merrill Lynch, Pierce, Fenner & Smith Incorporated. Further reproduction or distribution is strictly prohibited.

APPENDIX A   Conducting Your Own Research

1. Reprinted with permission.

Index

Obligations and risk, 198
Ohmae, Kenichi:
 The Mind of the Strategist, 55–56
 on strategy, 57–58, 59
Old school economic thinking, 129–130
Olympics (2008) in Beijing, 235
Opportunity cost of capital, calculating,
 41–43
Organization for Economic Cooperation
 and Development *Economic Outlook*,
 94–95
Overconcentration and risk, 65

P/E (price-earnings) ratio and comparables
 method, 17
PEG (price-earnings/growth) ratio, 209
Perception of world, 193–194
Performance and valuation methodologies,
 17
Personal computer (PC):
 empowerment of investor and, 69
 ETFs and, 3
 Internet and, 1–3, 175
 portfolio and, 64
Peterson, Peter G., *Running on Empty*,
 103–104, 124–125
Playing not to lose, 65
Plender, John, on hedge funds and banking
 system, 130
PMI (Purchasing Managers Index), 100–101
Political power, 79–86
 culture wars and, 80–83
 economic power and, 79–80, 87
 investment implications of shift in, 83–86
Porter, Michael:
 Competitive Strategy, 29–30
 Five Forces of, 30–34
 relevance of methodology of, 34
 Three Generic Strategies of, 34–36
Portfolio:
 concentrated compared to diversified, 196
 tracking, 177
Portfolio, effective:
 creating and maintaining, 6–7, 64
 ETFs and, 64–67, 166
 overview of, 63
 PC, Net, and, 64
 perception of world and, 193–194
 strategy groupings, 207–219
 See also Building effective portfolio; Core
 Plus portfolio process
Portfolio management, 8–9
Portfolio management tools, 2–3
Portfolio managers, 72–73
Power:
 buyer and supplier, 33
 economic and political, 79–87

empowerment of investors, 69, 163,
 221–222
 pricing, 101
Price-earnings/growth (PEG) ratio, 209
Price-earnings (P/E) ratio and comparables
 method, 17
Pricing power, 101
A Primer on Decision Making (March), 54
Principles, following, 9–10
Professional investor sentiment, 156–158
Profit:
 corporate, 98–99
 forecasting, 26
Profitability of economic sectors, 110–114
Purchasing Managers Index (PMI),
 100–101

Quality migration cycle, 158–160, 246–247
Quantitative strategy approach, 245–247

A Random Walk Down Wall Street
 (Malkiel), 143
Rate of return in 1980s, 49–50
Ratio analysis, 36–37
Real economy, 69, 139–142. *See also* Global
 economy
Real-time data, 224
Reflexivity, 49, 57, 140–141
Regret factor, 73
Research, conducting, 221–243
Return on equity (ROE) and Dupont
 formula, 38–40
Risk:
 asset allocation and, 197–198, 199–201
 beta and, 249–251
 calculating, 43–44
 change in circumstances and, 199, 205
 definition of, 250
 future assets and, 198–199
 incorporating, 203–204
 obligations and, 198
 overconcentration and, 65
 types of, 249
Risk/reward trade-off, 50
Rivalry determinants, 32
Roach, Stephen:
 on China, 235–238
 on deficits, 125–126
 Morgan Stanley web site and, 179
ROE (return on equity) and Dupont
 formula, 38–40
Roll, R., 251
Rosenberg, David:
 on consumer spending, 128
 on Federal Reserve Open Market
 Committee meetings, 231
 Merrill Lynch web site and, 179

Printed in the United States
By Bookmasters